GUESTS OF THE SHEIK

Elizabeth Warnock Fernea

GUESTS OF THE SHEIK

An Ethnography of an Iraqi Village

LIBRARY
BRYAN COLLEGE
DAYTON, TENN. **37321**

ANCHOR BOOKS

DOUBLEDAY & COMPANY, INC.

GARDEN CITY, NEW YORK

1969

71453

Guests of the Sheik was originally published in hardcover by Doubleday & Company, Inc., in 1965.

Anchor Books edition: 1969

Copyright © 1965 by Elizabeth Warnock Fernea
All Rights Reserved
Printed in the United States of America

For My Mother,
Elizabeth Warnock

TABLE OF CONTENTS

INTRODUCTION

I spent the first two years of my married life in a tribal settlement on the edge of a village in southern Iraq. My husband, a social anthropologist, was doing research for his doctorate from the University of Chicago.

This book is a personal narrative of those years, especially of my life with the veiled women who, like me, lived in mud-brick houses surrounded by high mud walls. I am not an anthropologist. Before going to Iraq, I knew no Arabic and almost nothing of the Middle East, its religion and its culture. I have tried to set down faithfully my reactions to a new world; any inaccuracies are my own.

The village, the tribe and all of the people who appear in the following pages are real, as are the incidents. However, I have changed the names so that no one may be embarrassed, although I doubt that any of my women friends in the village will ever read my book.

Without their friendship and hospitality, and that of other Iraqi and American friends too numerous to mention, this book quite literally would never have been written. I want to thank my friend Nicholas B. Millet for drafting the sketch-map which has been used on pages 20 and 21 in this book. I owe a special debt of gratitude to two people. Audrey Walz (Mrs. Jay Walz) read the incomplete manuscript and advised me to finish it. Her enthusiasm, together with her sound judgment and critical ear, have aided the book's progress immeasurably. My husband, Robert Fernea, first encouraged me to write *Guests of the Sheik*. His interest and his intellectual honesty helped me face the realities of living in El Nahra and, later, of trying to shape that experience into the book which follows.

CAST OF CHARACTERS

In the tribal settlement:

SHEIK HAMID ABDUL EMIR EL HUSSEIN (called Haji) sheik of the El Eshadda tribe

SELMA
BAHIGA } his wives
KULTHUM

NOUR his eldest son by a wife now dead

FEISAL } sons of Selma
ABBAS

HADHI son of Bahiga, at school in Baghdad

AHMAR } sons of Kulthum, at school or work-
IBRAHIM } ing in town

ALWIYAH } his older daugh-
SAMIRA } ters
SABIHA

AMINA servant of Selma

ABDULLA EL HUSSEIN older brother of Sheik Hamid

KHARIYA } his wives
BASSOUL

AHMED his oldest son, at school in Baghdad

JALIL his second son

MOUSSA EL HUSSEIN brother of Sheik Hamid

UM FATIMA his wife

FATIMA
SANAA
NEJLA } his daughters
LAILA
BASIMA
RAJAT

MOHAMMED a Sayid, or descendant of the Prophet

MEDINA his mother

SHERIFA his sister

ABAD } his brothers
ABDUL KARIM

FADHILA wife of Abdul Karim

SALEH a weaver

HATHAYA his daughter

MAHMOUD husband of Hathaya

ALI gardener of Sheik Hamid

SHEDDIR his wife

SAHURA his daughter

HASSAN his son

QANDA an old woman; tattoo artist and village beautician

HUSSEIN member of a clan of the El Eshadda tribe

SAJJIDA his wife

In the village of El Nahra:

JABBAR irrigation engineer

KHADIJA his sister, who keeps house for him

SUHEIR his fiancée

ABU SAAD mayor of El Nahra

UM SAAD his wife, also a teacher in the girls' school

SITT ALIYAH principal of the girls' primary school

HIND her sister, also a teacher in the girls' school

AZIZA the new teacher

DR. IBRAHIM the village doctor

NADIA his wife

KHALIL teacher of Arabic in the boys' primary school

SALIMA his wife

UM KHALIL his mother, also the village wise woman

In Karbala:

DR. YEHIA cousin of Moussa el Hussein

SITT NAJAT his wife, also a nurse

In the nearby village of Suffra:

SHEIK HAMZA

GUESTS OF THE SHEIK

PART I

1

Night Journey: Arrival in the Village

The night train from Baghdad to Basra was already hissing
and creaking in its tracks when Bob and I arrived at the
platform. Clouds of steam billowing from the engine hung
suspended in the cold January air as we hurried across,
laden with suitcases, bundles, string bags and an angel-
food cake in a cardboard box, a farewell present from a
thoughtful American friend. We were on the last lap of
our journey, and I found myself half dreading and half
anticipating the adventure we had come almost ten thousand miles to begin.

"Diwaniya! Diwaniya!"

"Those are the coaches we want," said Bob, taking my
arm and steering me down the platform past crowds of
tribesmen arguing heatedly or sitting in tight quiet groups,
their wives swathed in black to the eyebrows, with children on hip and shoulder; past the white-collar Iraqi
effendis in Western suits and past the shouting German
tourists.

An attendant in an ill-fitting khaki wool uniform helped
us board and guided us to a compartment, where he
dusted the worn leather seats with his coat sleeve. We sat
down. I found my stomach was churning and I glanced
quickly at Bob to see how he was taking the long-awaited
departure.

I knew he was nervous about my reception in El Nahra,
the remote village where we were now headed and where
he had been living and working as an anthropologist for
the past three months. He was no more nervous than I,
who knew little of El Nahra except that no one spoke
English there, that the people were of the conservative
Shiite sect of Islam, and that the women were heavily

veiled and lived in the strictest seclusion. No Western woman had ever lived in El Nahra before and very few had even been seen there, Bob said, which meant I would be something of a curiosity. I wasn't sure I wanted to be. And we were to be guests of Sheik Hamid Abdul Emir el Hussein, chief of the El Eshadda tribe, who had offered us a mud house with a walled garden. Our first home, said Bob—a honeymoon house. But who had ever heard of a honeymoon house made of mud?

"Hil-la! Diwaniya! Samawa! Bas-ra!" bawled the conductors. "*Yallah!*" The train began to move past the station and the line of waiting taxis and horse-drawn carriages.

"Well, we're off," announced Bob, a little too heartily. He motioned to the hovering porter and ordered some beer to celebrate our departure. "Maybe we'll have some rain before we get to Diwaniya." He stood up to peer out of the window.

I looked out, too—expecting what? A friend to wave goodbye? Three months ago I had come to Baghdad as a bride and the city had seemed strange and alien to me then, a place so far removed from my experience that I had nothing with which to compare it. Now, headed for an unknown tribal village, I did not want to miss my last glimpse of Baghdad, which seemed a dear familiar place.

Clouds hung low and dark in the bit of sky I could see between the buildings and the townspeople and tribesmen, carriages, cars and donkey carts that moved more and more quickly past the train window. The winter night was coming fast, and as we left the Tigris River behind, the lights were on in all the hotels along its banks—the Semiramis, the Zia, the Sindbad. We passed rows of mud-and-mat *serifa* huts with kerosene lanterns flickering in their doorways, a series of smoking brick kilns, a mosque with a lighted minaret, more serifa huts, and then there was nothing to see but the dark horizon and a few date palms and the wide, empty plain.

"Aren't you excited?" asked Bob. "I can't understand you at all. Here we've been waiting and planning all these weeks for you to come down, dear, and now that we're on our way at last, you sit there as calmly as though you were going shopping or something."

At least I look calm, I thought; that's good.

"Yes," I brought out. "I am excited." We sipped our beer. And also scared, I added to myself. I had to get along well in El Nahra so I could help Bob with his work. But would I be able to? Bob had warned that we could certainly expect the women to be friendly at first, in the customary hospitable Arab way, but he couldn't be sure how they would react after the initial period.

In the dining car I was the only woman, and the men stared at me curiously. We went back to our compartment and watched the dark landscape while the train pushed slowly south. I had thought, and Bob had agreed, that the women might accept me more readily if I met them on their own terms. Thus, although I had balked at wearing an all-enveloping black *abayah*, I had elected to live like the women of El Nahra—in relative seclusion behind walls, not meeting or mixing with men. But what if, in spite of my efforts, the women shunned me and left me to myself, more of a hindrance than an asset to my husband? Two years alone in a mud house, I reflected. Hardly an enchanting way to spend a honeymoon.

The weather was certainly not welcoming; a midnight rain in Diwaniya poured down as we ran from the train to the waiting room with its single wooden bench. I sat by the luggage while Bob looked for a taxi or a carriage to take us to the government rest house; even if the weather had been ideal, we could not have continued on to El Nahra that night. The village lay only ten miles southeast but there was no regular transportation except for occasional trucks and taxis which did not travel after dark.

While I waited, people gathered to stare at me again, and I slowly became aware that, among the crowds of middle-class Iraqis and townspeople, I was the only woman without an abayah. I began to be self-conscious. This is ridiculous, I told myself. Why should I have to wear that ugly thing—it's not *my* custom; the arguments with Bob about the abayah returned in a rush. Bob said I ought to wear it, since everyone else did. Since we were guests of the sheik, he added, it would make everything easier if I wore the abayah; the sheik wouldn't have to punish people for insulting me. Insulting me! I had been indignant. "They say an uncovered woman is an immoral woman," Bob had explained, "and the tribesmen ask why a woman should want to show herself to anyone but her husband." I remembered my furious reply: "If they can't take me as I am—if we have to make artificial gestures to prove we are human beings too—what's the point?" Now, although I hated to admit it, my principles were weakening before my embarrassment as more and more people gathered to whisper and point and stare. I wished from the bottom of my heart that I had borrowed the abayah offered by a Baghdadi lady friend and could bury myself in its comforting anonymity.

After half an hour's carriage ride through splashing mud we were ushered into a side wing of the rest house, the place where women were allowed to stay if accompanied by their husbands. I broke out our angel-food cake to eat with the tea Bob had ordered before we lay down to sleep with the rain dripping into the puddles outside our curtained window.

Although the sun was shining in the morning, the taxis were still not able to move on the muddy roads outside the city, so I was deposited in the home of one of Bob's friends to wait. The lady of the house was called Um Hassan, mother of Hassan, her oldest child, "like my husband is called Abu Hassan," she explained slowly and patiently in Arabic. Um Hassan was a perceptive woman. She took a long look at my tweed coat and red scarf.

"You're going to live in El Nahra?" she asked incredulously.

I said that I was.

Without another word she produced an abayah. "You wear this, dearie," she said (or the Arabic equivalent thereof), "and you'll feel a lot better." As I began to protest, she stopped me in midsentence. "You can borrow it. I'll have one made for you here."

Her son brought samples of black silk; a dressmaker

came and measured me. The abayah would be sent by taxi next week, said Um Hassan, and I could return hers then. Well, it seemed I'd capitulated; I was going to wear that servile garment after all. I discovered that my principles were not as strong as my desire to be inconspicuous and well thought of in my new home.

Um Hassan and I drank several glasses of hot sweet tea and I was urged to eat lunch while I waited for Bob to return. My mood was hardly improved by the long face Um Hassan pulled when I struggled to ask about El Nahra in my scanty Arabic.

"You won't stay," she prophesied. "You won't be able to stand it. No cinema, no paved streets—and the food! No chickens—if you get one, it's nothing but bones." To make sure I had understood, she rattled in their dish the chicken bones I had picked clean at luncheon.

Bob finally arrived at dusk, tired and annoyed; we would be sharing a taxi with six other people and he had had to pay double to assure that he and I would have the front seat to ourselves.

"The driver can't even promise we'll get through, the road is so bad," he admitted. "But I think we'd better try it; we can't sit in Diwaniya for the next three days."

Um Hassan showed me how to keep the black silk abayah on my head and around my body by clutching the two sides together under my chin. At the doorway I turned to shake her hand, stepped on the hem of the abayah, and it slipped neatly off my head into a little pile on the doorstep. The men in the waiting taxi stared popeyed, and one of Um Hassan's little boys stifled a giggle while Bob helped me recover the abayah and I tried to maneuver myself and the unfamiliar cloak into the taxi without losing it again.

Bob looked at me. "I do think you'll be more comfortable," he said. I knew he meant the abayah but I was beyond discussion of the matter at this point.

"We'll soon be home," he said. "Don't worry." He put his arm around me comfortingly, but he'd forgotten the abayah too, and only succeeded in dragging it off my head again. "Sorry," he muttered, and together we dragged the silly thing back up.

Home. Home indeed. I could not even see a track in the mud ahead of us as the old Ford taxi slid around through puddles in the growing dusk.

"After we pass the shrine of Abu Fadhil, the local saint, we pick up the El Nahra road," Bob was saying, and although I didn't believe there could be anything ahead of us in the muck, a single electric globe gradually became visible, high up; it was burning on the very top of the shrine's brick dome. The mud-and-thatch houses nearby were shut tight and darkened by the rain; they rose up on either side of us like deserted tombs. Only a donkey braying within indicated life. Night was coming; already the huts were merging into the flat landscape, and as we passed them and edged forward into empty fields of mud, the horizon itself slowly merged with the dark sky.

We drove on into nothing. No lights were visible in any direction; no other taxis, people or animals were on the road. In the back seat the men were quiet, and we could hear, very loudly in the silence, the splash of mud against the sides of the car and the ominous bangs and creaks as the undercarriage hit the ridges of ruts. Wind swept in through the windows, empty of glass panes. Even in my borrowed abayah and overcoat and sweater, I shivered in the damp air.

The ten miles took almost two hours, but we were stuck only once. The driver sighed, the men in the back seat got out and tied their long garments or *dishdashas* up, and Bob rolled up his trouser legs. Directed by loud shouts from the driver, the seven of them, shin-deep in mud, rocked the car back and forth in the slime, and finally, when it would still not budge, literally lifted it up and over the bad place, the driver gunning the motor as hard as he could to help. We finally got to solid ground, the men emptied their shoes of water, and Bob looked ruefully at his mud-soaked khakis. Everyone climbed back in the car and we drove on.

Eventually the men stirred. Bob was pointing ahead to where a faint light could be seen. Dark shapes of palm trees loomed in front of us, and we rounded a bend and rolled over the last rut onto pavement and into a blaze of fluorescent lights: the main street of El Nahra. Bob indicated the jail and the school and the mayor's house. The street was deserted, but the fluorescent street lights burned brightly all the way to the bridge, where we stopped at an open coffee shop. The back-seat passengers got out and a few men sitting drinking a late-evening cup of coffee raised their hands in casual salute to the taxi. We crossed the bridge and turned right onto a mud road, which followed the irrigation canal past dark walls and a lean-to coffee shop. "This is the tribal side of the canal," said Bob, "where we live." Here there were no fluorescent lights, only old-fashioned street lamps glimmering dully in the muddy waters. I could make out big trees next to the water.

A dog began to bark, and another. Within minutes what seemed to be hundreds of dogs were howling furiously around us.

"It's only the watchdogs of the tribal settlement," Bob told me. "They always bark when a stranger comes near. That's what they're for."

We turned left away from the canal, the dogs still barking, and the taxi stopped at a high mud wall, where Bob unlocked the padlock on a wooden door and carried in the bags. I gathered my abayah around me, picked up my purse and the angel-food-cake box and went through the door into a garden, following Bob up a narrow path to a small dark house as the rain spattered down onto the leaves in a sudden shower.

As Bob wrestled in the dark with the padlock on the house door, the trees in the garden around me rustled and sighed, and my shoes squished in deep mud. I shifted my feet, transferred my parcels to one hand so that I could get a firmer grip on the abayah. Water dripped from my bangs down my forehead and into my eyes.

The lock snapped open. "Don't expect too much," warned Bob as we stepped over the threshold. He flicked a switch and a single bare electric globe went on, illuminating a small, dusty, incredibly littered room.

"I've been living in one room," he offered, "but now you're here we can fix up the other. In fact you can probably fix this one up better too."

I stood by the door. Books, papers, clothes, blankets and dishes were piled on an old wooden table covered with dirty oilcloth, on a broken-down sofa, on a single iron cot which stood against a stained and cracked whitewashed wall. Among the dusty papers stood a tin can; the label stated that Robertson's strawberry jam had been or still was inside. Most of the earth floor was hidden under woven reed mats which in turn were covered with a dusty rug. Above my head I heard a strange sort of twittering and I looked up to the high beamed ceiling.

"What's that?" I found I was almost shouting.

"Only a few birds, for heaven's sake," answered Bob in an exasperated tone.

I looked at him and he looked back blankly. At that point, somewhere inside of me, I knew what I should do. For it had been hard for Bob too; he had searched for this village for months, gone through all the preliminaries that were necessary for us to settle down here: asked for permission to stay, found the house, moved into a strange place all by himself, and prepared the way for me. His Arabic wasn't very good either, but he had gone right ahead. I could have made a lighthearted joke about living in a mountain, no, *desert* cabin (loud, foolish laughter), with all the mountain, no, *desert* greenery (more silly laughter), where God paints the scenery, etc., etc., etc., and we could have laughed it off together, the tense journey and the staring, pointing people and the exhausting drive through the mud. We could have had coffee and talked about the abayah and kissed each other and it would have been all right.

But I couldn't do it. I felt only a flood of irrational resentment against my new husband for bringing me here, where not only was the bed not big enough for two, but the ceiling was full of birds' nests!

"Do you want to see the other room?" he asked. We went outside into the rain and mud again. "No connecting doors in this hotel," he added lightly.

He unlocked a second padlock and the door swung in, releasing a dank and musty odor. He turned on another bulb, lighting a bare room that held a camp stove, a table with a canteen of water on it, and more birds whirring in the beams.

"Shall we finish the tour with a quick turn around the garden, ending at the outhouse, which, experience has shown, is the best outhouse in the whole damned neighborhood?" Bob was trying his best to buoy up my sagging spirits, and I tried to answer in the same vein, but nothing came out.

"My dear B.J.," he said gently, "you don't need to wear your abayah in your own private garden."

I was still clutching the despised abayah tightly under my chin.

"Never mind, it keeps off the r-rain," I stuttered, feeling stupid and miserable and annoyed with myself for acting like the bride arriving in the palazzo and finding the plumbing unsatisfactory.

The outhouse was simple—mud walls and roof and a brick-lined hole in the ground. Bob had given me a flashlight so I could pick my way back through the muddy garden to where the door of the house stood open and the single light shone out.

When I got back, he had cleared a passage through the boxes and bags and straightened the bedclothes. We lay close together on the narrow iron cot and I clung to Bob, who slept almost immediately. I lay awake remembering my bachelor cousin, who had toasted Bob and me at our wedding. "Here's to the roving life!" he had said, raising his glass of champagne punch. "Here's to adventure and the non-stuffy approach. Your very good health!" It seemed years, rather than months, since that bright June day in my aunt's suburban Chicago garden when we had said goodbye to our families and friends and set off, in a shower of rice, for Georgetown University to study Arabic. That, too, seemed long ago after the boat trip to Beirut, the ride over the desert road to Baghdad, the months of waiting and working until Bob found the right area for his research in social anthropology. The lawns and towers of the

University of Chicago and the faces of my family against the June garden faded slowly as I listened to the strange birds chirping softly above my head, to the rain falling on the thatched roof of our mud house and to the sound of Bob's regular breathing; finally I, too, slept.

Loud knocking at the door awakened us.

Bob turned over and nearly fell out of the narrow bed. "That must be Mohammed," he said.

"Mohammed," I muttered sleepily. "Who's Mohammed?"

"The servant the sheik assigned to us; he's a nice boy. Brings water and shops and cleans a little and does the dishes. You can meet him after breakfast."

"But can't I shop?" I asked. "I'd enjoy going to market."

"Heavens, no. The women don't appear in the market."

The knocking continued while I thought of something to say to that, but before I got it out Bob was up, pulling on his trousers and shouting through the door in Arabic, "Good morning, Mohammed. I'll be out in a minute." To me he said, "You stay here. I'll get the stove going and fry some eggs, if Mohammed has remembered to bring them."

I dressed by electric light, for although the clock said eight-thirty, the window of the room had no glass panes and the wooden shutters were tightly closed. Overhead the birds were also waking up, and when I opened the door one flew out in a rush and I found myself staring at Mohammed, a tall thin man in what I was to find was typical tribal dress: white dishdasha, wool sport coat, tan *aba* or cloak, and black-and-white head scarf. (The scarf was called a *kaffiyeh*, Bob said, and the heavy rope which held it in place was an *agal*.)

Mohammed smiled broadly, showing a row of beautiful white teeth. "*Ahlan wusahlan*," he said. "Welcome."

Bob came out of the other room. We all smiled at each other awkwardly until Bob broke the impasse. "Come on and eat," he said. "Mohammed, please heat some water so I can shave."

We set the plates of eggs and the cups of Nescafé down

on the table. I tried to wipe the oilcloth, but it was caked with layers of dust. Bob turned on his radio to the BBC news, which came through sporadically between loud hums and bleats of static.

"That's Radio Moscow jamming," explained Bob between mouthfuls.

From the ceiling a feather wafted down onto the eggs. I snatched it off.

"Those blasted *birds!*" I cried.

Bob reached over and took my hand. *Don't cry*, I warned myself. "Place isn't much, is it? But really it should be quite nice when we get set up. I've been counting on you to fix it. The roof is good. We could replaster the walls. What do you think we need?"

"A bigger bed."

Bob smiled. "Actually, I thought of that. John Priest, this young American engineer in Diwaniya, has a three-quarter mattress he's willing to sell us, and an apartment-sized refrigerator too. His company is providing him with everything, so he doesn't need the stuff he brought over."

"What about a stove?"

"We do have the camp stove, but it's true, it uses too much expensive gas. I'll see what I can find. What else?"

His eye followed mine to the big nail on the back of the door and another which had been pounded into the plaster wall; on these hung all of his clothes that weren't scattered about the room.

"Maybe a cupboard or a wardrobe to store things in."

"Yes, good idea. Well," said Bob, rising, "I'd better get moving if I'm going to do everything today."

"This morning? Now? You're going now?"

"I have to. Those two boxes we shipped with us, with the blankets and the folding table and chairs, must be in the Diwaniya station. I can't leave them there more than twenty-four hours. And the next taxi should be going in about nine-thirty."

"Don't leave me alone here the first day, please Bob."

"B.J.," said Bob, "be reasonable. I have to get those boxes. And you're not alone. Mohammed is here. See what you two can do with the place. He's shy, so take it easy with him. He can go to the *suq* and buy whatever you need."

"Okay," I answered. "I'm sorry. But don't be gone too long."

"I promise you I'll be back as soon as I can, okay?"

"Okay." He kissed me and I was left alone at the table with the wind blowing through the cracks in the shutters and birds flying about the cluttered room. Then, without warning, the electricity went off and I sat in darkness.

If Mohammed had not been in the next room, I probably would have thrown myself on the rumpled cot and howled from sheer self-pity. This wasn't what the romantic, roving life should be at all, I said aloud, and drained my cup of Nescafé in the dark.

A light knock sounded at the door. Mohammed. What would I say? More important, what would he say and how would I know what to reply if I couldn't understand him in the first place?

Mohammed gulped once or twice and adjusted his agal and kaffiyeh. Looking at him, I decided he was pretty scared of me, too, and this gave me new courage. I smiled. He smiled in return and held aloft an Iraqi sterling pound note. He pointed out the door in an exaggerated fashion. "Mr. Bob," he said loudly, and pointed to the pound and to the door again and enunciated, "suq, suq."

Aha, he was going to the market; Bob had given him the pound note. "What do you want?" he asked in Arabic.

That was a greater problem. I rummaged in the suitcase until I found the Arabic-English dictionary and thumbed through it, Mohammed watching me intently, until I found the words I wanted. I went slowly—nails, rope, tomatoes, onions, potatoes, meat.

"No," interrupted Mohammed, "no meat."

"Why?"

He launched into an explanation. I shook my head. Then he made an unmistakable sound and gesture as though he were about to cut his own throat and said, "Tomorrow, not today." They don't butcher today, but tomorrow, I realized.

Feeling quite pleased with myself at this small linguistic success, I smiled again at Mohammed. He smiled too, cleared his throat and adjusted his agal and kaffiyeh.

"Eggs, sugar, salt?"

"Yes, there is," replied Mohammed.

I pushed ahead. Matches, a broom, soap—struggling with the unfamiliar words, but Mohammed was too polite to laugh at my ludicrous pronunciation. During our entire stay in El Nahra, Mohammed never laughed at us, no matter how silly some of the things we did must have seemed to him. Occasionally, if we appeared about to make a serious *faux pas*, he might mildly suggest another course of action. But afterward he would always spread his hands as if to say, "Naturally whatever you do, whether you take my advice or not, is perfectly all right." And Mohammed never, apparently, gossiped about us, although the temptation must have been great. In the first weeks after we arrived Bob noticed Mohammed in the coffee shops as the guest of many men who had never bought him tea before; perhaps people were curious about the strange Americans and believed Mohammed to be the best source of information. But we learned on good authority that Mohammed politely drank the proffered teas and coffees (why not?) but never divulged a word about what the Americans ate and what they did when they were alone at home. Mohammed was a Sayid, one of the thousands of Moslems who claim descent from the prophet Mohammed. He was also a gentleman. Although he worked for us, he did not work only for wages. We became his special responsibility; he explained to Bob that our reputation had to be protected like that of his own family.

When Mohammed had set off for the market and I was finally alone, I flicked the light switch again and again. What had happened to the electricity? Only in the evening did I discover that the current was turned off every morning at nine-thirty and switched on again at four in the afternoon. This was to save wear and tear on the generator, which was underpowered for the needs of the village. Meanwhile I was in total darkness, and when I opened the shutters it was so cold in the room that I put on my coat. In a few days I learned to wear several layers of clothes all the time and leave the shutters open so I could see.

A stroll in the garden. Yes, I would take a stroll in the garden, although the phrase from Victorian novels seemed hardly appropriate in this setting. Yet despite its present sodden state, the garden was a pleasant place. The high mud wall gave us complete privacy and the very tall date palms would provide shade against the summer sun. There were patches of grass, a small vegetable garden overgrown with weeds, an apple tree, banana trees and many other shrubs and trees I did not recognize then, lemon and bitter orange and oleander. From the slight rise in the center of the garden where the house stood, a banked mud path ran down under a large grape arbor to the edge of the wall. Near the grape arbor was a mud-brick oven. I had never seen one closely before and went over to peer into the cylindrical interior, blackened by the daily bread baking of previous inhabitants.

In the farthest corner stood the outhouse and in the opposite corner some tangled rosebushes were blooming. Here, although I stood on tiptoe, I could see nothing but the cloudy sky and the tops of the palm trees in neighboring gardens. The sheik's beautiful young wife, for whom this house had been built, had been well protected here from prying eyes, I thought, and intruders would have had an uncomfortable time getting in over the prickly camel-thorn that was arranged like barbed wire, six inches high, all around the top of the wall.

From my corner of the garden I looked back at the house, mud-colored, rectangular, flat-roofed. Its two wooden doors, one for each room, had once been painted blue, the color to ward off the Evil Eye. The shutters, banging open in the wind, had once been blue too. A crack zigzagged down the wall from one window to the ground where the plaster of mud and straw was washing away from the baked-brick sides. The roof beams, jutting out at regular intervals like square eaves, were covered with a thatch of mud and reed mats that looked quite inadequate to keep out the rain. What kept the roof from leaking? I would ask Mohammed. How would I make him understand? Never mind; I would ask Bob later.

Mohammed banged on the gate several times before entering the garden. He was laden with parcels and I went up to the house to see what he had bought. He paused at the door of the living room to take off his muddy shoes, and I looked at my own, caked with mud from the garden walk, and took them off too. Mohammed said, in careful Arabic, "That's better." He pointed to Bob's slippers, dry and clean by the bed, and I put them on. How practical, I thought, and thereafter always took off my dirty shoes at the door and slipped into clean ones.

We spent the rest of the morning trying to bring some order out of the chaos in the living room.

Mohammed asked only one favor of me the first day. Half in sign language and half in simple Arabic, repeated over and over again, he asked me please not to tell anyone he washed our dishes or he would be shamed among men for doing women's work. I said of course I would not tell anyone. He brought a copper jug of water to fill our barrel canteen, he beat the rug, and swept the floors with a tool not much bigger than a whisk broom. I indicated I wanted a reed mat for the other room. He nodded, but said it would be a week before it could be made. He strung a clothesline in the garden, hammered nails for pictures, and announced he was going home to eat lunch. Lunch— I had almost forgotten lunch.

"Will you come and eat with my mother?" asked Mohammed.

"No—no, thank you very much," I said hastily. "There is food here." I suspected Mohammed had asked me out of token politeness, and that his mother would hardly have been prepared for a guest, but even if she had, I didn't feel I wanted to face any more new situations at the moment.

Mohammed left and I bent over to rummage for a can of soup in the boxes around me. My back was to the door and I heard no footsteps, but suddenly I was aware that someone else was nearby. I turned around to find a grizzled old man in a shabby aba standing just behind me at the open door. I jumped up, knocking over my chair, and the poor old man, as startled as I was, gestured wildly toward the round tin tray on his head, which he lowered carefully to the floor. It was food—hot lunch, in fact. He seemed to be struck dumb at the sight of me, or perhaps he was dumb to begin with, for he did not utter a sound but pointed toward the door, then toward the tray and to me, and backed out of the door. I heard him hurrying down the path, apparently upset by the encounter. He was no more so than I.

In a minute or two I managed to laugh at my fright and sat down to eat the chicken and rice, mashed greens and bread which someone (Mohammed told me later it had been the women of the sheik's house) had so thoughtfully provided for me. There was more than twice as much food as I could possibly eat, so I scraped the leftovers into storage jars, washed the plates and put them back on the tray. When the old man returned, presumably for the tray, almost creeping to the door this time, he stared in astonishment at the empty plates and then at me. With a heavy sigh, he shouldered the tray and left. It was not until many days later that I learned the Arab custom of serving much more food than they expect you to eat. The leftovers go to women, children, family servants and to the poor. In my jars I had probably saved several people's lunch, including the old man's. And he—I learned from Mohammed that it was Ali, servant and gardener of the sheik—thought I had eaten it all! So the first tale that went round the settlement about the American lady was that, although she was thin, she had a fantastic appetite!

After lunch the sun came out briefly, and then it rained. Mohammed warned me that if the rain continued, Bob might not be able to return that night. The clouds in the sky seemed to be shifting, and I looked to Mohammed for confirmation.

"*Enshallah* [God willing] he will come," he said.

Mohammed pumped up the camp stove and I peeled potatoes and tomatoes. Darkness fell, the electricity came on, and Mohammed indicated he would wait for Bob near the taxi stand in town. There was nothing else to do, so I sat down in the living room and pretended to look through my Arabic-English dictionary. We had cleared away most of the boxes and litter and had moved the table to the side of the room. I had scrubbed the green oilcloth with a brush, and a colored geometric pattern was now visible in the rug, thanks to Mohammed's sweeping.

From the tree outside my shuttered window many birds called, and the few who nested in our beams answered. Will he come or not? I looked outside again. It was not raining, but the sky was overcast. Back in the room the radio emitted static, bits of Arabic music and the deadening hum.

After eight o'clock I heard rain on the roof and my heart sank. But then there were thumps and the sound of an automobile revving near the wall. I ran down the path to open the gate.

"Go back in the house and stay there," called Bob. "There are a whole lot of men to help with the stuff and you shouldn't be seen."

I did as I was told, crouching by the living-room shutter, where, through the cracks, I could see boxes and more boxes and finally the refrigerator being carried into the other room. An English-speaking voice, not Bob's, was giving orders; that must be John, the American engineer. Would we have company for dinner?

"Put on your abayah now and come out," Bob shouted, "so the men can put the wardrobe into the living room."

Again I did as I was told, slipping on my muddy shoes as I went out the door. With much grunting, the men edged the big wardrobe through the narrow door. Bob paid them off and they left.

John said he would be delighted to stay for dinner. Originally from Cincinnati, he was on an exploratory water-drilling trip for an American firm under contract to the Iraqi Government. It was his first job since graduation from engineering school.

"A small contribution," he said and produced a bottle of beer, which we split three ways and drank while we looked over the loot. The refrigerator was small, but

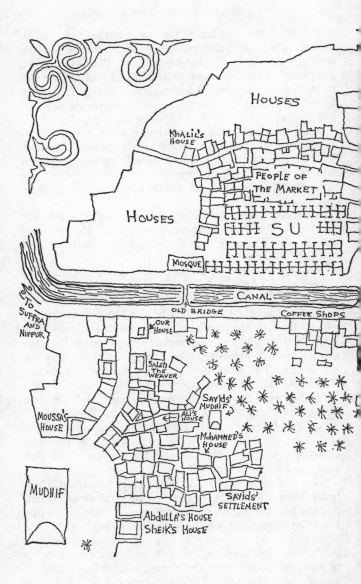

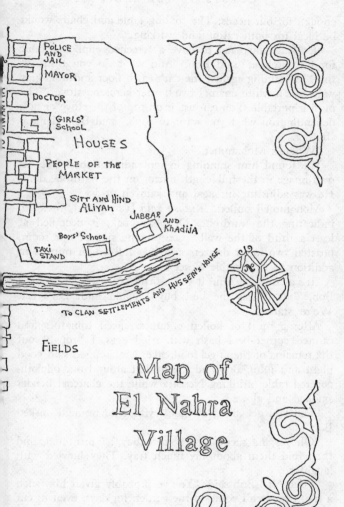

POLICE AND JAIL

MAYOR

DOCTOR

GIRLS' School

HOUSES

PEOPLE OF THE MARKET

SITT AND HIND ALIYAH

JABBAR AND KHADIJA

Boys' School

TAXI STAND

TO CLAN SETTLEMENTS AND HUSSEIN'S HOUSE

FIELDS

Map of
El Nahra
Village

enough for our needs. The folding table and chairs would be ideal for both eating and working.

"I asked Abu Saad to have a screened cupboard built for the kitchen," said Bob. "And what do you think of that?" Gleaming against the dark earth floor and mud-gray walls was a white enamel two-burner kerosene stove. "The oven is portable. You can use it on top of the stove or not, depending on what you want to cook," said Bob, demonstrating.

"Where's Mohammed?"

We found him standing in rapt admiration before his own image in the full-length mirror on the wardrobe door. He was adjusting his agal and kaffiyeh.

Mohammed smiled. "*Kullish zein* [very good]," he said, indicating the wardrobe. Of heavy oak, it occupied at least a third of the wall space on one side of our room, boasted two lower drawers and two full-length mirrors in addition to the double closet space.

"It's awfully big, and it was a little expensive," confessed Bob, "but it was the best buy I could find. Let's eat. We're starved."

After a meal of boiled potatoes, sliced tomatoes and canned corned-beef hash with fried eggs, I brought out the remains of the angel-food cake. Mohammed said good night and John, Bob and I were left around our oilcloth-covered table, drinking Nescafé while the charcoal brazier smoked and glowed.

"Did you get along all right with Mohammed?" asked Bob.

"Oh yes, he seems a very nice boy," I answered, and then told them about my lunch tray. They howled with laughter.

"Poor Ali," Bob said. "You've probably given him such a fright he won't come to the garden for days, even to cut grass for his sheep."

John stood up. "I'd better go," he said. "It'll take me at least an hour to get back to Diwaniya on that damned mud road. But thanks for dinner. I can't remember when I've had angel-food cake."

"Thank you for all your help," we answered, practically in unison. "Come see us any time."

He nodded and looked around him, at the beamed ceiling, the worn but bright rug, the outsized elegant wardrobe. "You know, I didn't believe it when Bob told me," he confided. "Mud hut, earth floors and all that jazz. But you've really got quite a nice little place here."

Bob saw him to the gate and I collected the empty coffee cups and carried them into the kitchen. The rain had stopped and a cold wind had come up, clearing the sky so that a few stars were visible. Shivering, I stepped back into the living room, which was still warm from the dying charcoal fire. Well, I thought, I suppose we could build a bookcase of boards and bricks and cover up the sofa and chairs with something. The mattress really does make the bed bigger. It won't be bad, I decided, and realized to my surprise that I was actually looking forward to fixing up our first home.

2

The Sheik's Harem

An invitation to lunch with the sheik was delivered early next morning. This meant that Bob would eat with the men in the sheik's *mudhif* or guest house and I would lunch in the *harem,* or women's quarters. The harem. What would it be like? What would the women be wearing? What should I wear?

"Something attractive," said Bob promptly.

I stared at him.

"And try to be natural," he counseled.

"Well, I wasn't exactly planning to be unnatural," I retorted.

He had not even heard me. "And keep your eyes open and try to remember everything you do and see."

"Yes, dear."

"You might write everything down as soon as you get home if I'm not here."

"Really, Bob, stop fussing so. I'm nervous enough as it is."

"I'm not fussing," he said, and then he looked at me. "Well," he explained, "I've been here for two months and the sheik's family, which is the word they use to refer to the womenfolk, hasn't even been mentioned in my presence. So I can't help but wonder about them. And it's a rather important occasion for you, too—your debut into local society."

Mohammed came with a jug of water and announced that Ali had been commissioned to fetch us.

"Hmmmm," said Bob. "It's just up the road, but of course we walk right through the center of the settlement from our house to the sheik's mudhif. Sheik Hamid is probably sending Ali to make sure the children don't bother you."

"Bother me? Even in the abayah?"

"Well, you've been here two days without anyone's having a look at you except Mohammed and Ali. If you're curious about the sheik's women, think how curious they must be about you!"

By the time Ali came for us, I couldn't decide whether I felt like a debutante being presented at court or Joan of Arc going to the stake. And since it had been dark when I arrived, I really had no idea of what lay beyond our gate. The sun was shining and the mud on our path was drying fast. As Ali opened the latch a group of small boys in dishdashas jumped away from the gate and stared and giggled until Ali shouted and flourished his stick at them, whereupon they ran ahead, turning back at every other step to look at us again.

"Ali says he is sorry for the boys' rudeness," Bob said. "Actually, the women probably sent them out as scouts and they're running back to the harem to tell them you're on the way."

No one else seemed to be on the mud-rutted road, however, which was bare of trees or greenery of any sort and was lined on both sides with mud houses set close together. Only high walls and blind fronts of mud brick faced the street; I was to learn later that the doors were usually on the side or in back, to allow the family more privacy in their comings and goings. All the walls, like mine, were topped with several inches of prickly camelthorn.

"Why isn't anyone else out?" I whispered to Bob, and, as if in answer, a woman emerged suddenly from one of the alleys between the houses, balancing on her head a tray of what looked like round gray pancakes. Seeing us, she uttered an exclamation and pulled her abayah over her face.

"Why did she do that?" I asked. "Does she think I have the Evil Eye or something?"

"Oh, no," said Bob. "The women always seem to cover their faces quickly when caught unawares by strange men. She's carrying camel dung," he added matter-of-factly.

"Camel dung?"

"They make it into cakes like that and dry it in the sun for fuel," he explained.

And when I looked back, that was what the woman was doing, arranging the dung cakes in geometric regularity on the sunny side of the road.

"Just keep walking," said Bob.

"But this empty street is kind of eerie," I answered. I simply could not resist looking around once more. As I did, a kind of whispered laugh or exclamation went up and down the street, where women in black abayahs stood by the walls or peered out of the doors of nearly all the houses, looking after me.

"The women are all standing at their doors, staring," I said to Bob.

"Never mind, it's not much farther. Look, there's the sheik's mudhif!"

Ahead was a clearing, at the edge of which earth had been built up to form a large square platform. On this stood the sheik's guest house or mudhif, framed by a grove of date palms, green and lustrous in the dun-colored landscape. I had not expected the guest house to be so big. The tribesmen near the entrance were dwarfed by the thirty-foot arch of the mudhif, which looked like an enormous quonset hut open at both ends. Great bundles of swamp reeds, arched over and anchored in the ground, formed the ribs of the structure which stretched at least 150 feet back toward the palm grove. Only in the entrance arch was the bunching visible for overlapping reed mats covered the sides and roof. We heard afterward from archaeologist friends that the plan and structure of the mudhif have origins in antiquity and that some of the earliest Sumerian temples may have been of just this shape.

Flying from the capstone of the entrance arch was a white flag with a crescent and star appliquéd upon it in red.

"I think that may be the tribal flag, or perhaps the sheik's personal flag," whispered Bob.

A few horses were tethered near the mudhif and more men, in aba and agal and kaffiyeh, were gathering in the clearing. As we approached, a tall man disengaged himself from one of the groups and came toward us. Bob turned off to meet him. "Good luck," he whispered, and I was left alone to follow Ali, who bore left, away from the mudhif, toward a large square mud-brick building which I had not noticed before.

This must be the harem, I told myself; it was here that all of the sheik's family lived, though Bob had said that in the past it had been used as a fortress in tribal wars and later against Ottoman and finally British soldiers. The gun emplacements could still be seen on the roof and the thick mud-brick walls were honey-combed with holes just large enough to accommodate a rifle barrel.

Ali led me all the way around the fortress to a narrow opening and motioned me through. I was standing alone in a large open courtyard, the hard-packed earth of which had been carefully swept just that morning, for I could see the marks of the broom in wide swathing arcs on the ground. The only visible object was a central water tap with a small brick wall around its base. To my right, to my left, and in front of me stood low, square houses built out into the courtyard from the shelter of the compound's high mud-brick walls. These, I was to discover later, were the apartments where each of the sheik's wives lived separately with her children. Through the entry-ways of these flat-roofed apartments, arched and plastered with mud, I could see daylight in other, small inner courts.

Where was everyone? The entire compound seemed empty. I turned back, but Ali was gone and I faced the courtyard alone, where now, from doors all around the court, women and children began to emerge. Little girls in long-sleeved print dresses and boys in candy-striped dishdashas ran and leaped toward me, then ran away giggling only to turn in a wider circle and come forward once more. The women—it seemed like hundreds of them—advanced more slowly, in their flowing black abayahs, their heads coifed and bound in black, all smiling and repeating, "*Ahlan wusahlan* [welcome]. *Ahlan, ahlan. Ahlan wusahlan.*" Most of them came at a dignified pace, but the younger women could not contain their excitement, it seemed, for they would caper a bit, look at each other, choke with laughter and then cover their faces with their abayahs as the woman with the dung cakes had done. I stood still, not certain whether I should advance, until an old woman came close and put a motherly hand on my shoulder. She looked into my face and smiled broadly, which warmed her deeply wrinkled face with a kind and friendly expression despite the fact that many of her front teeth were missing. She had three blue dots, tattoo marks, in the cleft of her sun-tanned chin. She nodded and, still with her hand on my shoulder, steered me across the court.

We went in procession, the women closing ranks around me, the children still jumping and leaping on the outskirts of the group, past the water tap, to a shorter mud wall. Here, at an open doorway, a lovely, quite fleshy young woman awaited us; she was a startling contrast to the women about me, for she wore no abayah, only a dress of sky-blue satin patterned with crescents and stars. She had tied a black fringed scarf around her head like a cap, leaving her long black curly hair free to fall loosely around her shoulders.

"*Ahlan wusahlan*," she said and shook hands with me, laughing in a pleased way, to show perfect teeth. Her dark eyes were outlined heavily with kohl.

"Selma, Selma," called the children, "let us come in too."

"Away with you," she said good-naturedly, but made no attempt to back up her words as she led the way, through her small inner court, to a screen door where I was ushered into what seemed to be a big bedroom.

"Go on. Out! Out!" she said to the children, but they crowded in anyway after the women. There was only one chair in the room and Selma motioned me to it. I sat down and found myself face to face with a roomful of women and children, squatting opposite me on the mat-covered floor and staring up at me intently.

Selma had taken my abayah and hung it on a peg near the door. "You won't need it here," she said, pointing to herself, although she was the only woman there without it. She sat down at my feet. I felt uncomfortable sitting in a chair while everyone else sat on the floor, so I got up and sat down on the floor with them.

Selma looked upset and leaped to her feet.

"No, no, the chair is for you," she said and took my hand to pull me back up. "You are the guest."

I sat down in the overstuffed chair once more.

There was a brief pause.

"*Ahlan wusahlan,*" said Selma in the silence.

"*Ahlan, ahlan wusahlan,*" chorused the roomful of women.

I cleared my throat. "You are Selma?"

"Yes," she said, laughing again in that pleased and very attractive way. "How did you know?"

"Everyone knows because you are the favorite wife of the sheik," replied an admiring young girl, and tweaked at Selma's blue satin skirt. She was a bit embarrassed, but pleasantly so, and swiped mildly at the girl, who ducked successfully and then giggled.

"And what is your name?" Selma asked me politely.

"Elizabeth."

"Alith-a-bess," she stumbled over the unfamiliar combination of syllables, and several others tried out the word and failed.

Selma laughed. "That is a difficult name. We can't say it."

"I have another name," I offered, knowing that diminutive names were often used here. "It's B.J."

She picked that up as "Beeja." "She is called Beeja," she said, and so I was named.

I asked the name of the girl sitting closest to me.

"Basima," she answered and pointed to her neighbor. "Fadhila. Hathaya. Fatima. Rajat. Samira. Nejla. Sabiha. Bassoul. Sahura. Sheddir. Laila. Bahiga." How would I ever remember who they were? They looked that day so remarkably alike in their identical black head scarves, black chin scarves, and black abayahs. It was months later that I began to notice the subtle differences that the women managed to introduce into the costume: Fadhila always wore a fringed scarf, Laila's abayahs were edged with black satin braid; Samira's chin scarf was fastened on top of her head with a tiny gold pin in the shape of a lotus blossom.

But the dominant presence in the room, watched by

every eye including mine, was the dazzling Selma, of ample but well-defined proportions, her air of authority softened by laughter. Mohammed had told me that Selma had five children. From her face, I guessed she could not yet be thirty, but childbearing had already blurred the lines of what once must have been a remarkable and voluptuous figure. The blue satin dress was cut Western style, but longer and looser; it moved in several directions when she moved, for Selma apparently felt that corsets were unnecessary. Her feet were bare (she had left her clogs at the door), but each slim, bare ankle bore a heavy gold bracelet. Gold bracelets were on both arms, several heavy gold necklaces swung against the blue satin dress, and long dangling gold filigree earrings caught the light when she moved. In her gold jewelry and blue satin and black silk head scarf, her eyes gay and almost black in her white face (whiter than that of any other woman in the room), she was attractive by anyone's standard and must once have been startlingly beautiful. I felt quite dowdy in my skirt and sweater and short-cut hair, and was only glad I had put on fake pearls and gold earrings.

Selma offered me a long thin cigarette, which I refused; she pressed me again, but I said I did not smoke.

"It is better not to smoke," said the old woman who had guided me to Selma's door. "Haji Hamid does not like women who smoke."

Selma looked at the old woman. "Kulthum," she said, "Haji Hamid is my husband as well as yours," and then deliberately lit cigarettes for herself and several others. In a few minutes the room was full of sweetish smoke, unlike any cigarette smoke I had smelled before. Kulthum said nothing, but I noticed she did not smoke.

I looked around me at the scrupulously clean room. Its mud-brick walls were newly whitewashed. I pointed upward, trying to indicate that the beams here were the same as the ones in my house. This was a fairly complex idea to get across, for at first the women thought I had seen something lodged in the beams and everyone peered and whispered. One woman stood up to get a better look. When they finally realized what I was struggling to communicate, they laughed, no doubt at the simple-mindedness of the conversational tidbit I had contributed. Later I found that every house in the village was built in exactly the same manner, so obviously my house had beams like this one!

"Haji Hamid's bed, the sheik's," said a girl, pointing to the large double bed.

"And Selma's," said one of the girls, snickering. She showed me in mime how they lay together in a close embrace. Everyone laughed and Selma blushed with pleasure. I glanced at Kulthum, but her wrinkled face showed nothing.

The intricate ironwork of the high-posted bedstead had been gilded, suggesting an opulence which was reinforced by the bright pink satin spread falling in flounces to the floor. The same pink satin had been used to cover a small radio on the night table. Over the bed hung an oil painting of a mosque; above that was a large faded photograph of Emir Feisal, father of the Iraqi dynasty, on horseback. A pair of large crossed Iraqi flags topped the king.

Selma noticed me looking about and got up to identify the many photographs and pictures which covered the walls. The man with the strong bearded face was Abdul Emir, Hamid's father. I had heard of Abdul Emir, for he was a famous warrior in Iraq who had led the 1933 insurrection of the Diwaniya tribes against the British-backed Iraqi Government. The rebellion had been so nearly successful that the British had been obliged to cut the area's water supply in order to put the tribesmen down. According to Bob, people in Diwaniya still spoke of this event, and it was whispered that the government continued to punish the tribal confederation by refusing to pave roads and by delaying electricity and other modern services as long as possible.

In another photograph Abdul Emir sat in a chair in a garden, flanked by nurses and surrounded by well-dressed tribesmen. He looked thin and ill, but he sat rigidly forward, gripping his knees with long, bony hands. The men in the picture were leaders of the tribes united in the confederation led by Abdul Emir, Selma told me, reading aloud their names from the caption and thus demonstrating her education, for—although I did not realize it then—she was the only woman in the room who could read fluently. Selma added that Abdul Emir had died soon after the picture was taken, and Hamid had succeeded to the sheikship. Four portraits of Hamid, taken at various periods in his life, attested to his present eminence.

Selma now began to rummage in a wardrobe, the only other large piece of furniture in the room. There were two chests with padlocks and, against the far wall, mats, blankets, rugs and long narrow pillows were piled nearly to the ceiling.

"For the mudhif," said Kulthum, following my eye. "Many tribesmen stay at the mudhif when they come to market, and many strangers stop here too."

Tradition decrees, Bob had said, that any guest may expect food and a bed for three days without any questions asked. Since these tribal guest houses are the only hotels on the bare southern plain, two or three guests an evening was usual. But from the pile of bedding it looked as though Sheik Hamid could easily sleep thirty or forty people.

Selma, who had gone out, returned now with a tiny cup of coffee which she presented to me on a green cutglass plate. I sipped it slowly and set it down on the plate. Selma took it from me and handed it out the door to a waiting servant.

After the coffee, conversation lagged. A baby began to cry, a thin baby with horrid-looking red sores on its face and neck, and the mother pushed aside her *foota,* or chin scarf, pulled out her breast and gave it to the child. The women regarded me fixedly. I smiled. They smiled. A very small girl with tousled hair and tiny gold earrings got up and touched my skirt, then buried her head in her hands in confusion. The women laughed. I laughed.

For some reason this set off a convulsion among the children, who all along had been fidgeting but subsiding at slaps from the nearest woman. But now they were stirred to greater pummeling and quarreling—so much so that Selma rose, took a stick and set about them in earnest.

"Out, out, out!" she cried, and several ran out with mock screams and yelps of pain.

"They are so difficult, children," said Selma, and sat down near me again.

She offered me another cigarette and I declined. When was lunch, I wondered? I had been in the room more than an hour and simply could not think of another thing to say, even if I had been able to remember any more Arabic. I crossed my ankles; a dozen pair of eyes followed the movement. I uncrossed my ankles; there was a short silence. My hostess flung herself into the breach and asked me how much my nylon stockings had cost, whether my skirt was ready-made and if my earrings had come from my family or were a present from my husband. I unscrewed them and handed them around; one of the women scratched to see if the gold would come off. All of these questions took time and had to be repeated again and again so I could understand. When my faltering replies came out in Arabic the women could not help laughing, but, out of politeness, they did so behind their abayahs.

I asked Selma how much her ankle bracelets cost.

"Forty pounds," she said proudly, "for one," and pulled out the pin so that it could be taken off and examined. It must have weighed at least half a pound. "All gold," she added.

The women began pointing out her individual necklaces and bracelets, telling me the cost and the Arabic name of each. Later I estimated that Selma wore on her person at least $1000 worth of gold. She said that the pieces of jewelry had been presents from her father and from the sheik, and repeated, "It's mine, my own."

This was literally true, I found. A woman's jewelry is her own insurance against disaster, and the community may take action against men who attempt to seize their women's gold.

At the door a great commotion was under way, as a maidservant tried to break through the crowd, stepping over women and children to bring me a copper basin and ewer, soap and a towel. She indicated that no, I was not to put my hands in the basin, she was to pour the water *over* my hands. Slight giggles at my clumsiness were silenced by a look from a tall girl with many gold teeth, who introduced herself as Alwiyah, the sheik's oldest daughter.

After I had finished washing, Selma rose with Alwiyah and handed me my abayah.

"It is time for lunch, *ahlan wusahlan*," she said.

In my abayah I followed Alwiyah and Selma across her little private courtyard to another larger room where a table, covered with a white cloth, was laden with plates of food.

Selma shut the door ostentatiously but the children and women clustered around the windows to watch. One chair was drawn up to the table. "Am I to eat alone?"

Selma and Alwiyah nodded and smiled.

"Oh, no," I protested, "this is too much—you must eat with me."

Selma and Alwiyah exchanged startled glances, whispered together and then Selma called for two more chairs. She sat down opposite me and Alwiyah sat at the side. Selma shook with inner laughter, and the crowd at the windows roared, for what reason I could not fathom. When, afterward, I had sat on a mat to eat and felt foolish myself, I realized why the women had found Selma's and Alwiyah's first venture at table amusing. Traditionally, to eat alone, served by one's host, is an honor, but Selma, sensing my discomfort, was doing things my way. She nibbled a bit of meat, taking a spoonful of this and that, enjoying herself and the audience reaction hugely. Alwiyah did not; she smiled regularly and made polite remarks, but was apparently too bound by custom to eat a mouthful.

The table was covered with ten or twelve different dishes: kebab and grilled kidneys; a salad of hard-boiled eggs, potatoes and beets; half a chicken in tomato sauce; mashed greens; two kinds of rice, one topped with a crisp crust, one mixed with nuts and raisins, chopped carrots and bits of chicken liver. There was a pitcher of watered yogurt to drink, and for dessert I was offered a soup plate of heavy white cornstarch pudding with an odd, but not unappetizing, flavor. "It is rose water," said Alwiyah.

Every time I paused, Alwiyah would urge me to eat more, but I finally laid down my spoon.

"You have eaten nothing," scolded Alwiyah, and Selma put another kidney on my plate. But I was determined, and in spite of haranguing from the women (a matter of form, I discovered later) I stood up and we returned to the bedroom where the servant brought the washbasin and ewer again.

The crowd had already gathered for the second round, and the air seemed more relaxed now as I successfully finished washing. We were just beginning to nod and smile at each other again when the sound of a man's voice outside sent the women and children scurrying away like a flock of frightened chickens. I was left alone in the room with Selma, who hurriedly donned her abayah and ran out the door, leaving me alone in the room.

I had no idea what was going on, or what was expected of me. Should I, too, don my abayah? Should I leave? Should I get under the bed? Before I had time to rise, Selma was back, rummaging in the cupboard for a heavy rifle and a full cartridge belt, which she handed out the door. The man's voice said something else, and she returned to me.

"The sheik and your husband are going partridge hunting," she said. "Do you want to go home now or stay until they come back? Do stay," she added.

I wasn't sure what arrangements were involved, but staying seemed the easiest course of action. The man's footsteps died away and in a moment the women and children trooped back in and Selma took off her abayah once more.

"*Ahlan, ahlan wusahlan,*" they repeated.

The silence was broken by the arrival of the servant with a tray of tea glasses. Selma served me herself, and then offered tea to Kulthum and to Bahiga, the other wives of the sheik. Both were much older than Selma: Bahiga light-skinned with big wide-open gray eyes, her face beginning to show wrinkles, Kulthum wrinkled and old enough to be Selma's mother.

"Where is your mother?" Kulthum asked. I told her she

was in America far away, and when Selma repeated this in a better accent, the women clucked in sympathy.

"Poor girl," they said. "Poor child."

To be alone without any of one's womenfolk was clearly the greatest disaster which could befall any girl. I rummaged in my wallet . . . unfortunately no picture of my mother, but I came on one of Bob and handed it to Kulthum. She seized on it and passed it around to the other women, who examined the picture from every angle and finally pronounced him *hilu* [handsome].

"But why didn't he let your mother come with you?" persisted Kulthum. I was at a loss to explain, but Selma interrupted with another question.

"Do you have any children inside you—here?" she pointed to her stomach.

"No."

"No?"

I said I had only been married for six months.

"*Enshallah*, you will have one soon," said Kulthum, and patted my hand. "Children are gifts of Allah. I have five sons and two daughters, thanks be to God."

"How many do you have?" I asked the other wife, Bahiga.

"Five living," she said. "Two died."

"Selma?"

"Two sons, three daughters," she replied.

"When you have children, you will not feel so alone without your mother," prophesied Kulthum.

The room was small and getting progressively more stuffy and smoke-filled by the moment, for the population, although it changed regularly, never numbered under twenty. Women were coming and going all the time. A few would get up and leave, those remaining would shift position and more would come in, greet me, and sit down. I had the feeling that runners had been all around the settlement, and women were coming from every house to look me over. I was suddenly overcome with weariness and my face felt hot. Selma looked tired too, but the women sat on, smoking, nodding, and murmuring, "*Nitwannes* [we are here to enjoy ourselves]." I looked at my watch;

it was after six but I knew I could not leave until the men came home.

I cleared my throat and told Selma the browned rice at lunch had been very good. How had she prepared it?

Selma looked pleased and began to explain.

"Eat more rice, Beeja," advised Kulthum. "You are too thin."

"Yes, yes," cackled an old woman, "does she have any breasts at all?" grabbing her own dropped bosom and then pointing at me. There was a loud burst of laughter.

"I certainly do have breasts," I began indignantly, but Selma, always the polite hostess, was ahead of me.

"It is pretty to be thin," she said.

"No, no, Selma! It is better to be fat."

"You are very pretty."

Selma stood up unexpectedly, took in both hands the loose roll of flesh around her waist and said, "You call this hilu [attractive]? No. I eat too much rice."

She looked to me for confirmation or denial. I was torn; what should I say—no, Selma, you are pretty, ergo I am ugly and thin and have no breasts, or yes, I agree you are too fat and you should go on a diet immediately? Fortunately the women intervened before I even had time to form my sentence in Arabic.

"No, no, Selma, you are pretty," they said, and one added, "without all that rice you wouldn't have such fine breasts and such a good big behind," illustrating her meaning quite graphically. Selma tossed her head and laughed and sat down again.

"That," shouted another, "is why Haji Hamid loves you more than Kulthum and Bahiga."

I looked around quickly, but Kulthum and Bahiga had gone. The conversation seemed about to take an interesting turn when the servant girl banged on the screen, hissed something to Selma I did not catch, grinned at me and wiped her face with her dusty black veil, all at the same time.

Selma rose. I'm sure she too was relieved. "The men are here and your husband wants you," she said. "The servant will go with you, because it is getting dark."

I donned my abayah, trying to wrap it around me as the women did, but not succeeding very well. Selma said kindly:

"Soon you will know how to wear the abayah."

"Don't they wear the abayah in America?" asked a woman in surprise.

"No, no," said Selma.

"Why not?" she said to me.

Again I could think of no reply but Selma was saying something to the woman.

"Then why does she wear it here?" persisted the woman.

"Because she is polite," said Selma, and nudged me gently toward the door. The group followed, repeating the traditional farewells, "*Ahlan wusahlan*," "*Tiji daayman* [come often]," "*Allah wiyach* [God go with you]." Selma bade me good night at the door of her own courtyard, but the other women and children walked to the entrance of the compound, where Ali waited to accompany me home.

In the mudhif, lanterns had been lighted, and the tribesmen going in and out were silhouetted in the shadowy arch. Stars were coming out in the vast sky above the mud houses and walls. Women passed us, silently padding down the path, bearing jugs and cans to fetch the nightly supply of water from the canal. I could see no faces, but several spoke to me. Ali and I stood aside while a flock of sheep, baaing and snuffling, shuffled along past, raising a fine cloud of dust into the evening air as the boy shepherded them home.

Bob was waiting at our gate.

"How did it go?" he said.

"Fine, I think," I answered. "I was obviously the biggest curiosity to hit the compound in years, but they were nice about it. But I'm really tired out."

"Come tell me everything that happened," he said, and we walked up to our house together. It seemed very cozy and calm and peaceful after the hubbub and strain of the afternoon.

When I mentioned Selma's eating with me, he said that was a very good sign.

"Twenty years ago," he said, "a Shiite Moslem here would not eat food which had been touched by Christians, and any dish from which a Christian guest had eaten or drunk was smashed so that the infidel wouldn't contaminate the faithful."

Although he knew this was no longer true among most of the men, he had feared the women might still feel this way, since they were relatively more isolated.

"Selma was very friendly, and a good hostess. She's been to school, you know."

"No, I didn't. What is she like?"

"Selma?" I considered. "She seems very good-natured; runs the compound, I'd say; laughs a lot; is intelligent."

"Yes, but what does she *look* like?"

"She's beautiful," I replied promptly, "running to fat, but still beautiful."

"I thought so," Bob said.

I looked at him. He had never seen Selma but assumed she was beautiful. Because he had heard stories about her beauty? That was unlikely, since men did not discuss women in public. Because her inaccessibility had surrounded her with mystery? Then the abayah and the seclusion were an asset to Selma, for they only increased her attractiveness. And they did not seem to hinder her much in her private life either, for she had seemed to me a happy and contented woman.

But I was still curious.

"Why did you assume she was beautiful, Bob?"

"Well, I hear that the sheik gave her family 1500 English pounds when he married her, and she is his fourth wife. Wouldn't you assume from that that she was pretty special?"

"Yes, Bob, of course." I couldn't help laughing at his male naïveté.

"Why are you laughing?"

"Oh, nothing," I said. "Let's have some more coffee before we go to bed."

3

Women of the Tribe

In a day or two Bob resumed his interviews and suggested I might start visiting the women regularly and begin to keep a journal. To help him complete his picture of tribal and village life, I was to record observations about women and children and activities within the home, areas which he had no opportunity to study.

"Just go," he said. "The sheik has told me several times that you will be welcome in any house in the settlement."

"No one has come to visit me," I pointed out.

"Never mind; it may not be the custom here," said Bob. "You make the first move."

I was too shy simply to knock on every door along the path, but fortunately during the first days my reluctance did not matter. Mohammed invited me to call on his mother, and in his house I met many of the Sayids, six families who were not members of the El Eshadda, but who lived with the tribe in a sort of *noblesse oblige* relationship. Because of their descent from the Prophet, the Sayids are bound to be treated with some respect, and are used as mediators in tribal disputes. In return for their services as peacemakers, the Sayids receive the protection of the tribe, and they had been given parcels of land when they first came to settle with the El Eshadda. The ancient practice of giving other special privileges to Sayids—plowing their land free, grinding their grain without payment —was less observed now than before. But the Sayids still received alms on religious festivals, and Laila, the local seamstress, later told me she always sewed without charge for Mohammed's sister.

The Sayids had their own small mudhif on the edge of the settlement, around which their houses clustered wall to wall. The first time I visited Mohammed's family, he called for me after supper, carrying a kerosene lantern to light the way. We turned off the main road into a dark and narrow alley which wound among the low mud houses, each marked by one or two lanterns hung inside the walls. Electricity was expensive, and only the sheik and his brothers could afford it. At the end of the alley the Sayids' mudhif loomed, also lit by lantern light, and, framed within its shadowy vault, a few men sat cross-legged, smoking and playing backgammon. The slap of the wooden pieces on the game board came to us distinctly over the sound of their voices.

Ahead, in a doorway, stood the figures of two women, tall, straight and thin like Mohammed—his mother Medina and his sister Sherifa. Medina held a second lantern high. "Ahlan wusahlan," she said, and we crossed their dark court, where I could hear the cow munching in the corner, into a tiny room, swept clean and almost empty. I sat on a mat covered with a rug and a white sheet. Sherifa insisted that I make myself comfortable with a long pillow also covered with clean white linen. She then brought in a charcoal brazier and we sat around it, warming our hands against the cold.

They served me fruit on that first occasion, which I knew was a great extravagance for them, but afterward when I went to visit I was offered, like all their other guests, a glass of lemon tea made by brewing the skin and seeds of dried lemons (numibasra). Medina made it especially well.

I spent many such evenings in Mohammed's house, where I was treated almost as a relative, and where the atmosphere was relaxed and the conversation gay. The family, once well-to-do and highly respected in the community, had retained a general air of taste and dignity in spite of misfortune. They still owned 200 acres of land, but because of soil salination, a mounting problem in the area, less than twenty acres could be cultivated. Their present poverty-stricken state was mitigated by Mohammed's job with us. They were "gentility in straitened circumstances" but they were cheerful about it, and that made all the difference.

When the family land had first begun to salt up, Medina's husband had left El Nahra to find work. He had not found it, but in Kut he had found a rich sheik whose personal charity was the support of Sayids, so he had settled there, and only visited El Nahra when he was sick or needed help. Medina made the best of it. She was only forty-five, but she looked seventy, so thin that every bone in her hand was visible. Her skin was seamed and wrinkled by years of work in the hot, drying sun, her mouth shriveled into empty gums. Her black garments had been new many years ago, but she wore them as though they had been bought yesterday; she still hennaed her fingernails and outlined her eyebrows with dull blue kohl. When she was feeling poorly, which was often, she lay on a mat and her voice became the dry, cracked whine of an old, old woman. But when she felt well she sailed down the alley like a queen, her black garments flowing behind her. In the afternoon sessions in the sheik's house she was always treated with courtesy and respect. She talked animatedly and smoked, one after the other, the cigarettes offered by Selma—she was too poor to buy them herself. The women listened to her attentively and laughed at her jokes; she had a way of gesturing with a cigarette and tossing her head back as she talked—she had style. I never met anyone who disliked her. Women would bring her food from their own limited stores and visit her in droves when she was too sick to get up from her pallet.

Sherifa carried herself like her mother, with a dignity not always seen among the poorer people in the settlement. I was told that when Sherifa had been younger, she had been very handsome, and her husband had bought her much gold jewelry. But the man went bad, no one could explain why; he had deserted Sherifa after her baby boy died; she was now neither widow, virgin, nor divorcee, and hence had no future. Yet she was intelligent and industrious and her advice was much sought after by other women and girls. She kept chickens and sold eggs; she raised lambs in the spring and sold the meat and wool. She helped keep the family alive.

The younger brother, Abad, was twelve, ambitious and

clever. He was in the sixth class at the local primary school, and at night he sat on the path under a street lamp to study his lessons, for the two lanterns in his house were not strong enough to read by.

There was an older brother, Abdul Karim, who seemed to have been born without energy. Theoretically he was a sheep trader, but few people had seen him at work. His wife, Fadhila, was vigorous and attractive, with strong arms and bright eyes; she laughed from deep inside, a loud, healthy laugh which infected even the dourest old ladies. Her greatest sorrow was that she had no children. According to local beliefs, it was always the wife who was at fault in these matters. In a society where childlessness is grounds for divorce, Fadhila, despite her health and energy, was judged inadequate as a woman and as a wife.

Fadhila and Abdul Karim lived in their own room, across the court from that of Mohammed, Medina, Sherifa and Abad. Each household was economically separate, but Fadhila and Sherifa shared the chores, bringing cans of water from the canal several times a day, sweeping the court, feeding the cow, the lamb and the chickens, baking the barley bread and doing the cooking, the dishes, the laundry. Fadhila preferred the dishes and the laundry because it gave her an opportunity both morning and evening to exchange gossip with the other women of the village who squatted along the canal, scouring their pots with the gritty silt of the bank and scrubbing their families' clothes in the muddy irrigation water.

Down the alley lived the sheik's gardener and servant, my guide, Ali, with his wife, Sheddir, and their grown son and daughter. Their house was even more modest than Mohammed's. A small court where Sheddir cooked on a Primus stove, a lean-to for the cow and chickens, an oven for bread, and one tiny rectangular room where the entire family slept on mats on the floor because they could not afford a bed. One wooden chest, its blue paint peeling, contained their few possessions. A lantern hung on a nail, and on the mud-and-straw walls of their room pictures had been pasted or tacked—pictures cut from magazines of

Mohammed the Prophet, of a traditional Arab beauty in abayah and fringed head scarf.

Ali's salary as the sheik's gardener and servant was minute; most of what he earned was in kind. He had access to the garden to cut grass for his cow, and he always received a small share of the sheik's grapes which he could trade in the market for barley flour or rice. Ali was saving money to help his son get married. Since Ali was a poor man, only twenty pounds was needed for the bride price, the sum set by custom within the tribe and paid by the groom's father to the bride's father. The bride's father uses part of the money to help his daughter buy furniture, household goods and her trousseau. But twenty pounds was half of Ali's annual income. How, then, to hurry up the procedure? Ali's daughter was of marriageable age, too, and since paternal first-cousin marriage was the preferred marriage in any case, Ali was negotiating with one of his brothers who also had a boy and a girl. If the fathers could simply exchange children, two marriages would be made for the price of one and the family line would be assured of continuance. A fair exchange. This was the kind of strategic arrangement which many poor *fellahin* families strove for. Otherwise a man might wait ten years to get married, for it took at least that long to save the required amount.

Sheddir, Ali's wife, while cutting grass in the garden one morning, invited me to visit her, and I did, twice. After that I did not feel as free to do so, for each time I came they spent an embarrassing amount on delicacies, fruit, coffee, sweet biscuits. I knew that wherever I went in the settlement, except perhaps for the houses of the sheik and his brothers, my arrival was bound to put a strain on the family's finances. Their traditional sense of hospitality always struggled with their slim budgets, and usually hospitality won. I would protest vigorously when this happened, but it did no good, for I was only following the accustomed pattern: a guest always protested at the honors done him to show his host how much he appreciated them. So I made excuses to Sheddir and asked her to visit me instead.

Occasionally, when I passed the house of our next-door neighbors, a family of weavers and dyers, the gate would be ajar and I could see bright yarns and rugs displayed in the court. I had been debating whether or not I might call on the weavers unannounced when one morning Bob came to tell me to drop everything and come at once. Saleh, the weaver, had been in the mudhif that morning. Bob had expressed interest in his loom and Saleh had promptly invited him over, adding that I would be welcome to come and sit with his family.

Since Bob was with me and the men of the family would be around, I fully expected to be ushered into an inside room and served tea behind a closed door while the men disported themselves in the court. But when the gate was opened, the women in their abayahs were sitting in full view at one end of the court; they beckoned to me. That was one of the few occasions when Bob and I visited within sight of each other, although we did not speak. The men sat in another corner, far from us, and the women covered their faces with their abayahs whenever Bob passed near them. Still, the weaving paraphernalia was spread all over the court, and there was a good deal of covert peeping through the abayahs as Bob and Saleh walked around, looking carefully at everything.

I recognized one of the women immediately by the thin, scab-covered baby she carried on her hip; it had been she who had given the baby her breast during my first visit to Selma.

"I am Hathaya, Saleh's daughter," she said. "*Ahlan wusahlan.*" I sat down with the group of black-garbed women who served as background for the vivid display in the court. A swath of bright red wool six feet long and nearly three feet wide splashed across the court from the pit loom near the family house almost to the mud wall. Looking closer, I saw that this was the woof of a rug in the process of manufacture; long strands of red yarn were stretched taut and fastened to wooden pegs driven into the hard-packed ground. Already a geometric pattern of black and red pyramiding squares and rectangles was emerging from the pit loom, where Hathaya's husband Mahmoud sat and threw the shuttle. I could not understand why he seemed to be sitting on the ground until I was told that the loom was set in a dugout nearly three feet deep and pedals controlling the woof were operated from below. All around us newly dyed yarn was drying in the morning sun. Yellow, red, orange, green, the skeins were draped over the wall, spread across the roof of the lean-to and hung on makeshift frames of sticks, covering every available inch of the dun-colored walls with gaudy loops of twisted color.

Fluffy piles of raw sheep wool had also been spread out to dry. Hathaya picked up a soft handful and tossed it to another woman, who produced from the pocket of her dress a spindle and showed me how she twisted the bits of fleece into strands of yarn, which were then spun on the wooden spinning wheel and finally woven on the loom. In addition to rugs the family made abayahs, which were dyed black for the women but left the wool's natural color for men.

"How much does one cost?" I asked.

An old woman held out the corner of her abayah for me to finger the rough homespun.

"For this kind, half a pound," she said, "if you bring your own wool. But a fine one, very warm, for winter, costs three pounds."

"How much wool does it take?"

"The wool of two or three sheep, washed and dried, will make one abayah," she said.

While Saleh took Bob around I drank tea with the women, who talked to me so fast I could scarcely understand a word, and who laughed hilariously at my stumbling answers. In this house there was no restraining presence such as Selma, no protection such as that offered by my special relationship with Mohammed's mother and sisters. These women had me to themselves, to do with as they pleased. The children plucked at my abayah and touched my shoes; the women would call them off, then draw near enough to touch the material of my abayah themselves. They talked loudly about me, indifferent to my presence or possible comprehension. However, I caught a few comments: my heavy shoes (horrible); my skin (white); my husband (not bad); my skirt, visible when I sat down even though I kept my abayah around me (good

wool, but too short); and my cut bangs (really strange,
quite awful in fact). They wondered audibly what I had
on under my skirt; when they asked me outright, I pretended that I couldn't understand.

One old woman, who talked the loudest and the fastest,
kept insisting that I should drink another glass of tea
(good for the blood), patted my hand and told me not to
worry (about what, I was not sure), yet she simply could
not restrain her mirth. Every time she looked at me she
would go off into a good-natured cackle which was in itself so infectious that the children and women would
automatically join in. Somehow, in this situation I was
not upset at being considered an amusing object, as I sometimes was on later occasions. Perhaps it was the sun on the
bright yarns, the lovely rug spread in the court, the men
and the women so proud of their industry and so pleased to
be able to show it off. Or perhaps it was the naïveté of
the women's unashamed curiosity and amusement. They
did not laugh simply to observe my reactions. They poked
me and pinched me and laughed in all sincerity, simply
because they were curious and found me terribly funny.
After a while the waves of mirth became contagious; I
began laughing too, at nothing in particular, and soon we
were all guffawing together.

When the men sat down in the opposite corner to have
their tea, I was given the tour of the loom and the spinning wheel. Would I like to see Hathaya spin? I would.
She did. Everyone was pleased. But the baby, in the arms
of another woman, began to wail and Hathaya picked it
up and gave it her breast. Would I like to see their house?
I would. A small, dark room, reminiscent of Ali's house,
then another larger, airier room where Saleh slept, which
was filled with neat piles of folded rugs and abayahs.

"Tell your husband you want one of these beautiful
rugs," said the old woman slyly; she was Saleh's wife and
no fool. She had decided, and rightly, that I might very
well be a profitable source of business as well as a divertisse-
ment.

I said I certainly would. "Are these for sale?" I asked,
indicating the piles.

"No," she said; these had been woven on order and were now waiting payment. The people would come in about a month after the harvest, when the fellahin were paid for their grain by the merchant in El Nahra. "But don't worry," she added quickly, noticing I was turning away. "Just save the wool from five sheep, and we will make you a special rug in beautiful colors."

Hathaya pointed out that we had no sheep.

The old woman looked thoughtful for a moment. "Ask Mohammed," she said. "He will find you some wool to buy in the autumn, after the sheep are shorn. And then bring it to me, and we will draw a fine pattern and . . ."

She was interrupted by a shout from the court. Bob was leaving and nodded to me to follow.

"You must come visit us every day," said the old woman, and went off into a final paroxysm of laughter. I said she must come and visit me; the women looked at each other and smiled. Would they come?

"God willing," they replied, and I picked my way past the yarns and the bright rug to the gate where Bob waited.

"*Ahlan wusahlan,*" said Hathaya. Her baby was wailing again; she turned from us and helped it to find the breast. The gate shut and we were again on the dusty path, which was drab compared with the gaiety and color we had left behind.

4

Women of the Town

Across the canal from the tribal settlement of mud-brick houses lay the village itself—more mud-brick houses, shops, a small covered bazaar, and a mosque distinguished from all of the other mud-brick buildings only by a small mosaic. "There is no God but Allah and Mohammed is His Prophet" was spelled out in faded blue tiles above the door. Date palms and a few eucalyptus trees gave shade along the bank of the canal. The urban side of El Nahra was reached by a new cement bridge which had recently replaced the pontoon footbridge; the old bridge had risen and lowered as the canal filled and emptied, but the new one arched proudly over the canal, oblivious of the water or lack of water underneath.

The American Point Four engineer who advised the Iraqi Government on the construction of this new bridge had suggested it be built of cement blocks; it had been. He had neglected to allow for the fact that it is difficult to get onto a high cement bridge from a dirt road without proper approaches, which did not of course exist in El Nahra. Hence, although the villagers were pleased with the new bridge, many of them cursed it in the winter, for when the dirt roads turned to mud, the horses and donkeys and even the cars would slip and slide and skid, trying to gain enough purchase to get onto the slick cement of the arch.

The engineer had also pointed out that the old bridge was really very badly situated—down the canal from the main street, where it joined the tribal settlement with the mosque. What was needed, he said, was a central location. Accordingly, the bridge was built to accommodate such modern ideas; it was moved up the canal and now spanned the hub of the village, joining a group of busy coffee shops on the tribal side to the bazaar entrance and taxi stand on the other, urban bank. What the engineer did not know, and of course no one dreamed of telling him, was that the old bridge was inefficiently situated for a very good reason: to allow the women to pass over, unnoticed, to either side of the canal, to visit friends or pray in the mosque without being exposed to the stares of the strange men who always filled the coffee shops or lounged at the entrance to the bazaar.

Now the new bridge facilitated social intercourse among the men, it was true, and it was certainly a time saver for the taxi drivers who had to deliver passengers to the tribal side, but it considerably cut down the social life of the women. They could no longer slip across the bridge to see a friend and slip back without their absence being noted. They could no longer wind through alleys to the back entrance of the bazaar, make a small purchase and return home discreetly. With the coming of the new bridge, each foray across the canal became a major undertaking. Who knew who might be sitting in the coffee shop who might remark that so-and-so's family was running about town these days. For a model wife stayed at home, cared for her children and for her house, prepared good food for her husband and his guests, and kept out of sight of strangers. So, although few people really noticed it and only one or two of the women even remarked on it, in fact the women went out much less often after the new bridge was finished and the old bridge was dismantled and sold for firewood.

The main street of El Nahra, neon-lighted, was a continuation of this new bridge. Here were the offices of the government officials assigned from Baghdad to administer the village and its immediate area. A boys' primary school (400 pupils), a girls' primary school (175 pupils), the mayor's office, the jail, the government dispensary with its resident doctor, the police station, and the post office lined the street. On a side road facing the canal was the office of the irrigation engineer, the one indispensable man among the government officials, for on his authority the floodgates which channeled water from a branch of the Euphrates River were opened and closed. The village and the surrounding farm community depended on the water supply for life.

Along this bank, near the irrigation office, were the most modern dwellings in El Nahra, two or three well-built houses of fired brick, with tiled floors and carefully cultivated gardens. This was the fashionable, the "right" side of the canal, and the tribal settlement was obviously on the wrong side. Why on earth didn't Bob and I, foreigners and not destitute, live on the right side of the canal, I was asked by the women schoolteachers, the mayor's wife, the engineer's sister and the doctor's wife, the handful of middle-class ladies in the town who entertained me at lunch and tea, polite, pleasant, and quite puzzled as to our presence in this remote village and our house among those of the tribal fellahin.

Khadija, the engineer's sister, was from a tribal group herself and could hardly contain her curiosity about the women of the sheik's house; she had never visited them, as they were not of her social group. Paradoxically she would have liked nothing better, for she enjoyed visiting the hut of the man who cultivated her beautiful garden. In the gardener's one-room shack she could sit on the floor with his wife and daughter, drinking tea and gossiping. This kind of visit was all right—the gardener and his wife were her servants; she was expected to be kind and visit them occasionally, bringing small presents of tea and sugar. But the sheik's house? Never. She was above that sort of thing now. Her brother Jabbar, the engineer, was a self-made man. An attractive, intelligent and ambitious boy, he had graduated highest in his class from the time he entered his village primary school until he finished secondary school in his provincial capital. His achievements brought him a scholarship to the engineering college in Baghdad. Now he was an effendi, a white-collar worker; he had risen higher than any member of his family before him. His younger sister, brought to El Nahra to keep house for him, had assumed his social status without his education and intelligence; unfortunately, she had not even Jabbar's good looks in her favor. She worked at dressing smartly and learning to make crème caramel, she obediently visited the teachers and the mayor's wife, tried hard to keep up with the latest song successes of Abdul Wahab and Um Khalthum, and asserted that she wanted to learn to read and write, but she was equipped for her role neither by training nor by native intelligence.

Jabbar wished her to become accustomed to conversing with men so that she might be a companion as well as a housekeeper for her husband; accordingly he invited Bob and me to his house and insisted that the four of us sit and eat together. Khadija was painfully embarrassed and could not even look at Bob; she kept her eyes cast down and occasionally giggled nervously. Jabbar decided I could teach her to bake cakes and cookies like the upper-class Baghdadi women; I tried hard, but she had neither talent nor interest.

Khadija seized on me out of loneliness and curiosity, for I was so odd a figure in the village even she felt comfortable with me. But the friendship was a difficult one. Unless I spent every afternoon with her, which was impossible, she complained to Jabbar that I did not like her; since Jabbar was one of Bob's closest personal friends in the village as well as a key figure in his irrigation study, this made life troublesome for all of us. I finally limited myself to a weekly visit with her, and Bob told Jabbar that I was busy at home and helping him the rest of the time.

Khadija dreaded marriage, she told me, because she would have to leave Jabbar and her family and go with her husband; I thought she feared more the burdens of cooking, child-rearing and entertaining in a white-collar household, activities at which she seemed bound to prove inadequate.

The teachers, the mayor's wife and the doctor's wife, all fairly well educated, tried to be kind to Khadija, and although she was pleased at their attentions, basically she resented them. Hind, youngest of the three teachers, a lively witty girl, tried to teach Khadija to read and write. At this time Jabbar was considering marrying Hind; though nothing had been said to Hind's family, she had heard the rumors. When he suddenly became engaged to another girl, Hind quite rightly tried not to visit his house so often. But Khadija was furious and told me over and over again that Hind had never liked her, that she only wanted to marry Jabbar, and that was why she had visited her before.

I did not believe this, for Hind was kind as well as sensible, much like her older sister Aliyah, who had come to El Nahra thirteen years before when the girls' school opened and had remained there ever since, teaching, in loneliness and obscurity, the girls of this remote area. At first, she told me, only a few girls, daughters of merchants and effendis, had come to school; Aliyah had not been discouraged. She visited the village families, not just once, but many times, until they became used to her presence and were no longer suspicious. She pointed out the importance of women learning to read, not only the Koran (the women *mullahs* were available to teach them that), but books about Islamic history, about sewing and cooking. When Sheik Hamid married Selma, Aliyah went to visit her and was welcomed warmly; they had mutual acquaintances among the teachers in Diwaniya. Gradually the tribal girls began to attend the school. First only one came from each of the wealthier families, then the poorer girls, and finally more and more of the villagers. The school had grown slowly, but it had 175 girls now, and only three teachers. Inspectors from the Ministry of Education had expressed several times to Aliyah herself their amazement at the large enrollment in such a conservative area, but knowing Aliyah and the high personal respect she enjoyed in El Nahra, I was not surprised.

The town fathers knew that Aliyah was no modern upstart, come to teach the girls to take off their abayahs and learn the wicked, immodest ways of the city. Her family was from Baghdad, it was true, but was known to be conservative and religious; Aliyah wore the abayah herself and lived quietly with Hind, their mother and another unmarried sister who cooked and kept house. Jabbar once explained to Bob, "They have no man to protect them, but their good reputation is protection enough."

Aliyah was anxious that I teach English part-time at the school; she had asked the Ministry repeatedly for another teacher to help handle the growing enrollment, one who could manage English. But she was constantly disappointed, for young girls did not want to come to a village as remote as El Nahra, where there were no decent living facilities for single women, few congenial companions, and not even the cinema to distract them from the hard work, low pay and bleak atmosphere. I would have liked to help Aliyah; we both wrote letters and I was interviewed by the Ministry. They offered me a job as an English teacher in the boys' secondary school in Diwaniya. "After all," said the deputy Minister, "boys need to learn English more than girls," but I declined. So nothing ever came of the project; I was sorry for Aliyah's sake, but in the long run it was better for Bob that I not be tied down every morning.

I admired and liked the two teachers and enjoyed their company. They were intelligent enough to have some grasp of why we were there, and they accepted us without many questions. I would have visited them more often except that we all had our own work to do. But when I was depressed I would put on my abayah and walk across the bridge to Sitt Aliyah's house. There I would drink tea and try to improve my Arabic by talking and listening to Aliyah, Hind and their visitors (they always had visitors, from every economic stratum of the village) talk of books and movies and the place of women in the new Iraq. It was comforting to know that even in El Nahra there were women who cared about such things, who worked subtly to improve conditions around them, but always from a position of strength and acceptance in their own community.

Um Saad, the mayor's wife and the third teacher, was another sort altogether. Highly educated, bearing the name of a wealthy and ancient Baghdadi Shiite family, she was held slightly in awe by the other teachers. In spite of her origins, or perhaps because of them, Um Saad was slight and unassuming. The moment I entered her house, I was aware of taste and education. There was not a garish object or a wrong color or texture. The pictures were old and good; the bookcase—the only one I ever saw in El

Nahra with one exception (in the house of Khalil, the bright young man who taught Arabic literature in the boys' school)—covered one whole wall of the dining room.

The mayor, Abu Saad, was something of a poet and Um Saad read and criticized his work; she knew a great deal about Arabic poetry of the past and present. Their relationship was a close one: they had three sturdy boys, they were intellectually companionable, they seemed very happy. But there was one problem. Abu Saad confessed to Bob that he knew the wearing of the veil and the hiding of women in the house were old-fashioned and out-moded customs, that his wife was as intelligent and sensible as he was and that he should encourage her to enjoy the world as he did. But all of his background warred against it; his father had been a mullah, prominent in the business affairs of one of the most important mosques in Baghdad. His grandfather had written books well known throughout the Islamic intellectual world, urging limited education for women but warning of the dangers of a too liberal interpretation of women's role. Abu Saad tried to overcome this, but he could not; Um Saad tried to understand and sympathize with his conflicts, but she could not. She remained a devoted wife and mother, but she was quietly disappointed that her husband did not have the strength to live according to his own rational convictions.

The doctor's wife never visited Um Saad; they had nothing in common. Her name was Nadia; she was voluptuous, well dressed, very coarse and very wealthy. Her husband, a Christian, had renounced his faith and become a Moslem in order to marry her. Dr. Ibrahim hated the village and despised the tribesmen and fellahin; he told Bob at their first meeting that the fellahin were animals, not human beings. After that Bob avoided him whenever possible. He kept his dispensary open only when he felt like it, and treated with contempt or indifference the men and women who trooped to the government clinic, racked with one or several of the diseases endemic to the area—tuberculosis, bilharzia, malaria, amoebic and bacillary dysentery. Although the sulfa and other medicines provided by the government were supposed to be free, Dr. Ibrahim charged for them. One night when Mohammed's mother was very ill, the doctor refused to go to see her in his own car (it was raining and he didn't want to get it splashed with mud) and forced the distraught Mohammed, in addition to the medical fee, to pay half a pound for a private taxi to take him across the canal to the tribal settlement. The tribesmen were silently contemptuous of the doctor. "No man who changes his religion can be trusted," they said, and dosed their bilharzia and dysentery with caraway tea, buying aspirin in the market for the pain.

This little group of civil servants and civil servants' wives—Um Saad, Aliyah, Hind, Nadia and Khadija—were always pleasant and always hospitable to me. Their lives were remote from those of the tribal women I knew: their upbringing and training, their aspirations and hopes were different, for they were from the cities, which have developed separately from the rural areas in the Middle East for generations. But as I visited back and forth between the two societies, sitting in a deep maroon plush armchair at Um Saad's or squatting on a reed mat at Mohammed's, I was struck too by the similarity in these women's values. Though the town and the country are worlds apart, a good woman is the same in both spheres: her reputation for fidelity is above reproach, she is hard-working, a devoted wife and mother, a good cook and housekeeper, and a quiet, obedient companion to her husband. And in spite of the relative obscurity in which these women lived, I came to realize how much they influenced men, their husbands and especially their sons, and even—indirectly, by silent example (as did the teachers)—men they never saw or met. Not only did the women influence, but in many cases they helped to determine events: whom their sons would marry, whom their daughters would marry, whether or not a child would go on to school and university. And they did this without coercion, without publicity, and above all without reproach.

5

Gypsies

Gypsies! I had heard the word several times in the houses of the women recently. "Do they dance?" I asked. "Tell fortunes?"

"Of course," said the women. "They are gypsies."

"Have you ever seen them?" I asked. They looked at me.

"No," they said.

Bob reported that a troupe of traveling gypsy entertainers was camped somewhere in Diwaniya province and, one sunny winter day, out for a drive with Jabbar and Khadija, we saw them on the move, thirty people or more in a caravan of donkeys and camels.

They were unmistakable, distinguished from all other nomads on the road, not only by their bright clothing and gaily saddled animals but by the arrangement of the caravan. The men were in front, as is usually the case, but these men were on foot rather than on horseback, and instead of kaffiyehs and abas and heavy rifles, they wore tight black trousers and gaudy silk shirts and carried drums and pipes and batons. Next came the younger women on donkeys, but again there was a difference. The gypsy girls rode astride and their abayahs were tucked artfully around them to good effect, showing here a décolleté flowered dress, there a printed silk petticoat or a gold-braceleted ankle. On the camels at the end of the procession rode the old women and men and children. The pots and pans and striped blankets were tied to the camel saddles. But even the children were different, the boys in tight pants and silk shirts like their fathers, the little girls in shiny silky flowered dresses.

Almost as soon as we saw them, the caravan moved over to the side of the road and stopped. The young men turned to prance toward us and two children jumped down from the camels and proceeded to turn somersaults and cartwheels on the road, directly in front of our oncoming car.

"Stop, Jabbar, please," said Khadija, "so Beeja and I can see," and when Jabbar put on his brakes, the men snapped into formation. The children wove, tumbling, among the *oud* players, the drummers, the men with pipes and nose flutes, occasionally even upstaging the leader, who had produced a handful of small balls from his pocket and was now twirling and tossing his baton and juggling the balls, all at the same time. The camels stayed by the side of the road, but the girls brought the donkeys round to serve as a backdrop for the performers and musicians, and, like bareback riders in a circus, reined in the beasts with one hand and gestured coquettishly toward us with the other. They shouted and called to us, but we could not understand what they were saying.

Slowly the little tableau moved toward us on the empty road, until the gypsies were so close we could see the flashing gold teeth of the men, their embroidered skullcaps and the single gold earrings in their ears, the gold pendants about the slender necks of the children. Smiling and calling to us still, the girls turned the donkeys slowly around, jingling their gold bracelets and switching their black abayahs like the trains of ball dresses. I had already begun to think of the abayah as a sheltering cloak, a symbol of modesty. It was a shock to see it used in this way, at one moment framing the girls' pointed faces and tightly laced bosoms, and then flipped toward us provocatively as they turned in time to the music.

Now the music increased its tempo, the children twisted their narrow bodies in a frenzy of backbends and somersaults, and to the accompaniment of a long roll on the skin drums, the leader flung his baton high into the desert air. While it twisted and turned in a dazzling series of circumlocutions, he deftly juggled the balls, caught the baton, then the balls, tossed his black head triumphantly and sank to his knees in a sweeping bow. He landed almost directly beneath the car window, and while we clapped, Jabbar produced some coins, and the leader, with a brilliant smile, peered into the car where Khadija and I sat, in our abayahs, in the back seat.

Would we like one of the girls to dance? he asked.

"Oh yes," said Khadija, who had stared fixedly at the gypsy girls during the entire act.

"Not today," said Jabbar. "That's enough."

He waved off the leader and we drove on, while Khadija sank back against the seat and proceeded to sulk.

"See, Khadija, they are still waving after us," I said, looking myself at the group which receded quickly into the distance until finally only a few tiny sticklike figures and animals stood on the empty road under the wide blue sky. Khadija did not turn her head, and though even Jabbar tried to tease her, she did not respond. We rode home in silence and spoke no more about the caravan.

A few days later Bob reported that the gypsies had camped again, this time near El Nahra and we had been invited to visit them by Abdul Razzak, a friend of Jabbar's who was irrigation engineer in a neighboring village. Abdul Razzak was going to take presents to one of the dancing girls, who, Jabbar claimed, was Abdul Razzak's mistress and very beautiful.

Khadija did not go with us, for reasons which remained unexplained, and I was alone with the three men. It was a cold day, the sun darkened by a thick cloud which looked ominously like an impending sandstorm. As we left El Nahra, the wind whipped up the silt in clouds around us.

The dust was worse farther out, blowing so hard that we almost passed the gypsy camp before seeing it. I had looked forward to entering a low black camel-hair tent, like those the Bedouin pitch on the plains in their seasonal wanderings through the Euphrates Valley. But I was disappointed, for these were old army tents, tattered and faded and stained, arranged in a small semicircle around a larger central tent with a cross of wood at its peak.

"Does the cross mean the gypsies are Christians?" asked Bob.

Abdul Razzak said no. "I think it is just their radio aerial."

Even before we stopped, the watchdogs had set up a

fierce barking; they jumped on the car with teeth bared, scratching and growling. It was hardly an auspicious welcome, and we decided to stay where we were until someone came to greet us. At least five minutes went by, with the dogs snarling and jumping at the windows; finally a man, wrapped in an aba against the cold and wearing only a skullcap on his head, looked out of the central tent. Through the fog of dust he recognized Abdul Razzak and called off the dogs. He was full of apologies for not coming sooner; he had been asleep, he said. They had entertained all of the provincial police officers the night before, and everyone was very tired. Abdul Razzak said we would come another time, but the man brushed aside this suggestion. He ushered us into a side tent, which was higher than it looked from the outside, but was dark and cold. No one was up and about, but at a sharp word from our host, two women in abayahs arose from mats and padded silently out in bare feet to prepare our tea. We were seated on boxes covered with old blankets and rugs; Abdul Razzak offered cigarettes and the host made an effort at polite conversation, but he looked exhausted and even talking seemed a strain.

I looked around me in the gloom. From the entrance flap, which had been staked back, a thin stream of light illuminated the bare earth in the center of the tent. This was empty. But the edges and corners of the tent, shrouded in darkness, seemed full of bundles and boxes, and people lying on pallets. When one of the bundles moved and a child emerged, I began to wonder how many men and women lay around us in the darkness, too weary and cold to bother about visitors.

Only the women who had been summoned by our host were moving about. One placed a small charcoal brazier at our feet and sat down beside it to warm herself; the other was making tea near the entrance. The child who had awakened wandered over, tousle-haired and dirty and thin, and crouched near the brazier. The rest of the company slept.

"I am sorry," said the man. "Everyone is tired and it is so cold."

Abdul Razzak tried to be gay and Jabbar laughed help-fully at his jokes. Bob joined in the conversation occasion-ally, but I sat in silence clutching my abayah under my chin. Finally Abdul Razzak could not stand it any longer. "Where is Fatima?" he asked. "I have brought her some presents." The man called out and one of the bundles answered back; in a few minutes a girl came over, yawning and smoothing her hair down under her abayah. Even in the gloom of that miserable tent she moved beautifully, drawing her abayah about her with ease and grace. With-out a glance at us, she bent over Abdul Razzak's hand, kissed it perfunctorily and sat down at his feet, one arm resting on his knee. He produced the presents, a bottle of perfume, a scarf, and some English biscuits in a painted tin box. She thanked him, not very graciously, and mut-tered something at which both Jabbar and Abdul Razzak guffawed. Jabbar translated into English. "She is asking Abdul Razzak why he didn't bring her some hashish so she can forget her troubles," he said, and proceeded to stare at her admiringly.

Fatima sank back into a cross-legged position and asked for a cigarette. While she smoked she looked us over, ap-parently decided that we were not worth her while, and looked away. She was young, with enormous black eyes and fine high cheekbones, but her face was wasted and pinched by illness. Her eyes were dull and had dark circles beneath them, her skin was yellowed like the skin of malaria patients, and she was so weary she seemed to have difficulty even stubbing out her cigarette. Abdul Razzak was teasing her; she responded with a faint smile, rested her elbow on one knee and began to pick her teeth. The host spoke sharply to her, but she continued to pick her teeth. "You must forgive her, Abdul Razzak," said the host. "You know how sick she is, and she was such a suc-cess last night the officers didn't let her stop dancing until nearly five o'clock this morning."

Another girl had joined our circle; she looked much like Fatima, and Abdul Razzak said she was her older sister. The sister nodded at Jabbar and Abdul Razzak and Bob, and jerked her head in my direction. "Who is that?"

she asked. Jabbar explained. She stared, came over and sat down nearer to me, and stared harder, then stared at Bob. Then she laughed, a short dry laugh and whispered something to Fatima. Fatima repeated this to Abdul Razzak, who looked slightly embarrassed.

"What does she want?" I could not help inquiring.

"Nothing, nothing," said Abdul Razzak, but I insisted.

"She says she will dance for you if you like, but it will be very expensive since she does not usually dance for women."

"Tell her I didn't come to see her dance, just to visit," I said. The sister stared at me again, a shrewd hard glance, then looked away indifferently. Fatima was seized by a fit of coughing, and when she had finished, she rested her head in her hands. Her shoulders were trembling.

The tea, in a china teapot with a bit of aluminum wound around its broken spout, had been brewing in the charcoal at our feet. Now the older woman poured it out into glasses, served it, and sat down, looking at us with her one good eye; the other was whitened and sightless with trachoma. After we had drunk tea, the girls had some, and Abdul Razzak passed around cigarettes again. Fatima declined, punched Abdul Razzak playfully on the knee and asked for something else. He smiled, produced another cigarette and gave it to her. "Hashish," explained Jabbar, laughing. "She will become more jolly after she has smoked it."

Gradually, as the clink of tea glasses signaled refreshments and warmth, more and more people had risen and come over to join the group. Men, women, children, they were all thin, and after glancing at us fleetingly, they would turn to conversing with each other in low-pitched tones. The one object in the room that seemed to interest them was a child of about two. She was very plump, fatter than anyone else in the tent, with the deceptive milk fat which is the ominous and ironic sign of serious malnutrition and almost certain death. Her hair was matted around crusted sores, which covered her head and face and disappeared down into the neck of her filthy shift.

"See how lovely and fat she is," the older women said proudly, and picked her up so I could see her better.

I nodded politely.

Fatima and her sister, who had indeed become more lively since the tea and cigarettes, were chattering volubly with Abdul Razzak. As the child was being exhibited, they looked at me in an almost friendly fashion and spoke to Abdul Razzak.

"The girls asked if you have any children and I said no, and they said they think there aren't many children as fat and healthy as this one. They are all very proud of the baby, so you must praise her." I did as I was told and Abdul Razzak translated my remarks.

All the women looked pleased, and the one who was holding the baby at the moment got up and brought the child over to me, trying to get her to sit on my lap. The child did not realize what was required of her, but obediently held out her arms. I took her and everyone murmured with delight.

I looked at the child in my lap, the deceptive fat hanging in gray rolls about her neck, wrists, and ankles. She smiled, but through the layers of filth, the unhealthy flab, the scabs and the oozing of the open sores on her face, it was a grotesque gesture, hardly human. I was suddenly violently revolted and found myself, to my horror, utterly unable to lean down and kiss the small face turned up to me. The women pushed her at me; I simply could not. I smiled wanly, patted the child's matted head, and handed her back.

Apparently the women had not noticed my distaste, for the child tottered off, and they laughed at its uncertainty on the flabby legs. I tried to think of a pleasantry to offer in the conversation, but none came. Our host had lapsed into silence, but Fatima was sitting on the box beside Abdul Razzak, talking to him in a low, urgent voice. Her sister smoked, resting her elbows on her bent knees and staring straight ahead at nothing. Some of the women had gone off, and Jabbar said he thought we should leave.

He nudged Abdul Razzak, who was nodding absentmindedly to Fatima as he rose. She continued her plea, whatever it was. The host rose with us, but the women stayed where they were and the girls huddled together, lighting still another cigarette in the dying embers of the charcoal fire. The child had disappeared.

At the tent flap the man bade us goodbye, and we walked in silence to the car, followed by a hound sniffing hungrily at our heels. I looked back at the tents, which were almost the same shade as the dun-colored earth, at the shivering man wrapped in his aba, his hand raised in a gesture of farewell as the dust swirled around him. And I remembered the proud, gay procession we had seen along the road, the drums, the pipes, the flashing eyes of the women as they jingled their bracelets and swished their bright-colored petticoats. I was glad Khadija had not come with us.

6

Housekeeping in El Nahra

In a few weeks our life in El Nahra settled into a working routine. After breakfast, Bob and I would listen to the BBC news and drill on Arabic, adding to each other's vocabulary new phrases and words we had heard for the first time the day before. By nine-thirty he had gone off for his morning interviewing and I began the household chores. My afternoons, like his, were given over to regular visits, he with the men, I with the women of the tribal settlement. The evenings we spent together, reviewing the events of the day, writing in our journals, reading or playing chess.

Most of the problems posed by everyday living in the village had been solved fairly easily. Our stove, refrigerator, new cupboard and the aluminum work table and folding chairs filled the bare kitchen. The dirt floors were covered with new reed mats, and we had screens made for the windows. Bob and Mohammed dug a garbage pit for tin cans and we burned refuse in the cylindrical oven. After many days of delicate negotiations, Bob finally found a man who was willing, once a month, to clean out our mudbrick toilet. We arranged to have our heavy laundry done in Diwaniya, as no one in El Nahra wanted to do a Christian's laundry, even at a price; the rest of the clothes I did by hand. We even became accustomed to taking baths out of two pails of water, one for washing, one for rinsing.

The preparation of food, however, was a major occupation. Shopping had to be done each day, for we were out of reach, literally as well as financially, of the luxuries of canned and frozen foods. Bob bought jam, dried yeast and coffee in Diwaniya, and otherwise we ate what was available locally: the vegetables and fruits currently in season, rice, eggs, yogurt, and, since we were rich by village standards, meat every day.

Mohammed did the marketing, and with his help I soon learned what every merchant had to offer, although in all the months in El Nahra I never visited them in person. Only women of very low status ever appeared in the public bazaar; rather than go personally, a woman sent her children, her servants, even her husband to buy groceries, pick up mail, or carry urgent messages to friends.

The village butcher slaughtered a goat or a sheep daily, and if Mohammed got to the market early, we had lamb kidneys for lunch, or liver, or the tenderloin which lies along the backbone. But if he was late we got a kilo chunk of unidentifiable meat, which might take one or four hours to cook, depending on the age of the animal. With Mohammed's help, I learned to strip off the tough membranes, and then he would either grind the meat or cut it into minute pieces suitable for stews of various kinds, which we ate with rice.

Onions and garlic to give flavor to the stringy meat were cheap and plentiful, and Mohammed brought me a fine supply of spices, cinnamon bark, whole nutmegs, turmeric root, peppercorns, saffron, dried celery leaves and mint. Whenever I needed spices for cooking, he would pound them fine with an old brass mortar and pestle which belonged to his mother.

Homemade tomato paste was the other ingredient essential to local cuisine. In the summer, when tomatoes glutted the market, every good housewife bought a supply, spread the tomatoes on flat tin trays and carried them up to the roof of her house. There, in the summer sun, the raw tomatoes dried and thickened, and salt was added every other day for about two weeks. The resulting tomato paste was then ready to be packed into earthenware jars to be kept throughout the winter. This paste had a delicious and distinctive flavor—the women asserted it was the combination of salt and summer sun.

We used locally made *ghee*, or clarified butter, for cooking, and after experimenting with a few tins of tasteless imported margarine (specially treated to maintain its texture in tropical climates!) we turned to local butter for all uses. One or two women in the tribal settlement specialized in making butter and selling it to the market to be clarified into ghee. If we ordered in advance and paid slightly more than the market price, we could usually get part of the supply. Many months after I arrived, I was visiting the butter-and-egg woman one day and asked the purpose of a shapeless leathery mass which lay near us on the ground. The woman demonstrated that it was her butter churn, a young lambskin which had been cleaned and dried in the sun, then greased for easy handling. The cream was poured in, both ends of the skin were securely tied, and then my neighbor simply shook the "churn" back and forth till the butter came. Occasionally the butter we bought was topped with a film of dirt, undoubtedly from the inside of that old and fragrant "churn." When this happened, Mohammed would simply scrape off the dirt and return it to the woman, explaining that we only paid for clean butter.

I made yogurt from water-buffalo milk, which was richer than the thin milk yielded by the settlement's undernourished cows. The *jamoosa*, or water buffalo, huge black slow-moving animals, were much better adapted to the local climate than were cows. They seldom contracted tuberculosis. Their milk was in demand and even the meat could be eaten, but, though the buffalo herders were prosperous by local standards, they did not enjoy a comparable social status. A cow was an animal conferring prestige, but a water buffalo was not. Still, several tribesmen owned buffalo, and from one of our neighbors Mohammed would buy a quart of milk each evening. Still foaming, the milk was put on to boil. It cooled during the night. In the morning we skimmed off the cream, a rich, thick butterlike substance (*gaymar*) which was delicious with jam on toast. To the rest I added a spoonful of yogurt starter, wrapped the pan in a towel to keep it at a constant temperature, and by late afternoon we had yogurt, for cooking, for eating, or for drinking if we diluted it with water.

We always got good rice, rice grown in Iraq, or the

famous long-grain "amber" rice which supposedly came from Iran. When potatoes were available, we often buried them in our charcoal brazier and baked them. Other vegetables were seasonal; for weeks we might eat marrow squash, then spinach would come onto the market, followed by broad beans and okra. In the fall there were eggplant and carrots. The winter fruits, oranges and bananas, were excellent and in summer we ate watermelon and grapes.

For special occasions we could buy a chicken, which was, predictably, very skinny and outrageously expensive, but had a good flavor if parboiled or marinated before roasting. On some nights we returned home to find by our doorstep a brace of small partridges which had been shot by one of Bob's friends. Plucked and cleaned and sautéed, they made a fine change of diet.

The local bread, flat round cakes made of barley or wheat flour, salt and water, was healthful and good when hot, but usually it was dry and often tasteless. Finally I tried baking my own bread in our portable oven and soon I was baking four fairly presentable loaves a week.

So we ate well, if monotonously, slept a reasonable amount and were seldom sick. We were finding people generally pleasant and helpful, and our painfully meager Arabic showed signs of improvement. Gradually we began to feel more or less at home in El Nahra, although new problems kept arising, some more serious than others.

First there were the birds, which absolutely refused to leave. We shooed them out of the house several times a day, and tried to keep the windows and doors shut lest they swoop back in. Bob had screen doors made with tight latches, and we crept in and out of the house, shutting the doors quickly against the flocks of swallows that filled the yard, perched on the roof or in the lemon trees, waiting for the door to be opened the smallest crack.

One night I awakened, coughing, for a feather had fluttered down into my face. What would come next? "This must stop," Bob said, and in the morning he and Mohammed set out to "do something definite about the birds," I was not sure just what. Mohammed returned with a long bamboo pole, and every night thereafter before we retired, Bob would probe in and around each of the beams, routing out the sly swallows who had hidden there during the day, waiting for the peace of the night to recommence their mating and nest building! After a month of nightly probing, most of the swallows retired in defeat, but the next spring they came again, small groups which camped in the lemon tree, twittering sadly and obviously unable to understand what had happened to their haven.

Bob was also in some perplexity about horses. Much of the visiting of tribal clan settlements in the back country had to be done on horseback, as there were no roads. Bob enjoyed this, for he had always liked to ride, and he found it another area of common interest with the men of the tribe. For these occasions the sheik insisted on lending Bob one of his good Arab stallions. They were valuable and beautiful horses, worth at least 500 pounds, and Bob lived in fear that, while he was riding the borrowed animal, it might trip and break its leg, and then what would we do? It was not only that we could not afford to replace the horse, but that the sheik would probably not allow us to do so (after all, we were his guests) and this would have been even worse.

One morning the gate opened and Bob and Mohammed led a horse into our garden. He was small and light brown and slightly sway-backed.

"I've bought him," Bob announced.

"Bought him?"

"Yes, what do you think of him?"

"Well—"

"I know he's not too beautiful, but he was only thirty pounds, and it seemed the best way to avoid borrowing the sheik's horses all the time."

I nodded. It did seem reasonable. But who would feed him and water him?

"I've already thought of that," said Bob. "I'm paying a man to feed and water him every day, and he can be tethered at the mudhif."

So it was. Bob was very pleased to have his own horse,

and except for occasional visits to our garden to crop grass, the horse was completely cared for at the mudhif.

Meanwhile I was having my own troubles. These were serious, but they were hard to define, and I could not at first describe them even to Bob.

At this time we had been in El Nahra for two months. Bob had made many friends, not only among the tribe, but also in the town. He felt his study was going well, and he was enthusiastic and full of plans.

But I felt I was getting nowhere. I had conscientiously visited a number of houses in the settlement, some of them several times, had been welcomed and treated to tea and gossip in each. But not a single woman had come to call on me, and even in my own visiting, the women and I were still saying to each other approximately the same things we had said on the first occasions. My direct questions on subjects in which Bob was interested were parried by polite remarks. As my Arabic improved, I could often get the drift of conversations and understand occasional fragments. It seemed to me that many times the women were talking about me, and not in a particularly friendly manner. If I could have been certain they were talking about me, and understood exactly what was being said, then I could have dealt with it, replied to the comments and brought it out in the open. But the terrible thing was that I could not be certain. Were they talking about me or not? What errors in etiquette or custom had I committed? What in heaven's name were they *saying*? My uneasiness grew in this atmosphere of half-hearing and part-understanding.

I tried to tell myself that the women did not come to see me because they were busy with household chores and children, and that they seldom went out anywhere; this was all true. I realized that my novelty value was wearing off, and I was not developing any close relationships with the women which might have replaced it. Why? I did not know.

Finally I talked to Bob about it. He tried to help, pointing out that among the men, tradition prescribed how strangers were to be greeted and treated, but that this was not true of the women, who did not see a stranger from one year to the next, and were certainly not accustomed to dealing with them for long periods of time. Bob and I rarely visited together, so we had little opportunity to compare impressions of the same situation, which might have corrected my judgments and dispelled some of my doubts. He suggested that he speak to the men about having their wives visit me, but this I vetoed. I felt that if the women had to be forced by their husbands into coming to see me, they might better not come at all.

We discussed the situation very rationally, and I could even explain it to Bob, saying that of course the language barrier made all communication doubly difficult and was bound to exacerbate the situation in which I found myself. There was no doubt that the women did not answer direct questions. There was no doubt that they did not come to see me. But was there actual hostility? Unfriendliness? Coolness? I felt definitely that there was, but I had to admit that my isolation and loneliness might very well be magnifying this unfriendliness into a ridiculous and unrealistic bogey. But it was there, nonetheless, and I came to dread the daily visits, the tea drinking among the whispering, the smiles which now seemed artificial and insincere. And the giggling behind the abayahs. Twenty women, giggling, with their eyes fixed on me. Or were they?

Bob took me into Diwaniya, and we went to the movies. He stayed home in the evenings to read and play chess when he should have been in the mudhif, interviewing. He knew how miserable I was and he did his best, but in the end it was a problem I had to solve myself. We were very happy together in our little mud house. If only I could make some kind of breakthrough with the women, I thought. For one thing, I spent at least four hours a day with them. They were a major factor in my life, whether I liked it or not, and my only company, except for Bob and Mohammed. I felt very strongly that we must have some common humanity between us, although we were from such different worlds. But how to find it?

Things reached some sort of climax when Bob was invited on a long trip to visit one of the farthest-outlying clan settlements. The sheik's brother and his oldest son were going across the fields thirty miles on horseback, and would be gone at least two days and one night. I did not mind spending the time by myself, but the sheik decided it was not proper or safe that I stay alone at night, and decreed that Amina, Selma's servant, would sleep in the house with me. At that particular stage in my relations with the tribal women, a servant from the harem to watch my every movement as I brushed my teeth, washed my face and went to bed was the last thing on earth I wanted. But there was no help for it. The sheik said she was to come, and she came.

Poor Amina. I think she relished the night with me even less than I did, but there was no recourse for her either. She came at suppertime, and sat on the floor beside me, watching me as I ate. Then followed the hour when I usually read or wrote letters. Amina continued to watch me. A half hour of this intense, silent scrutiny was enough. I gave up, made tea and offered her some, and tried to talk. She was not very communicative, but she drank the tea. Mohammed came to set up a camp cot in the living room, beside the bed where I slept. Amina was to sleep on the cot and I was to wake her at five, so she could go and milk the cows. Mohammed bade us good night and departed. I wanted to undress and climb into bed but, feeling shy, went into the kitchen to change into my nightgown. Amina followed me. I came back to the living room; she did likewise. Apparently the sheik had warned her that things would go badly with her if she let me out of her sight for a single moment after darkness fell. I wondered whether she would accompany me to the toilet. She started to, but stopped halfway down the path to allow me some privacy. I came back, undressed as I had seen my grandmother do, putting the nightgown on over everything and gradually discarding clothes from beneath its protection, while Amina watched. I got into bed. Amina wrapped herself in her abayah and lay down on the cot, pulling up the blanket which I had offered her. Once more I got up to turn on the light and check the alarm, and at this point Amina spoke.

"Is your husband kind to you?" she asked. I said yes. She sighed, and burst into tears. I was appalled. I was trying to make up my mind whether to go over to her when she stopped dead in the middle of a sob, sat up cross-legged on the cot, dried her eyes on a corner of her tattered abayah, and launched into the story of her life.

How I wished then that my Arabic were letter-perfect! For the story poured out of her in a torrent of words, punctuated by occasional sobs. I caught perhaps a third of what she actually said, but she repeated so much that the outline was finally made fairly clear to me. As the tale emerged, I was tempted to break down and cry myself.

Amina was a slave, but she had not always been one. As a girl of fifteen, she had been married to a sixty-five-year-old man. Not even her father thought it was a good match, but there were twelve children in her family, and never enough barley bread and dried dates, the diet of the very poor, to go around. Her marriage brought her nothing but grief, for she nearly died delivering a stillborn son, and then her husband died, leaving her penniless. Her own family was destitute. Most of the members of her husband's family had died, and those who were alive did not want another mouth to feed. No one wanted her. What was she to do? At this point Sheik Hamid heard of her plight. He had then been married to Selma for three years; she had two sons and needed a servant. Hamid bought Amina from her father for twenty pounds, and gave her to Selma.

"And never have I had such a good life as since I came here," she averred. "Why, I can have as much bread as I want, every day, and rice, and sometimes meat. Selma even gives me cigarettes. And Haji—" here she raised her hands and her eyes to heaven and launched into a flowery eulogy of the generosity, the greatness, the goodness which were peculiar to Hamid's character.

"Do you ever see your family, Amina?" I asked, knowing that even through woe and poverty and separation, family ties are not soon severed in this society. The question was a mistake. Amina began to cry again, and between sobs she said she had not seen her family for seven years.

"But oh, Haji, he is a good man. There is no sheik in the Euphrates Valley as good as Haji." She went on and on like this until she finally ran down. She was worn out and so was I. The recital had taken at least an hour. I suggested we might sleep, and she agreed. But when I turned out the light, the sound of muffled sniffling came to me through the darkness.

"What is the matter, Amina?"

"Nothing," she replied, but the sniffling continued.

"If your husband is really kind to you," she said inexplicably, "get a lot of gold jewelry from him while you are still young. You never know what will happen."

And before I could reply she was snoring loudly, fast asleep.

Bob came back at 6:30 the next evening. I had no time to recount the tale of Amina, for several members of the clan had returned with the men, and were eating in the mudhif. Bob was expected to make an appearance, and he changed his clothes and left. Not more than five minutes after he had gone there was a loud pounding at the gate. I thought he had forgotten something and ran to open it. Not Bob, but seven or eight black-veiled figures greeted me—the women! They had come at last. They marched up the path, giggling and whispering to each other like a bunch of schoolgirls on a field trip to the zoo. Not until they were all inside the house and had removed their face veils did I know who had come: Selma—yes, Selma, the social leader of my little settlement—and Sheddir, wife of Ali; Laila, one of the sheik's nieces; Fadhila, sister-in-law of Mohammed; two women I did not know; and Amina, my roommate of the night before. Aha, I thought, the business with Amina was not a waste of time, perhaps she has told them I am not such an ogre after all. I smiled at her in gratitude, but she was talking to Selma and did not respond.

No one paid any attention to me. They gazed around them, at our wardrobe with its full-length mirror, at the postcards and the calendar I had pinned up, at Bob's brick-and-board bookcase, at our narrow bed against the wall. I decided to let them look, and went to make tea, returning with seven glasses on a tray. Everyone refused. I offered it again. Again I was refused. Suddenly I was angry. This was a great insult, not to accept tea in a house where one was visiting, and they knew it and I knew it and they knew I knew it. I said, as sweetly as I could, "How is it that you receive me into your houses and insist that I drink your tea, but when you come to see me, you only want to look, and not accept my hospitality?"

There was a shocked silence.

Selma rose to the occasion. "The women are shy," she said. "They know your ways are different from ours, and think they should refuse the tea, since it is their first visit to your house."

She knew I knew she was making up every word she said, but I once more appreciated her tact and kindness in a difficult situation. "But," she said grandly, "I have been to secondary school in Diwaniya and have read about the West, I know your ways are much the same as ours, so I will drink some tea."

The crisis passed. Sheddir also accepted a glass, and Fadhila, but the others still refused. I passed around cigarettes. As I had thought, this was too great a temptation to resist, and everyone, even those whom I had never seen smoke, took a cigarette.

"What do you do all day here by yourself?" asked Fadhila.

"I cook, and clean the house."

"Why don't you do your washing in the canal as we do?" suggested Sheddir.

"Because I like to do it in my house," I said.

Then in a whispered conversation which followed, I distinctly heard Sheddir say that she often came to our garden to cut grass for their animals, and had never seen much laundry hanging on my line. She allowed as how I must be very lazy. I felt myself bristling, readying a tart reply to that one, but Selma intervened.

"You say you cook," she said. "What do you cook? I thought Westerners ate all their meals from tin cans."

I told them what we had for lunch, and added that I had baked bread that morning.

"Bread like ours?" asked Sheddir.

"No," I said, "Western bread."

Selma explained to the group that this was a high loaf called "toast." Haji ate it all the time in Baghdad and had told her about it.

"Let us see some," they clamored.

I ran to the kitchen, proud that I was good for something, and returned with several slices of fresh bread, cut into quarters.

"You taste it, Sheddir," Selma instructed.

Everyone stopped talking and watched as Sheddir, very flustered indeed at being chosen the group guinea pig, picked up one of the squares of bread between thumb and forefinger and stuffed it in her mouth. She masticated a moment, then made a terrible face and spat it out on the floor. The ladies exploded and laughed till the tears ran down their cheeks. I was close to tears myself, and not humorous ones, but I realized that Selma was watching me.

"Sheddir is not accustomed to your bread—she finds it strange," she offered kindly, but she could not help shaking with laughter at this huge joke. At the height of the mirth, Sheddir thought of something else that was screamingly funny, and launched into a long tale which I did not understand, but which seemed to have something to do with me, for she kept watching me out of the corner of her eye as she talked.

"Do you know what she is saying?" Selma asked me. I shook my head. "Sheddir says you do not know how to cook rice, and because your rice is so bad, your husband comes to eat at the mudhif."

I admitted I did not know how to cook the rice in El Nahra because it was different from the rice in America.

Even Fadhila laughed at this. "Rice? Rice is the same everywhere," she asserted and people nodded. I was obviously slow-witted as well as lazy.

My face must have shown what I was feeling, for Selma changed the subject.

"Do you and Mr. Bob both sleep in that little bed?" she asked. I said yes.

"What fun they must have, I'm sure!" croaked Sheddir and the ladies were off again. I knew this was a good-hearted joke, but I had been tried too far that evening. Selma saw it too. She stood up and pulled her abayah around her, announcing that Haji Hamid would soon be back from the mudhif, and if he found her gone—she made an unmistakable gesture.

"Oh, no, Selma," protested Sheddir. "Haji would never beat you. You are too beautiful." Selma arched at this, but she did not deny it. The attention had been diverted from the strange American and the women's attitude changed. They rose and prepared to take their leave. I saw them to the gate, voicing the traditional farewells, and got a few halfhearted ones in reply. Then I shut the gate and burst into tears.

Six months before, I would not have believed that I could be so upset at being accused of laziness and in-competence by a group of illiterate tribal ladies. But there was no question but that it was a real and very terrible snub now. Not only the practical difficulties of continu-ing the visiting and maintaining good relations bothered me. It had now become important to me to be accepted by these people as a woman and as a human being. And tonight, when I had thought success was near, the eve-ning had turned into a fiasco. I was indignant first, and told myself they were nothing but a group of curiosity seekers. Then I began to feel righteous. After all, they had insulted me by refusing my tea, spitting out my food, and telling me I was lazy and a bad cook. I felt hurt. They did not find me sympathetic or interesting or even human, but only amusing as a performing member of another species. I tried to feel tragic, superior, ironic, above it all—but failed utterly and wept again.

When Bob came home he told me to forget the whole incident, to remember that we were in El Nahra to do some specific work, not prove any romantic theories about humanity being the same everywhere. But this did not satisfy me. Bob said I should simply try to relax, and continue the visiting on a businesslike basis. I said I would try, but I was not convinced.

Next morning, after Bob had gone off to the mudhif, I was unreasonably depressed. Bob had suggested I should charge out and visit immediately one of the women who had been at our house the night before, apparently on the theory that if you get thrown from a horse, you must get back on it right away or you'll lose your grip forever. But I could not force myself out. I started lunch and then wandered into the garden, stopping to inspect a large hole in our mud wall where dogs sneaked in at night to raid the garbage pit. I bent down to look through the hole, and drew back in alarm as my gaze met three pairs of eyes, three black-framed faces looking in at me from the other side of the wall.

One of the women smiled. "Good morning," she said through the hole.

"Good morning," I replied.

"We hear you can't cook rice," she said.

I almost threw a rusty tin can at her, I was so annoyed.

But the third one said, "If you will open your gate, we will come in and show you how to cook rice, so your husband will be pleased with your food."

For the second time in twenty-four hours I was close to tears, but this was quite different. I opened the gate and let the ladies in (one was Laila, the sheik's niece; the other two I did not know). They marched purposefully up the path and into my kitchen, where they did indeed show me how to cook rice.

We picked over and washed the rice, covered it with cold water, then sat down on the floor to drink tea while it soaked. A large pot of salted water was put on the stove to boil, and the rice was cooked in the boiling water until the grains were separate and tasted right. When the rice was drained, clarified butter was put in the dry pot over the fire until it sizzled. Then the rice was poured back into the pot and stirred quickly until each grain was coated with the boiling butter. Then we covered the pot, turned down the heat, and let the buttered rice steam slowly. We drank another cup of tea, and I thanked the ladies profusely.

"We don't want your husband to beat you," said one. "After all, you are here alone without your mother."

"Come to see us soon," said Laila, as the gate closed behind her.

Lunch was quite a gay meal that day. Even Bob remarked on the rice, and when Mohammed came, he tasted it and pronounced it all right—the final seal of approval, I knew, for though Mohammed did not eat much, he was very particular about his food.

That afternoon I marched up the path to the sheik's house almost triumphantly. The rice-cooking lesson had reassured me, and I felt I could take on the whole harem. Mohammed had been sent to tell them I was coming, but apparently he had forgotten, for no one was at the door, and I crossed the courtyard to Selma's house without seeing a soul. At the door Amina met me.

"Oh," she said, obviously startled, "*ahlan wusahlan*," and quickly led me into the sheik's bedroom, where the rugs were rolled up and the bed stripped. General housecleaning seemed to be under way. In yesterday's mood I would have gathered my abayah around me and departed, but not today. Amina hurried out to find someone, leaving me alone in the bedroom for the first time. The biggest chest was open, spilling out sheets and pillowcases, tablecloths, antimacassars and towels. Also I saw, to my amusement, that despite the splendor of the gilt bedstead and the satin spread, Sheik Hamid, like every other person in the village who could afford a bed at all, slept on bare boards covered with a cotton mattress. I was just screwing up courage to take a closer look at the contents of the open chest when Selma hurried in, in an old house dress.

"*Ahlan wusahlan!*" she said. She was flustered and preoccupied and I apologized for arriving unannounced, explaining that I thought Mohammed had told her of my coming.

"Never mind," she said, "stay and have tea. But you must excuse me, because I have to make Haji's bed before he comes back from the mudhif."

I said I didn't mind at all, and she shouted for Amina, who came in and grinned at me as she helped Selma beat the mattress and lay it back carefully on the boards. By this time word of my arrival had spread and a few women and children straggled in. They joked with Selma as she puffed over the mattress, and nodded at me. Selma dug into the chest for sheets and pillowcases, heavy white cotton elaborately embroidered in bright colors. The bottom sheet was tucked in all around, but the top sheet had a wide border of embroidery which was draped down over the bedside. The pillowcases were skinned tightly over the long, narrow pillows, and tied in fancy bows at each end so the colored pillow covering (pink to match the bedspread) showed to good advantage. Mottoes were embroidered over the pillowcases—for good luck, said Selma, translating them for me. The most popular motto was "Sleep here and good health."

"Can you do embroidery like that?" asked Samira, the daughter of Kulthum, pointing to the complicated pattern which followed the border of the sheet.

"Not as beautiful as that, but I can embroider," I replied, remembering the few doll clothes I had painfully cross-stitched long ago under the watchful eye of my aunt.

"Why don't you embroider some nice pillowcases for your and Mr. Bob's bed?" continued Samira.

I was up to anything that day. "Oh, I'm already planning to," I lied airily. "Mr. Bob is bringing me some cloth and embroidery thread from Diwaniya."

"You can buy the cloth here," said Samira.

"Yes, I know," I answered, knowing absolutely nothing about it, "but the cotton is cheaper in Diwaniya and the selection is much better."

Another woman interrupted to say that cloth was cheaper in El Nahra, and there was no need to go all the way to Diwaniya for it.

"It may be cheaper," admitted Selma, turning from the bed, where she was applying a final pat to the satin spread, "but it is not as good quality as the cotton in Diwaniya. I know, because that was my home before I married, you remember."

That silenced them.

"What kind of pattern will you embroider?" asked Laila,

the sheik's niece who had come to my house the evening of the bread episode.

"I haven't decided," I answered, quite truthfully this time. "I think I would like to do one like that"—and I pointed to the flowers and leaves and the good luck mottoes on Haji's clean pillowcase—"but I don't have any patterns."

"Oh," said Laila. "I have many, many patterns, because my sisters and I embroider all the time. Come to visit us when you get your cloth and you can choose one of ours."

I was suddenly unreasonably elated at the invitation. "I will," I promised. "I will get the cloth tomorrow, so I'll come day after tomorrow."

Selma had finished and locked the chest again. She sat down to rest, untying her *asha* and rearranging her hair under it. "Amina," she called, "bring us tea." Amina brought a tray of three glasses, one for me, one for Selma and one for the oldest woman in the room. I had been sitting on the floor the whole time, but no one had commented on it. Selma was too occupied with other things to think much about me and the proprieties of entertaining a guest. We all drank our tea together.

It was late and I felt that I should go, but we sat on. When I rose, Selma said, completely unexpectedly, "The sheik would like to meet you."

I looked blank.

"Would you like to see him here or at your house?"

The suddenness of it caught me off guard. I thought fast. I had been in purdah ever since I arrived and had neither spoken nor sat with any tribal men other than Mohammed, who didn't count as he was considered "my family" now. Yet Sheik Hamid was our host. What was the best thing to do?

"I must ask my husband," I said, and Selma nodded. It was apparently the answer they expected.

When I got home I was in good spirits, and related to Bob all the details of the cleaning and weekly bed changing, the big chestful of linens, and my plan to embroider pillowcases. He looked surprised. "Do you know how to embroider?" he asked.

"Oh of course. I learned when I was seven years old."

He laughed. "All right," he said. "Do what you like."

Then I exploded my bomb. "The sheik wants to meet me. What do we do?"

He looked really surprised then, and a little puzzled. I told him how the question had been put to me, and he nodded thoughtfully.

"We'll see," he said. "We'll have to think about it."

But I was destined to meet Sheik Hamid far sooner than either of us expected. Completely unforeseen circumstances demanded it.

7

Problems of Purdah

News of our residence in El Nahra had spread quickly throughout the area. Almost every week visitors came to the sheik's mudhif to look over the American strangers: schoolteachers from neighboring villages anxious to practice their rusty English; rural civil servants who had brothers or cousins at school in the United States; relatives and tribal brothers of Sheik Hamid who wanted to talk politics with the foreigners that Hamid had imported. Often Bob would ask the visitors down to our garden for tea; they were always men and I never appeared.

But one afternoon when I was alone in the house I heard a loud knocking at the gate. Bob had gone hunting with the sheik's eldest son, so I knew it could not be he. And Mohammed always opened the door himself. Who would be visiting so early after lunch?

I had strict instructions not to let in any man whom I did not know. For we had, after all, taken great care to avoid my being seen by the tribal men whose guests we were. If some passing stranger should be admitted when Bob and Mohammed were absent, it would make a mockery of our avowed desire to abide by local custom.

I peeped through a crack in the wooden gate and saw a brand-new aqua-and-white Buick parked in our alley. A portly figure was barely distinguishable in the back seat. "I am the driver of Sheik Hamza, who has come to visit you," said a man's voice.

"I am sorry. My husband is not at home," I replied.

The driver relayed this message, then I heard the Buick's window being rolled down and another voice said, in badly pronounced English, "Good afternoon. I visit you."

I swallowed. Hamza was the sheik of a tribe settled

about twenty miles to the west; Bob had spoken of him as a spendthrift and wastrel who lived most of the year away from his village, neglecting his tribal duties and leaving his fields in the care of relatives while he spent the share-croppers' money in Lebanon or Europe.

"I'm sorry," I replied. "My husband would be glad to see you, but he will not be home before six o'clock."

A torrent of Arabic followed, in which the sheik and the driver argued. The driver rattled the gate and said to me in Arabic, "You do not understand. Haji Hamza wishes to visit *you*."

I repeated the little speech about my husband, some-what shakily this time, but not knowing what else to do. There were more angry words, and I wondered fleetingly whether they might be so bold as to break the flimsy gate latch, but the sheik's voice spoke peremptorily, the car window was rolled up, the driver backed out the Buick and they drove away.

Five minutes later Mohammed hurried in, breathing hard. Sheik Hamid had seen Hamza's car at our gate. Knowing Bob was not there, he had sent one of his sons to fetch Mohammed from his afternoon nap in case I needed help. I told Mohammed the story, and he nodded approvingly. "Hamza is not a good man," he said. "You did right not to let him in. He was not even polite enough to come to the mudhif and greet Haji Hamid. He just drove away."

When Bob came I told him of the incident, but he had already heard it from three other people, including Mo-hammed. He too was relieved that nothing had happened, and then told me that some time ago Sheik Hamza had conveyed through Jabbar an invitation to us to lunch at his house on the tribal lands near Suffra. Bob had told Jabbar that he would be delighted to come, and that I would like to meet his women. He had heard no more from Hamza. "We have to be consistent," he said. "It would be very poor if Hamza, who has a bad reputation anyway, went around the area boasting that he had seen you and talked with you, while in El Nahra we insist we are following local custom."

"Besides, it might be interesting to see another sheik's harem," I said. "I think I'd rather do that than eat with Hamza."

Bob looked at me closely. "You're in good spirits," he grinned. "I never would have thought embroidery could have such a therapeutic effect."

I smiled. I *was* feeling better. The embroidery project had worked out well. I had gone to Laila's house and she had traced a pattern onto my length of cloth. After that I took my pillowcase with me whenever I went visiting. The women all remarked on it, but after the first few minutes I found I could sit quietly and stab my needle through the cheap cotton, and little by little the group would forget my strange presence and talk on as though I were one of them. I had a place in the circle and something to do; I didn't have to make conversation every single minute and, as my Arabic slowly improved, I found I was learning a great deal by simply listening.

We forgot about Hamza, but after a week he relayed his luncheon invitation again. He told Jabbar that I would be welcome in his harem. So, looking forward to the change, we set off one pleasant afternoon in Jabbar's Land-Rover. We followed the traffic heading up and down the canal bound for El Nahra or Suffra—women carrying fuel on their backs, groups of donkeys bearing grain, and men riding horseback. Suffra was only a tiny clearing in a palm grove, but a sheep market was in progress near the suq, and we had some difficulty making our way through the crowds of bleating animals who ran backward and forward in terror as the car approached. From Suffra we took a track across the fields, and after an hour of driving came in sight of a large square three-storied house with a red tiled roof and yellow stone walls. It stood at the end of a wide paved driveway lined with date palms and orange trees, and was set squarely in a fenced garden.

"Quite a palace," Bob said. I remembered the modest mud-brick fortress of Hamid and his guest house of reeds, and silently agreed.

Jabbar laughed bitterly. "Hamza lives in style," he said,

"and he takes such a large share of the crops from his fellahin that they are the poorest in the countryside."

"Mind you," he continued, "I can't say I dislike being entertained here—he always has good food and lots of liquor, and life is pretty dull in El Nahra—but when the revolution comes, men like this must go." Jabbar was a passionate believer in the need for Iraqi national reform, like many young, first-generation educated men and women who knew from personal experience that conditions were deteriorating in the rural areas. Bob met many of these young men, and they all believed firmly that the Nuri Said government would soon be overthrown. Diplomats and foreigners, seeing only Baghdad's economic boom, pooh-poohed such talk when we met them at parties. The revolution, when it did come one year later, appeared to surprise almost every embassy in Iraq.

"It will be interesting," Jabbar was saying, "to find out whether Hamza has spent any money on his women's quarters. You can tell us later."

The Land-Rover paused at the entrance to the house, and a servant came out to greet us. Jabbar explained that I was to go to the harem. Could he drive me there, or would the servant accompany me? The man looked puzzled.

"The harem?" he said, looking at us, and at me in my abayah.

"Yes, the harem," repeated Jabbar somewhat testily. The servant conferred with another servant who had come up to the car, then excused himself for a moment and came hurrying back.

"The women are not here," he said. "The sheik would like you all to come in."

"Not here?" echoed Bob, and forgot his customary politeness in such matters, he was so annoyed. "Where are they?"

"They have gone on pilgrimage to Karbala," the man replied.

At this point Sheik Hamza emerged, fat and middle-aged, in well-cut robes, fingering his worry beads and smiling broadly.

"I am so sorry," he said. "My wives and daughters have been plaguing me for weeks to let them go to Karbala, and when they asked this morning, I could not persuade them to stay."

We had been tricked. "This is impossible," Bob said to Jabbar in English. Jabbar agreed, but said that we really could not just turn around and go back to El Nahra; Hamza would already have prepared food for us, and if we were to refuse his hospitality now, it would be a grave insult.

"We must go in," he told Bob. "An insult like that would damage my reputation in the area as well as yours. Hamza may go to Baghdad and no one will ever hear of it. And if gossip does get about, explain it yourself to Sheik Hamid. He knows Hamza and will understand."

Bob was silent. I could tell he was furious.

Hamza stood by the Land-Rover, still smiling and fingering his worry beads. "Please do come in and be comfortable, you and your wife," he said.

We had no choice but to act as though it were a perfectly normal occasion. I would take off my abayah when we were inside the house, and we would lunch as pleasantly as we could under the circumstances, just praying that news of our visit didn't reach El Nahra before we did.

We walked up the neat gravel path between formal gardens, and into an enormous rectangular living room. Trying to be as dignified as possible with two menservants, Hamza and his teenage son standing by goggling, I took off my abayah and handed it to one of the servants. Then I crossed the room and sat myself down in an overstuffed sofa slipcovered in cretonne—orange and yellow dahlias of truly gigantic proportions on an apple-green ground. Bob sat down beside me, and Jabbar took an armchair nearby. Hamza just stood there, staring at me, clicking those worry beads and shifting from one foot to the other like an adolescent boy at the burlesque for the first time. I don't know what he expected, but I'm sure I was a disappointment, for I was wearing a high-necked wool dress (it was a cold day) and a brown sweater and thick-soled walking shoes. Hamza took a deep breath and came forward, still with his goggling smile.

"You must have a drink," he said in Arabic.

I smiled too. "No, thank you," I said.

"Oh, but you must. I have Scotch whisky and gin and beer."

"Perhaps some tea?" I suggested.

Hamza's face fell, but he shouted at one of the servants and then sat down next to Jabbar. Jabbar began talking of local affairs, but our host only half listened. He kept looking at me, then looking away and giggling to himself, still fingering his beads.

I was embarrassed at these covert glances, and tried to talk to Bob, who was still so annoyed he could barely speak. Jabbar gradually drew Bob into the conversation and I took advantage of the redirected attention of the three men to look around me at our host's "palace."

Covering the entire floor of the room was the largest and most magnificent Persian carpet I had ever seen, woven of muted blues and reds in a subtle and ancient pattern. I could not help asking Hamza about it. It had belonged to his grandfather, and was an antique carpet, costing thousands of English pounds even at that time. I stared at it, thinking of the beautiful room that could be built around such a carpet, and then looked at the gewgaws, odd pieces of bad, expensive furniture, pictures, posters and cheap statuary that covered the carpet and competed with it so vulgarly.

All around the room, armchairs, sofas and end tables had been placed against the walls. The one exception was the far corner, where stood a radio-record player combination with many shiny fixtures and luminous dials. The chairs were upholstered in mustard or scarlet velvet and gilt braid, or in different patterns of cretonne: birds, leaves and enormous flowers in a blinding selection of colors. Two layers of lace curtains screened the windows, which were hung with drapes of still another cretonne pattern (birds in birdcages as I remember).

And the walls, mercifully white, were plastered with airline calendars, beautiful examples of Arabic calligraphy, out-of-focus photographs in colored frames, whatnot shelves loaded with knickknacks and reproductions of Landseer-type English paintings. All the pictures were hung about two feet from the ceiling, so I had to crane my neck to look at them. Hamza, observing the direction of my gaze, got up in the middle of a conversation with Jabbar and Bob and began to identify the photographs: one of his father—an unpleasant-looking old man, but at least his face had bones and character in contrast to the formless fat of Hamza; countless pictures of himself: Hamza shaking hands with the young King Feisal; Hamza boarding a KLM plane for Lebanon, standing beside a pert airline hostess and grinning fatuously; Hamza bowing before Nuri Said, the Iraqi Prime Minister; Hamza kissing the hand of the British ambassador's wife, who wore flowered voile and a picture hat.

Then he started on the whatnot shelves: one had come from Germany, he said, and had cost ten English pounds . . . who would believe that such a small piece of wood could cost so much? For a moment I was afraid he might launch into the origin and price of every whatnot in the room (it would take hours) but fortunately the servant arrived with tea. Hamza sat down beside Jabbar again, and we were presented not with the strong tea of the tribe, but with an imitation of English afternoon tea, lukewarm and filled with canned milk and sugar.

A second servant brought in a large silver tray which was encrusted with baroque silver leaves. Hamza told me proudly it was a French antique tray; it may have been. Plates of tinned biscuits and pastries were passed around, and a huge bakery cake, complete with garlands and rosebuds of pink icing, was set down, together with a silver cake knife, in the center of the biggest coffee table. The tinned biscuits tasted like tinned biscuits, but the pastries were stale and hard, at least a week old, bought no doubt when Hamza was last in Baghdad. Even Jabbar, I noticed, waited until Hamza left the room for a moment and then surreptitiously wrapped his inedible pastry in a handkerchief for later disposal. While Hamza was out, I broached the subject of the cake. "Shall I cut it?" I asked.

Jabbar laughed, almost gleefully. "You can't," he said.

"I can't! Why not?"

He laughed again.

"It's made of plaster," he said, lowering his voice at the sound of approaching footsteps. "He just keeps it for show, and serves it to all his guests."

I opened and shut my mouth in amazement, and looked hard at the cake. Perhaps the pink rosebuds were a *little* dusty, but . . . I restrained a giggle in time to refuse a second cup of milk-sugar-tea.

Hamza was trying out his twenty-five-word English vocabulary on us. This was good for perhaps ten minutes of questions and answers.

"You visit Iraq for the first time?"

"Yes."

"How you find the weather in Iraq?"

"It's very nice."

"How is the weather in America?"

"Hot in the south, cold in the north, like Iraq."

"Did you visit Hollywood?"

"No."

"Is the weather hot in Hollywood?"

"Sometimes hot, sometimes cold."

"Do you see Marilyn Monroe?"

"No."

After this effort, Hamza lapsed into Arabic with Jabbar and I continued my fascinated inventory of the room. The whatnot shelves held, among other things, two pink-and-gilt cornucopia vases filled with bright paper flowers; Toby mugs from England; a Kewpie doll; a miniature German beer stein with a pewter cover; and several figurines (the shepherd embraces the shepherdess in baby-blue china; the Chinese man balances his eternal water buckets in red-and-black lacquer).

On the mantelpiece of the artificial fireplace stood, reflected in an oval gold-framed mirror, a full-size Coca-Cola advertisement (a girl in white shorts and sailor blouse lounged beside a bright blue sea and smiled before the pause that refreshes), a fine Turkish silver coffee service, a painted plaster Dutch girl, and two glass candlesticks.

In one candlestick stood a red twisted candle; in the other a green twisted candle; "Merry Christmas" was spelled out on each candle in vertical gold paper letters.

All of the end tables were covered with antimacassars, which were in turn covered with glass ash trays, brass ash trays, silver ash trays and vases stuffed with real overblown roses. The central coffee table, its three black legs supporting an enormous abstract kidney, held, in addition to the plaster cake, Hamza's favorite treasures: a Persian miniature on ivory, a beautiful inlaid Damascene cigarette box, and an enormous music box upholstered in pink silk. At the touch of a button on the music box a ballerina doll sprang up from a hidden recess and pirouetted, round and round, to the strains of "Tales From the Vienna Woods." Hamza pointed out the largest object on the table, a silver and gold globe, as big as a basketball. He pressed another button, and I started in fright. The world split open and cigarettes sprang out at us in all directions.

That was enough. I leaned back and nibbled a last tinned biscuit. Hamza thought I was bored and immediately suggested a tour of the house and gardens. We rose politely and followed him, tailed by the young son, still goggle-eyed. I decided privately that the boy must be not quite bright.

The gardens were lovely. Carefully tended rosebushes were in bloom, filling the air with fragrance. The grass was freshly watered and lush green, and rows of lemon and orange trees shook their leaves in the late afternoon breeze. At the edge of the gardens we could see the fields of green barley ripening in the gentle winter sun, stretching away as far as we could see to the edge of a palm grove. Small groups of Bedouin tents dotted the landscape and a man on a donkey, making his solitary way home, disappeared from sight as we watched. A flock of black-and-white crows rose, calling to each other from the tall grain. The sun had begun to set. I said to Hamza in all sincerity that with such a lovely scene to look upon every night, I thought he would never want to leave his house and go back to Baghdad. Jabbar agreed, pointing to the pale colors of the sky as the sunlight faded from the flat land and the dark palms, and said the country was very beautiful to him. Hamza seemed at a loss for words; after a moment he said he was lonely and bored in the house, and would leave again soon. We returned to the porch and sat on a lawn swing. As the twilight deepened, a faint trilling note came to us, and, as we waited, breathless, the full-throated song of a nightingale. It was a mournful song, clear and sweet in the quiet air. I had never heard a nightingale before, and was just deciding that I had been too harsh in my private judgments of Hamza's taste when a blast of music from the special combination record player drowned out the unseen bird. "Mambo Italiano!" screeched a sugary male Latin voice. Hamza chuckled with pleasure. "My son knows that we like music," he explained.

After "Mambo Italiano" we heard Elvis Presley on two badly cracked records; at the earsplitting volume Hamza's son had set, each nick in the face of the record grated doubly on our hearing. When Elvis Presley was finished, we heard "Mambo Italiano" again.

In half an hour we finally did accept a drink from Hamza. Anything to dull the noise, I thought, and asked for beer, which came with dishes of Greek olives, pistachio nuts, and canned English vegetable salad. At 7 P.M., starving and exhausted, we were summoned to lunch, five hours after we had arrived.

Hamza had spread his resources lavishly for us. I counted forty-three separate dishes of food on the table, centered by a whole roasted lamb. Unfortunately none of it was very good, and all of it was cold, the rice, the tomato sauce, even the good lamb meat clammy with a film of congealed grease. I was glad I was a woman then, for the delicacies of the table (sheep's eyes, roasted to lumps of fat) went to Bob and Jabbar. We picked at our food, doing our best, but it was heavy going. The cornstarch pudding was tinted bright pink and had the consistency of rapidly drying plaster. I barely got it down.

After our meal we returned to the living room, and as we sipped our coffee a sudden rainstorm burst around us. For fully two hours the rain poured down in sheets, and Jabbar looked worried. He told Bob in English that we could not leave until at least an hour after it stopped raining, for even with four-wheel drive we would not get farther than half a mile in the mucky fields. Of course, he added slyly, we could always spend the night at Hamza's. Spend the night? I looked in consternation at Bob, who was not too pleased at the prospect either. Hamza responded nobly to the sound of rain outside by turning on the record player again. We sat doggedly listening to "Mambo Italiano" and Elvis Presley over and over again until finally the rain let up.

At eleven o'clock Jabbar decided it might be worth trying the road. Hamza said he would send four men to ride in the back of the car and help us if we got stuck. Bob protested but Jabbar said he thought it was a good idea.

Hamza and his son stood at the door, bidding us a flowery farewell. We thanked them and shut the door of the Land-Rover. The four retainers, with rifles cocked, climbed into the back.

"Why do they bring their rifles?" I asked.

"Well," said Jabbar, "Hamza is not too popular with his fellahin, as I'm sure you can imagine. He sent the men along to help us out of the mud, but also he is taking no chances that someone might attack us."

"Surely that's not even a possibility," said Bob.

"You never know," answered Jabbar. "The share of the crop which the fellahin take is very small. Hamza gets the rest."

We inched through the mud in silence, for the presence of the four armed men in the back had dampened our conversational spirits. After two hours we reached the crossing to Suffra, and here we stopped, the men dismounted, said "God be with you," and turned to tramp home the ten miles through the muddy night.

"Thank you. God be with you," shouted Jabbar after them, and we started on again.

After perhaps another half hour Jabbar spoke.

"You mustn't think too harshly of Hamza," he said. "Oh, of course he wanted to see your wife—she is the only Western woman who has come into this area in years—but more than that, he probably was ashamed of his women's quarters. He wanted to entertain you in style, as he thinks Westerners entertain, and so he brought you to his house, to offer you the best he had. It's a compliment, in a way."

"He certainly was generous," admitted Bob.

"And Hamza is not really an evil man," continued Jabbar. "He is not like the sheiks on the Tigris who beat their fellahin and imprison them and treat them no better than pack animals. Hamza is just stupid.

"Yet," went on Jabbar, "because of his stupidity, many people are starving. No," he added, almost to himself, "it is not right. He must go, like all the others."

"But what about men like Sheik Hamid?" argued Bob. "They fulfill their tribal duties, they are hard-working and conscientious, they take only a fair share of the crop."

Jabbar was quiet for a moment. "Sheik Hamid is different, I agree," he said. "A hundred, even twenty years ago, he had a place, but not now. It is too bad, really; Sheik Hamid will fight in all sincerity because he feels he is right, and that sheiks and tribes are still important. He really believes that, you know. And when the revolution comes he will be hurt; he will never recover. I am sorry about men like Sheik Hamid. But Hamza"—he snapped his fingers in the air—"he will just run away and never understand what happened to him—if he gets away, that is."

And we were all silent, thinking of the foolish Hamza and his goggle-eyed son, his trick cigarette holders and Persian carpets, his plaster cake and his beautiful nightingale.

8

I Meet the Sheik

A week later I was presented to Sheik Hamid. The day after we returned from our visit to Hamza, Bob went up to the mudhif and invited the sheik to lunch. He accepted, and said his brother Abdulla and his oldest son Nour would accompany him. We decided that after lunch I would, minus my abayah, serve the tea; at that point I would be introduced, and the meeting would take place in our own house and on our own terms.

We were both extremely apprehensive about the lunch. It was the first time we had entertained our host, and we wanted to do it well. For days beforehand we discussed what might be appropriate to serve; finally I drew up a menu which Bob liked, and submitted it to Mohammed for his approval. He made only one change. "Five chickens would be better than three," he said. "After all, it is Haji Hamid who is coming."

And this is what we had:

Chicken and Noodle Soup
Grilled Kebab   Beef in Spiced Tomato Sauce
Lamb cooked with Beans and Onions and Fresh Dill
Whole Roast Chickens (2)
Fried Chickens, American Style (3)
Caucasian Rice (with raisins, almonds, onions,
chicken livers, butter and saffron)
Eggplant in Meat Sauce   Sliced Tomato Salad
Yogurt   Khubuz (flat wheat bread)
Homemade Western Bread
Butter and Jam
Strawberry Jello   Caramel Custard
Spongecake   Cookies
Fresh Fruit (Bananas and Oranges)
Tea   Coffee

We wanted to provide enough food to honor the sheik in traditional fashion, yet no more than he might provide for us if the situation were reversed. I wanted to prove, egotistically enough, that I could cook. Mohammed simply wanted, I think, not to be ashamed of us.

So for three days we prepared for the feast. The chickens and butter were ordered, and Mohammed's mother offered to make the *khubuz* and send it over hot, just before lunch. Mohammed visited four food stalls in the market to find amber rice. I baked bread, cake, cookies, made the desserts and the yogurt. Bob picked out the fruit himself, piece by piece, and Mohammed bargained for it. The night before, all three of us were in a state of nervous exhaustion.

The day of the lunch I was up at six, for there were many dishes to cook, and I had only two kerosene burners and the camp stove on which to work. Mohammed arrived at eight, and Bob fussed around the kitchen, watching us cut up the onions and the meat, fry the almonds and raisins and chicken livers in butter, and pound the spices. He kept going out and coming back, and made our feverish preparations no better by telling us that everyone in the settlement was aware that the sheik was lunching with us that day. "An hour after he leaves, every house will know exactly what we served them," he said. "So it better be good." I nearly lost my temper at that point, but Mohammed merely looked around him at the pots boiling on all the burners, at the cut-up vegetables, the fruit, and the sweets which lay piled on the kitchen table, and then looked calmly at Bob. "There is a great deal of food here," he said. Bob repented, and offered to make amends by cutting up the raw chickens, cleaned and plucked the day before by Mohammed, into American-style pieces. Mohammed thought this amusing but said it was not a bad idea, since it would make the chickens easier to eat.

The men were due at one and I felt I must produce the food fifteen minutes later, no more, no less. At 12 the camp stove sputtered out of gas; Bob was already at the mudhif, waiting to accompany the men personally to the house. Mohammed was making salad, but he dropped everything and ran to the market for gas.

At 12:45 Mohammed asked me for the tray.

"What tray?" I said.

"The big tray for serving," he answered, and explained that he should carry in all the food at once, in order to make the best possible impression.

"I don't have a tray like that," I confessed, panic-stricken.

"Never mind," said Mohammed, and ran out again, returning with an enormous tin tray like the one Ali had brought my first day in the village. "My mother's cousin's," he explained, and sat down on the floor to scour it. I noticed he had put on a clean dishdasha while he was at home, and that his kaffiyeh was freshly pressed.

I heard the gate open, and knew that the guests had arrived. Bob almost immediately came into the kitchen to check on the progress of our preparations, and, seeing Mohammed down on the floor scouring the tray, looked quite cross.

"Why didn't he do that before?" he asked. "It's one o'clock. They're here. We have to eat."

I explained. Mohammed, who had not understood what we had said, must have caught the tone. He suggested that it would be better if Bob did not leave our esteemed guests alone in the other room. Bob went.

Then Mohammed and I dished up the food, the chicken, the kebab, the meat dishes, the vegetables and salad and yogurt. Abad, his younger brother, appeared at the back door with the bread, still hot from the family oven. I began to spoon the rice out onto a platter, but Mohammed said he would do it, and proceeded to pack the rice down carefully so as to cover the entire platter with a neat mound, saving a few of the nuts and raisins and the crisp butter crust from the bottom of the pan to decorate the top. He looked quite pleased with his handiwork. We piled the platters, twelve of them, onto the tray. Mohammed mopped his brow, readjusted his headdress, then lifted the heavy, steaming tray to his shoulder and set out for the other room.

I sat down in the kitchen. The first part of my job was over. I listened carefully for voices from the living room which might indicate how the whole thing was going. After an interminable quarter of an hour, Mohammed came back.

"They are eating a lot," he said. "The rice is all right."

He looked as relieved as though he had cooked it himself. He carefully mopped his brow again, before returning to the living room to stand by in case he was needed. This was the signal for me to lock the door, change into my brown wool dress, and put on lipstick and earrings and my Baghdadi gold bracelet in honor of the guests I was about to meet.

Mohammed knocked, and I opened the door so he could bring in the tray of leftover food. I looked carefully at the dishes; the rice had indeed been a success. I had cooked enough, I thought, for fifteen people, and almost half of it was gone. The men had also seemed to enjoy the soup, the chickens (their plates were piled with bones) and the meat with tomato and spices. The eggplant and bean dishes had not been so popular.

Now for dessert! The tray of sweets looked quite attractive, I thought; Mohammed must have thought so too, for he went out to the garden and brought back a rose to stick into the spongecake. At that I was impressed. Mohammed shouldered the tray again, actually smiling as he went out.

Ten minutes passed before dessert was polished off. Mohammed came back with the partially eaten food. He would brew the tea now, he said—he knew exactly how the sheik liked it, with a bit of cardamom seed. I was glad to turn over this responsibility to him, for I found, as my meeting with Hamid approached, that I was as nervous as an adolescent debutante at her coming-out ball. I combed my hair for the fourth time and adjusted the earrings again. Bob came into the kitchen, looking quite pleased, saying the food had been good. "It's almost time," he said in a tone usually reserved for missile firings and atomic-bomb explosions.

Mohammed was carefully placing three spoonfuls of

sugar in each tiny glass, then he poured the tea—strong enough to float an egg, I thought, but it did emit a fine odor of cardamom. "Come on," said Bob. "Wait two minutes after I leave, and then bring in the tea." I did, wondering idiotically, as I traversed the short mud path from the kitchen to the living room, whether or not my stocking seams were straight.

I went in, my eyes cast down, less from modesty than from simple unadulterated stage fright. The men said good afternoon. I replied nervously, my voice cracking foolishly. I passed the tea around, somewhat shakily, and set down the tray. Then Bob introduced me formally and I shook hands with the three men, drew up a chair into the circle, and looked directly at my distinguished guests for the first time.

Sheik Hamid Abdul Emir el Hussein, honored with the title *El Haji* because he had made the *hajj* or pilgrimage to Mecca, returned my gaze. I cannot say exactly what I had expected this man to be like, whose lineage was one of the oldest and purest in southern Arabia and whose position had become synonymous in my world with romance, wanderlust, and mystery. But I didn't expect him to be quite so solid and dignified, exuding an air of middle-aged respectability and authority.

Sheik Hamid was a big man, portly but erect; his gray mustache was clipped, and his steel-rimmed glasses sat squarely on his nose. Superficially he resembled Sheik Hamza, in his sober well-tailored brown robes, British shoes, gold signet ring and wrist watch, fingering his string of amber worry beads. But there the resemblance ended; where Hamza shambled and goggled, Sheik Hamid was direct and businesslike. Seated firmly in his chair like a man who is reasonably successful and content with life, he regarded me in a forthright fashion, smiled and inquired briskly about my family. Was my father well? I replied that my father had been dead for many years. The guests clucked sympathetically, and the sheik's brother Abdulla said that it was difficult for a family when the father died. Was my mother well? Yes, I said, and turned toward Abdulla, a tall spare man with finely drawn features and deep-set eyes. He was murmuring condolences about my father, and as I listened to the mellifluous Arabic words, rounding and joining in a harmonious pattern, I lost some of my nervousness in the beauty of the language spoken so well by this gentleman.

Abdulla asked me if we were comfortable in El Nahra, and I said yes. Sheik Hamid said we were welcome to stay as long as we liked, that his house was our house, and his belongings ours. I knew these were the customary sentiments, uttered to every guest, but he said them sincerely and I believed him. Then Nour, his son, said something to his father in an undertone; I wondered why he had not participated in the conversation, and then I remembered Bob's saying that when a son, whatever his age, was in the presence of his father, he always deferred to him and did not speak until he was spoken to.

The sheik listened to Nour's whisper and then said to me, "Is there anything you need for your house that we might provide?"

"No, no," I protested. "We are grateful for what you have done already. Thank you very much."

We spoke of the weather, and Sheik Hamid and Abdulla and Bob discussed the condition of the crops. I brought in another tray of tea. Bob passed around cigarettes. Abdulla and Nour took one, but Sheik Hamid did not.

"You do not smoke?" said Sheik Hamid to me.

"No," I replied.

"It is better for a woman if she does not smoke," remarked Abdulla.

I smiled politely. He was paying me a compliment, I knew, but since I was not certain how to respond, I kept silent. My part of the conversation was apparently over and I looked at Bob, trying to convey that I felt it was time for me to leave; he understood and nodded.

I rose to collect the empty tea glasses, and asked the men if they would drink another tea. They refused, as is customary when food or drink is offered for the first time. Bob pressed them to have more, which is also customary, and Sheik Hamid said no, the tea was very good, but he had had enough. Once more Bob offered it, and they still refused; this was a sign they really did not want any more tea!

"You must excuse me. I have work in the house," I said.

Sheik Hamid chuckled, but the chuckle had no edge of salaciousness about it, as Hamza's had. It was an extremely fatherly chuckle.

I bade them farewell, apologizing for not shaking hands, for I was carrying the tray.

"You must always visit my family," said Sheik Hamid, and Abdulla repeated the sentiment.

"Ahlan wusahlan," I replied, and Bob held the screen door open for me as I departed.

When I got to the kitchen, I found I was perspiring from a combination of nervousness and relief. Mohammed was down on the floor washing the dishes, for he had gone home during the tea drinking and changed into his old dishdasha. The clean kaffiyeh was draped over a chair.

I told Mohammed how good the bread had been which his mother had sent, and he nodded, saying that his mother always made good bread. Sometime, he added, he would bring me *khubuz laham,* a special bread in which tiny cubes of cooked meat and onions and chopped celery leaves were added to the dough before the bread was baked. I began to put away the leftover food and tidy the kitchen, and the piles of plates and greasy pots were diminishing as Mohammed worked steadily.

I felt let down and disappointed. I suppose I had expected Mohammed to comment enthusiastically on the excellence of each dish which we had presented for the sheik's pleasure. He didn't. No one ever did such a thing, I found out later. If the food was good, it was obvious; people ate it, and there was little of it left. Why should one talk about it? I half realized this, even at the time, but I needed reassurance.

Finally we heard the men leaving, Bob walking to the gate with them, and then the sound of his footsteps running back up the path. He burst into the kitchen quite jubilantly.

"The food was good, B.J.," he announced, "and what

impressed them even more was that you cooked that dinner all by yourself."

"Mohammed helped, you know."

"Yes, but Sheik Hamid said it would have taken seven or eight women in his house to produce that much food. He was quite struck by your industry."

"Let's hope he mentions it to *his* women," I replied. "Maybe they will begin to think I'm good for something."

"Well, they'll hear it one way or another," said Bob. He stopped and considered.

"I think the whole thing went off all right, don't you?" he asked, and we sat down to review, play by play, the incidents of the great occasion. We were very pleased with ourselves. Mohammed continued to wash dishes, glancing up at us only occasionally with what I thought was an indulgent smile.

PART II

PART II

9

Ramadan

Ramadan, the Islamic month of fasting and penitence, fell in April that year. We had been well briefed about Ramadan by our friends in El Nahra, who described the strict fast—no food, water or cigarettes from sunup to sundown. After the breaking of the fast, regular religious readings (*krayas*) were held, conducted by mullahs, men and women religious teachers who served the segregated sexes. Gay evenings of visiting, socializing and tea drinking inevitably followed the krayas and the long days of abstinence. This year particularly, people welcomed Ramadan, for it was to come in a relatively cool month. As the lunar calendar, by which the Islamic feasts are calculated, moves forward through the seasons, Ramadan falls at a different time each year. When it comes in the summer, in the burning heat of July or August, it is a great hardship on the faithful fellahin who must work all day in the fields without a drink of water or a mouthful of food. Many of the old and sick die during a summer Ramadan, but if this happens, the souls are assured of immediate entrance to heaven, for death has occurred when the believer was fasting and hence in a state of grace.

The beginning of Ramadan is marked by the appearance of the new moon. The mullahs in the holy shrines of Khadhimain, Najaf and Karbala watch the sky for several days, and when the chief mullah announces that he has indeed seen the crescent moon, however briefly, the beginning of the month is officially declared from the minarets of the mosques. The news travels quickly by radio, by taxi and horseback throughout the surrounding countryside.

Two nights in a row Mohammed came with the evening jug of water to announce that he thought Ramadan would begin the next day; two mornings he appeared to say he had been mistaken. The third night the skies opened and it poured. Bob and I had considered waiting up to see if the new moon really would appear, but the rain discouraged us and we went to bed early.

In the middle of the night our doorbell began to ring. I heard it first, an insistent buzzing that went on and on, audible over the steady beat of the rain on the roof. I woke Bob. Who could be at the door at this hour? The bell went on buzzing. It was an eerie sound at three in the morning, in the darkness and the rain. Finally Bob got up, slipped on rubbers and a raincoat and went to investigate. No one was there, but the bell continued to buzz. After standing in the garden for a few minutes listening to the noise, Bob suddenly realized that the rain had short-circuited the bell. He tried to fix it and failed, and finally, drenched and furious, he simply ripped out the connection. The bell stopped ringing. He dried himself off and got back into bed, grumbling and annoyed. We fell asleep almost at once. Perhaps a half hour later we were startled awake by a thunderous noise of drum beats, rifle shots, shouts and a loud knocking on the door. Bob sat bolt upright in bed.

"Don't go out there," I suggested, quite frightened.

Bob deliberated for a moment. He too had been startled by the unaccustomed noises and also had just spent fifteen minutes in the muck trying to disconnect the doorbell, but finally he put on his wet raincoat and rubbers again. At the door he paused, rummaged in the cupboard until he found a hammer, and headed out.

"What's that for?" I asked.

"Well," he smiled sheepishly, and I realized he was probably a bit uncertain about what he might find. We had no weapon in the house.

Out he slogged into the pouring rain, while I sat in bed shivering, hugging the blankets around me, and listening for telltale sounds. The knocking had stopped, but the rifle shots continued and the drum beating became even louder.

In five minutes he was back, laughing. He tossed the

hammer on the table. "What is it?" I asked, but he sat at the table while the water dripped down his face, and laughed and laughed.

"It's Ramadan," he announced. "The mullah must have seen the new moon, and the old man up the alley is making sure that everyone knows it."

"But why the knocking on our door?" I persisted.

"He's knocking on every door," Bob answered, "to remind the people to get up and eat breakfast before the sun rises. He's the neighborhood alarm clock."

Bob dried himself once more and climbed into bed, still smiling to himself. "You were really frightened, I think," he chided me.

"Well, what did you carry that hammer out for?" I answered accusingly, and he laughed again. We fell asleep and didn't wake until Mohammed knocked on our door. It was half past eight.

"It's Ramadan," announced Mohammed.

"Yes, we know," said Bob.

Ramadan had been under way for a week when Mohammed asked me if I would like to go to an evening kraya with his sister Sherifa. It would be a big kraya, he said, held in the house of a distant relative who lived on the other side of the canal, with the *ahl-es-suq*, or people of the market. Bob had already been to several krayas for men, and I was eager to go, for the women talked about the krayas as great social as well as religious events.

Fadhila, Sherifa and several younger girls came for me. They were not wearing their face veils, which surprised me, as I knew we would be crossing the bridge and passing the suq, and the tribal women did not walk unveiled in that area. However, I had underestimated their ingenuity. They did not want, and did not need, to wear their face veils on the settlement side of the canal, so they waited until we reached the bridge before pausing to don their veils.

We crossed the bridge, turned right into an alley immediately in order to avoid the suq, and again into still another alley where we knocked on a dark door and were admitted into a large courtyard. Electric lights were strung along the mud walls which faced the court, illuminating the scene of preparations for the kraya. The earth court was carpeted, and mats were now being laid down in straight rows and covered with white sheets for the expected guests. Two women squatted in a far corner, filling with cigarettes a large plastic box painted with colored flowers. Sherifa and Fadhila went to the women and embraced them, kissing them on both cheeks. I shook hands, we were offered cigarettes and then led to a mat in the center of the court, near the chair where the mullah was to sit. Fadhila told me she and Sherifa were placed next to the mullah as a special honor, because they were descendants of the Prophet.

Against one side of the court which lay in shadow stood a rickety wooden bed where a woman lay, wrapped from head to foot in her abayah. She occasionally shifted position and moaned. Near the bed were five or six clay water jars, from which the young girls of the household were filling small aluminum bowls. These bowls of water were passed around, with the cigarettes, to the growing number of guests.

The kraya, Sherifa said, would begin about half past eight. It was still only seven-thirty, but fifteen or twenty women and numerous children were already present. I had never seen any of the women of ahl-es-suq before, the shopkeepers' and artisans' wives, and I watched them as they filed in, greeted friends, and kissed with deference the older women present.

Babies slept peacefully in their mothers' arms, babies wrapped in yards of white or printed flannelette, and the toddlers sat quietly, cross-legged and solemn beside their elders. Only one child was crying, its abnormally large head lolling against its mother's shoulder. She jostled it constantly, but it continued to howl. No one else seemed to notice, for the women were too busy talking to each other.

For the occasion, young and old had donned their best black. There were some beautiful abayahs of heavy silk crepe, and a few of the black head scarves were heavily fringed. Many wore a wide-sleeved full net or sheer black dress, which Sherifa identified as the *hashmiya*, the ceremonial gown worn for krayas and similar religious services. Underneath was a hint of color; as the women seated themselves cross-legged and arranged their hashmiyas over their knees, bright satin petticoats shimmered through the smoky net: green, blue, red. They wore black stockings, and the rows of clogs left at the door were almost all black.

This attractive yet austerely dressed company was suddenly jolted by a new arrival, whose abayah had been pushed back over her shoulder to reveal a sheer hashmiya surprisingly not black, but green and white over yellow. Heavily made up, all her bangles and necklaces jingling, the woman flounced in, looking defiantly from side to side. The young girls gathered around her to finger the material of the showy hashmiya, but the conservative old matrons, without jewelry and without eye make-up, continued to smoke or chat, not even lifting a hennaed finger in her direction.

There was a stir: the mullah had arrived, a tall woman with a hard, strong face, carrying worn copies of the Koran and her own Book of Krayas. Everyone made way for her as she strode across the court and seated herself ceremoniously in the chair near us, the only chair in the room. Sherifa and Fadhila rose to kiss her hand, and then she spied me and looked again, narrowing her eyes. I nodded politely, not feeling that it was appropriate for me to indulge in the customary hand kissing since I was an unbeliever. She addressed a couple of questions to me in a loud, shrill voice which I did not understand, but the hostess stepped in and explained that I was the guest of the El Eshadda; Sherifa added that I wanted to see a kraya and they had invited me. The mullah nodded, said "*Ahlan wusahlan*" perfunctorily and looked away. More women and children were pouring into the court; we were forced to move over and make room for two young women who were old friends of Sherifa and Fadhila. The four of them chattered together until the mullah interrupted rudely and asked Fadhila if she was pregnant.

Fadhila said no.

"Why not?" demanded the mullah.

Fadhila, obviously stricken, murmured, "God knows best," in a low voice.

I thought it a cruel question, for Fadhila had been married for seven years, and everyone in the village knew she was barren.

Finally, when it seemed that not a single person more could be jammed into the court, the mullah stood up and clapped her hands to quiet the crowd. The two young women who sat near us took their places on each side of her (they were novices, I later found out, in training to be mullahs themselves) and the kraya began.

The mullah sat down and the two young girls stood to lead the congregation in a long, involved song with many responses. Gradually the women began to beat their breasts rhythmically, nodding their heads and beating in time to the pulse of the song, and occasionally joining in the choruses, or supplying spontaneous responses such as "A-hoo-ha!" or a long-drawn-out "Ooooooh!" This phase lasted perhaps ten minutes, the girls sank down into their places, and the mullah arose to deliver a short sermon. She began retelling the story of the killing and betrayal of the martyr Hussein, which is told every night during Ramadan and is the beginning of the important part of the kraya. At first two or three sobs could be heard, then perhaps twenty women had covered their heads with their abayahs and were weeping; in a few minutes the whole crowd was crying and sobbing loudly. When the mullah reached the most tragic parts of the story, she would stop and lead the congregation in a group chant, which started low and increased in volume until it reached the pitch of a full-fledged wail. Then she would stop dead again, and the result would be, by this time, a sincere sobbing and weeping as the women broke down after the tension of the wail.

I sat silently, frozen by the intensity of it all, and hoping that none of the women, and especially the mullah, would notice that I was sitting without beating my breast, without chanting or weeping—in fact without participating at all. I contemplated throwing my abayah over my head,

as all the other women had done, so the hawk-eyed mullah
would not be able to tell whether I was crying or not,
but by this time I thought she was sufficiently carried away
by the force of her own words so that she wouldn't have
cared. I was right. Real tears were coursing down that
hard, shrewd face as she told, for the hundred thousandth
time probably, the story of the death of the martyr.

Abruptly the weeping stopped, the women were drying their eyes and everyone stood up. I nearly tripped
and fell as I tried to rise, for my abayah was caught under
me and one leg had fallen asleep in the cramped position
in which I had been sitting for the past hour. Sherifa caught
my shoulder as I stumbled—fortunately, for the mullah was
beginning the third stage of the kraya. Flanked by her two
novices, she stood in the center of the court rocking forward with her whole body at each beat, slowly but regularly, until the crowds of women formed concentric circles
around her, and they too rocked in unison, singing and
beating their breasts. Three older women joined the mullah in the center, throwing aside their chin veils so they
might slap their bared chests.

"A-hoo-ha!" sounded the responses.

All her veils flying as she rocked, the mullah struck her
book with her right hand to indicate a faster tempo, and
the novices clapped and watched to make sure that all
were following correctly. I shrank back out as the circles
of women began to move counterclockwise in a near-
ceremonial dance. A step to the left, accompanied by head-
nodding, breast-beating, the clapping of the novices, the
slap of the mullah's hard hand against the book, and the
responses of "A-hoo-ha!" "Ya Hussein," they cried. The
mullah increased the tempo again, the cries mounted in
volume and intensity, the old women in the center bobbed
in time to the beat, there was a loud slap against the Koran,
a high long-drawn-out chant from the mullah, and everyone stopped in her tracks. The three old ladies who had
bared their chests readjusted their veils, and many of the
women stood silently for a moment, their eyes raised, their
open hands held upward in an attitude of prayer and

supplication. But the mullah was already conferring with her novices. The kraya was over.

The women began to stream out, smiling and chattering, drawing their veils over their faces and bidding each other good night. Sherifa was laughing with one of the novices. Fadhila led me over to our hostess, where we sat down for a final chat and cigarette before departing. It was hard to believe that these decorous and dignified ladies were the same women who, five minutes ago, had thrown themselves into a ritual of sorrow for the martyr. I was quite overcome by the episode and found it difficult to respond easily to the conversational overtures being made by my hostess.

Finally we rose to go. It was ten o'clock. The old woman on the bed in the corner, I noticed, had not stirred throughout the whole ceremony. As we began to leave, a crowd of little girls surrounded me, grabbed me, pulled my abayah apart to see my dress and stared rudely into my face. "Haven't you ever seen a woman before?" asked the hostess, quite annoyed, trying to hustle the children out, but they would not go. Sherifa tried to push through, but the crowd of girls was too dense around me. At this the mullah became enraged, and shoved her towering, threatening figure through the crowd, setting on the little girls, beating them with her fists and with the Koran and sending them screaming and hollering, half in pain, half in excitement, out into the night. I thanked her. The women also were amused by this display of the mullah's temper, and talked about it on the way home, imitating to each other her gestures with the Koran and laughing among themselves.

"Was the kraya good?" asked Sherifa.

"Oh, yes," I said.

"This mullah is a strong one; she talks well," she said appreciatively, and I agreed.

Almost every evening during Ramadan I went to krayas —at the sheik's house, at Laila's house, at Abdulla's and Mohammed's. The tone of each kraya depended on the personality of the mullah, but the basic ritual remained the same: The *latmya* invocation with preliminary chant and breast-beating; the sermon, different for each day of Ramadan, but followed by the telling of Hussein's betrayal (*hadith*); the latmya again, at a faster pace, with the circles of women moving together in strict tempo, the spontaneous cries and wails, the profession of inspired penitence by the few women who join the mullah in the inner circle and finally the *da-a*, or moment of silence and prayer at the end. This final moment is considered to be the climax of the kraya, I was told, for then, in a state of purification, the women may ask great favors from Allah and expect to have them granted. Often these favors are requested conditionally. A woman may pray for a son, and vow that if her prayer is granted, she will hold krayas in her house during Ramadan for a stipulated number of years. Such vows are sacred, and if for some reason the woman cannot fulfill them, she may be released only by a gift to the mosque or to the mullah.

The krayas are comparatively recent innovations into Shiite ritual, dating from the sixteenth century, when the Ottoman Turks conquered Mesopotamia and imposed their sometimes harsh and unjust rule on the people of Iraq. The Turks were Moslems, but Sunni Moslems; they were hated doubly by the Shiites, as conquerors and as representatives of a rival sect. The krayas had begun as protest, and as they gained in popularity and acceptance throughout the Shiite world, became the means by which the Shiites asserted their religious differences from the Turks and, by implication, their dissatisfaction with the Ottoman regime.

Today the krayas still provide religious fulfillment for both men and women, and they also seem important as social occasions in the lives of the women, who seldom congregate in large groups. Women gather for two hours before a kraya is scheduled to begin, and stay long after the mullah has departed, talking and smoking. No refreshments other than cigarettes are ever offered.

Women consider it a great honor to hold krayas in their houses. Usually extra money is needed, to pay for the cigarettes and to offer a gift to the mullah for her services, and this money must either come out of the woman's own savings or be granted to her by her husband. Often the presents to the mullahs are made in kind. Laila told me that they always gave two chickens and a gallon can of clarified butter to the mullah on the two great feasts, and in return the mullah would officiate at several krayas, either during Ramadan or Muharram. But Sherifa and Fadhila might ask the mullah to come for nothing, for it is considered an honor for the mullah to hold a kraya in the house of a Sayid.

Mullahs are not necessarily Sayids themselves. However, the vocation of mullah is usually handed down within a family. Widows, or young girls who do not expect to marry, often choose to become mullahs. It is a highly esteemed profession, and profitable as well—a gifted woman can support an entire family.

Women mullahs receive their training from older mullahs in their native villages, going regularly for lessons from the time of puberty. They learn to read and write and recite the Koran, they are instructed in the ritual of the krayas, and begin to memorize the Koranic *suras*, the stories, the historical background which they incorporate eventually into their own Book of Krayas. An educated Shiite mullah has a sophisticated and well-documented source book which she uses to conduct her krayas. The tribal and village mullahs depend on legend and oral tradition to supplement the standard material employed in the sermons and rituals.

A Shiite friend of mine in Baghdad, a girl who was teaching in the College of Liberal Arts, once told me that her sister wanted very much to become a mullah, but their father would not allow it. He felt first, that it was old-fashioned, and also, with many educated Shiites, that such special vocations and ceremonies accentuated and aggravated the differences among the sects of Islam, and that only if the bitterness between groups in the Arab world, and particularly religious groups, could be dissipated would Arab unity be possible. My friend agreed with her father, but she admitted that she still attended krayas during Ramadan and Muharram.

Why did she go? The memories of childhood were still

very strong, she said, and she found the krayas a common meeting ground for herself, estranged from the old ways, and her sisters and cousins, who were still traditional. She enjoyed the reading of the Koran which followed the krayas. Each of the women present would take a turn at reading the suras, which gave everyone an opportunity to participate personally in the proceedings.

The krayas in El Nahra were not often followed by Koranic readings, simply because most of the women could not read. Only at Laila's house, where the two middle girls, Laila and Basima, were in the sixth class of the girls' primary school, did this take place. The women of the settlement told me that the krayas at Laila's house were always good, because of the Koranic readings at the end. It was considered a great treat: Basima would read, and Laila, and finally their mother, Um Fatima, would take the Koran and read a few of the most important suras. As a girl in her father's house, Um Fatima had been taught the rudiments of reading by a mullah, and she still retained this limited ability. Laila was competent, but Basima was better than either. More intelligent than Laila and better educated than her mother, Basima seemed to sense the power of the words she was reading. They were not just groups of characters to her, and as she sat on the mat and read sura after sura in a slow, expressive voice, women would shake their heads, murmur to themselves, or raise their open hands to heaven in the traditional gestures of supplication. When she had finished, there would be a pause, a sort of hush before the women sighed, gathered their abayahs around them, and prepared to leave.

10

The Feast

Ramadan was drawing to a close, and the three-day Iid el-Fitr (the feast of fast-breaking) drew near. This year the end of Ramadan coincided with the winter harvest, so the festival was to be celebrated in a season of plenty. Almost everyone would be able to afford new clothes, traditional for the occasion, and the three seamstresses in the settlement worked far into the night.

For the three days of the Iid the sheik's mudhif would be the scene of tribal feasting. All members of the El Eshadda were welcome, in fact expected, to visit the mudhif at least once during the Iid as a tacit demonstration of their loyalty to the sheik. Such large tribal gatherings took place only at this Iid and the Iid el-Adha, which follows Muharram. But then the men assembled, as they had in the past before wars and raids of conquest, to sing old songs of the tribe, and, in the measures of the ancient warriors' dance or *hosa*, reiterate their pride in the El Eshadda and its present chief. Climax of the gathering was an enormous noonday meal in the mudhif, provided by the sheik with the aid of contributions from other tribesmen.

The banquet, for from 200 to 800 men, was prepared by the women of the sheik's house, assisted by the daughters and wives and servants of his brothers. The women talked of nothing else for weeks beforehand, and when the first day of the feast dawned, I hurried up to the compound to see what was happening.

Inside the mud walls the women were already at work, but they rose to greet me, and we shook hands and exchanged the salutations of the day, "*Ayyamak sa'ida* [May this day be happy for you]." Hard candies were offered and *kolaicha*, the sweet cakes of sugar, oil, barley flour and cardamom seed made especially for the Iid.

"Come up above, we can see better from there," said Laila, leading me up a narrow stair to the wide roof covering one end of the compound which had been used as an observation post when the house had been a fortress. From the low battlements we could view discreetly the increasing activity around the mudhif. The clearing was just beginning to fill with men, and servants hurried about, filling the animal troughs with water and stacking freshly cut grass into piles for the visitors' horses. A thin ribbon of smoke spiraled from the mudhif entrance, signal that the coffeemaker, freed grandson of a Negro slave, was roasting beans over charcoal.

Since early morning tribesmen had been arriving from outlying clan settlements. Even now, from the roof we could see several small figures of horsemen on the flat horizon, outlined against the bright blue sky. They gradually assumed shape as they approached in twos and threes, and we could see the men's abas and kaffiyehs billowing behind them in the light breeze, and their saddle buckles glinting in the morning sun. Then there was a pause as the horses were hidden in the shady palm grove, a sudden clatter of hoofs as they burst out of the grove onto the hard-packed silt of the clearing, and shouts of recognition as the men dismounted, tied their horses and turned to greet the sheik, who was seated ceremoniously on a pillow just inside the entrance. Bright rugs had been laid on the floor next to the arched walls of the mudhif, and here the men took their places after exchanging traditional greetings with the sheik and the men already present. The coffeemaker brought them a sip of bitter coffee in a tiny china cup; they drank the coffee, and the arrival was officially over; the men settled themselves for low-voiced conversation with their fellow tribesmen, some of whom they might see only on these occasions.

Laila was very excited, and pointed out individuals to me—Hikmat, her mother's cousin from the El Jurayd clan; two brothers of Sheik Hamid's first wife; a gray-bearded

man riding up with his three sons, the subchief of one
of the original clans of the El Eshadda. There also, said
Laila, was Sayid Muhsen, descendant of a Persian family
which had settled in the El Eshadda area a hundred years
ago. Sayid Muhsen was well known for his progressive
ideas. I remembered that Bob had told me Muhsen had
built a school in his little settlement of fifty families and
had gone to Baghdad to beg a teacher from the Ministry
of Education. It was rumored that the girls and boys of
the settlement attended school together, which was almost unheard of in the Diwaniya area. There—Laila paused
—yes, she said, it was Urthman, one of the estranged uncles
of the sheik. The quarrel over the succession to the sheikship still smoldered between the two men, but on feast
days Urthman came to say his salaams to Hamid. Laila
predicted, however, that Urthman would not stay to lunch.

The crowd was growing, augmented by the men of our
settlement, who were emerging from the houses along the
path in new white dishdashas and freshly pressed abas.
Boys and girls dashed round the clearing, excited by the
activities of the festal day and dazzled by their own sar-
torial splendor, the new sandals or tennis shoes, the girls
in bright dresses, the boys in striped dishdashas. They
ran between the women's quarters and the mudhif, bearing messages in both directions.

"Haji wants tea now for him and three guests," announced Abbas, second son of Selma.

"Yes, yes," answered Selma, preoccupied with the rice
paste she was patting into shape for *kubbas*.

"Now, Mother," insisted Abbas.

"Who are the guests?" Selma wanted to know.

Abbas listed them, and within a few minutes every
woman in the compound knew that the mayor, the engineer and a visitor from Diwaniya had come to pay their
respects to the sheik.

The women had been at work since five o'clock, but
now at ten, instead of losing heart at the prospect of the
300 lunches to be served hot at noon, they were gayer than
ever. Even Kulthum who, as senior wife, was supervising
the preparations with seriousness and dispatch, paused in

her work to exclaim in surprise when told that Urthman had arrived and might stay to lunch. Laila translated, telling me Kulthum had remarked acidly that Urthman's winter harvest must not be too good if he found it necessary to cadge a free meal from the nephew whom he cursed in every coffee shop in the vicinity. But I gathered from the tone of the laughter and the blushes on the sheik's daughters' faces that Kulthum's comment had been a good deal more pungent than that.

For the feast, a cow and five full-grown sheep had been killed; Laila took me to the slaughterhouse behind the women's quarters where Abu Selman, the sheik's official butcher, had ceremoniously slit the throats of the animals and murmured the customary blessing over them. Abu Selman was now skinning the carcasses and removing the entrails. The kidneys, liver, heart and brains were set aside for special dishes; the head, stomach and feet of three of the sheep were turned over to the sheik's daughter Samira, who would clean them and make them into *patcha*, a local delicacy. The other two sheep were to be roasted whole over a charcoal spit and the eyes and ears offered as treats to the most honored guests. Abu Selman chopped the carcasses into great chunks and his son carried them on tin trays to Kulthum, who waited with her sharpened knife to cut the mutton and beef into still smaller pieces. The piles of fresh slippery meat were washed and washed under the water tap, then went into salted water to be boiled until tender over fires of dried palm fronds that were blazing all over the eastern corner of the court. This boiled meat and its broth, together with bowls of vegetable stew, mounds of rice and piles of wheat bread, formed the meal which would be served to the tribesmen.

The sun climbed higher, and the heat from the fires added to the general discomfort; the women were sweating profusely through their black garments. In one corner the sheik's daughters and their cousins were peeling squash, chopping spinach and cutting up onions and tomatoes for the vegetable stew, to be flavored with a bit of fat meat, garlic, salt, celery leaves and raw ground turmeric. Three women were mixing and patting barley dough into flat loaves; a small girl sat brushing the flies away from rows of plates of cornstarch pudding.

"More fuel, Amina," called Kulthum. "Samira! Sabiha!" Armloads of small sticks and fronds were brought and Amina stoked the open fires.

"Here, too," Alwiyah shouted. She stood at the door of the kitchen, wiping her eyes with her foota while smoke billowed white around her. "Quickly, Amina, hurry."

"Yes, yes," muttered Amina, depositing more fuel at the door.

"No, inside," and Alwiyah gave her a good-natured push.

Grumbling, Amina entered, dropped the fuel and re-appeared wiping her eyes.

"It's hot as hell in there!" she announced to the whole court, and everyone laughed as she elbowed Alwiyah and then ran like a naughty child from the sheik's daughter's outraged dignity.

"What are you cooking?" I asked Alwiyah, and she showed me into the kitchen, a long mud-brick room without smoke holes, where six or eight women were stirring and tending enormous pots cooking on open fires. The smoke hung in the room like dense fog, and the women would stir for a few moments, then walk to the door to wipe their streaming eyes and mop their sweat-streaked faces. Yet they laughed as they did so.

"These are the dishes for the sheik and the special guests," Alwiyah said. This explained the women's good nature despite the heat and smoke. They had been chosen as the best cooks, to prepare food for Haji's tray.

"Don't stay in here, Beeja—it's too hot," warned Alwiyah with a hand on my shoulder. But I wanted to see the food, so the pots were uncovered one by one: ground liver stewed with tomatoes, kubba, fried eggplant, patcha, saffron rice. Four chickens were being grilled over charcoal in the bank of round brick ovens along one side of the kitchen.

"Beeja, the hosa is beginning. Come on," called Laila.

Bob had told me to watch for the hosa, which in the past was always performed before the tribe went to war or set out on foraging raids into the desert. Now it served as a rally of support for the tribe and for its leader, reviving memories of the El Eshaddas' exploits and inspiring tribal pride in their collective glory.

"Come quickly," said Laila, and we hurried up to the roof again. The crowd was backing away from the front of the mudhif, leaving an open space for young tribesmen with rifles held high to assemble in a circle. The sheik stood near the entrance, the proper position for him during the songs of the hosa, which praised him and his lineage. Bob, I saw, stood beside the sheik.

The circle of tribesmen were shuffling slowly to the right, while one recited a rhymed poem in a high singsong voice. This was greeted by shouts of approval; the moving circle repeated the poem and added a refrain before stopping to fire guns into the air. With a shout from the audience, the cadence was resumed; another tribesman offered a poem, the circle moved and chanted to the refrain and the hosa was on in earnest.

"Hikmat is saying a verse about what a brave warrior Hamid's father was against the British," Laila told me.

Then came a loud paean to Hamid himself, "A great politician, a generous man," repeated Laila. The circle moved faster and faster, and the figures were nearly obliterated in clouds of dust raised by the shuffling men. One man and then another, exhausted by their exertions in the hot sun, dropped out of the circle and others took their places. As enthusiasm mounted, more tribesmen offered spur-of-the-moment poems and these were greeted by louder and louder shouts of approval. The staccato sound of rifle shots reverberated around us, and the verses came so quickly it was difficult to hear anything above the shouts and rifle fire. But I was almost certain I had heard some words in English, repeated over and over.

"What is that?" I asked Laila.

"Oh, that is an old poem," she said. " 'Elizabeth, great queen Elizabeth, you were always our friend before, why did you desert us in Palestine?' "

The women were calling us down to help load trays, for the sheik had ordered the food. Then we mounted the roof again, and as the first line of men servants emerged from the women's quarters, bearing large trays of steaming rice on their heads and followed by small boys carrying the plates of stew, the hosa stopped. The men fired one last barrage of rifle shots and disappeared into the shadows of the mudhif. Lunch was served.

None of the visiting tribesmen had brought his family with him, but one very old and poor woman had come with her son and was eating with the oldest inhabitant of the women's quarters, a crippled and half-blind wife of Hamid's dead father. Because of their age, these women had been served at the same time as the men; they squatted together by a tray of food in a shady alcove near Kulthum's apartment, eating slowly, without a word to each other.

In the compound, the women rested in the shade. At midmorning they had snacked on fresh bread and bits of meat and were content to sit until the men were finished and the platters returned, partially empty, from the mudhif. Then we would eat together from one of the big tin trays, and then, too, the women would know whether or not their efforts had been a success. There was no doubt that the poorer tribesmen would eat as much meat and rice and stew as they could, but it was the trays of delicacies which would be scrutinized carefully to see whether the kubbas and the patcha, the liver and grilled chickens, the eggplant and the pudding had appealed to the more sophisticated palates of the effendi guests, and, of course, to Sheik Hamid himself. No word of praise would be uttered, but every woman in the compound would be able to tell, from the amount left on the platters, whether Selma's special kubba was really so special, and whether the daughters were making progress in their efforts to prepare good patcha.

Amina burst in to announce that the men were bringing back the dishes; the coffeemaker was brewing tea in the mudhif, she said, and the men were talking quietly and belching politely to indicate their appreciation of the feast. Clean plates were filled with leftovers from the big trays and we began to eat. The children had been fed before, piecemeal, from the steaming pots, but they joined us anyway, nibbling bits of everything that was offered, sitting happily in their now somewhat wrinkled and dusty new clothes. The wives and daughters and servant girls ate and talked together congenially. Petty jealousies were banished today; from the look of the trays, things had gone well and the party was a success. Now the women were entitled to good food and tea in the shade. The dishes would have to be done after eating, but after that entertainment was scheduled. Sheik Hamid had sent word that the young boys were to dance for us as they had done for the men at the end of the meal in the mudhif. Laila told me this was a special treat in my honor, and the women smiled at me and touched my shoulder and nodded as we ate together.

First the dishes. Amina and the other servants brought soap and sand into the center of the court; hundreds of plates and bowls and spoons and pots and trays were piled high around the water tap, a seemingly endless task. Everyone helped, except the two old ladies, who had eased their bones down onto clean reed mats set out by Amina and were now snoring peacefully in Kulthum's open court. Twenty-two women can wash a lot of dishes in half an hour. The clean utensils were put away, hands and faces washed, black garments rearranged, and mats and pillows laid out against the far wall of the compound in the widening patch of shade. We sat down in two expectant rows, far from the kitchen and its smoky smells and memories.

Kulthum looked exhausted as she picked her teeth carefully with a straw. She also looked triumphant. With lunch successfully over, she could rest momentarily on the realization that it was her organization that had produced the meal. Even the thought that she would have to do it again tomorrow, for six or seven or eight hundred, and the day after that as well, did not dim the glow of self-satisfaction that brightened her lined and tired face. She was past forty and no longer bearing children for Hamid; her oldest son was in disfavor with his father; her personal fulfillment had to come from other sources.

Soon a line of little boys trooped into the court, headed by Selman, the butcher's son, who played the reed pipe to accompany the dancing. Crowds of children surrounded

the boys, sons of the women in the court, or their sisters'
and brothers' offspring. Selman picked out a song on his
pipe; he had learned his skill by listening to an old nomad
who earned his tea and meals by playing in the mudhifs
and coffee shops in the valley. As Selman's song gained
volume, the little boys formed a long line and put their
arms about each other's shoulders. They moved in an off-
beat shuffle, singing as they moved, back and forth, now
jumping slightly, now bending down for a concentrated
jump in the steps of the line dance or *dabka*. Kulthum's
youngest son, the leader, was gesturing with a handkerchief and leading the line around and inside itself, shouting to indicate the jumps and imitating very well the pro-
fessional dabka leaders I had seen in Baghdad and
Diwaniya.

The coffeemaker's daughter dashed off and returned
with an empty kerosene can, turned it upside down and
picked up the beat. The women joined in, clapping in
time. The plaintive notes of the reed pipe blended with
the childish voices as they sang of death by violence, of
love and betrayal, smiling at their mothers and aunts and
moving together, now slowly, now quickly, now jumping
high, now stamping to the beat of the kerosene drum.
The bright dishdashas and the white tennis shoes of the
little boys were covered with dust that spurted up in
clouds as they jumped, but they kept on as the women
urged them to one more, just one more song. A wail that
nearly split my eardrum was greeted by shouts of laughter.
Selman stopped briefly to shake the saliva out of his pipe
and the little boys giggled, for the wail had originated
with Kulthum, dignified, middle-aged Kulthum, who had
drawn her abayah over her face and let forth a truly momentous cry to indicate her pleasure in the occasion.

The ice was broken; several women began to wail joy-
ously as they clapped. Kulthum asked for "Samra, Samra,"
and the tired little boys, jumping more slowly now and not
quite together, started the old song of the beauty of the
brown-skinned maiden. They did not finish it, for the
sheik came striding across the courtyard on his way to his
afternoon nap. Selma scurried ahead of him to turn back

his sheets, but he made his way over to us, patted Selman on the head and spoke to me. His daughters and sons rose to give their father formal feast-day greetings. He bowed, they bowed and kissed his hand and stole away. Soon only Selma and I and the sheik and a few of the little boys stood by, and I made my excuses and said what a fine Iid it had been. Sheik Hamid, after another bow, headed for his bed, and I started home, ready for a nap myself after the excitement of the day's activities. As I passed the mudhif, I had a brief glimpse of many men resting on mats inside, while their horses munched grass in the growing shadows of the afternoon.

11

Moussa's House

The houses closest to the tribal mudhif were occupied by the sheik's brothers and uncles. Abdulla, the sheik's older brother and second in command, and his two favorite younger brothers lived in houses connected to the sheik's own by common walls and passageways. Brothers with whom he was not so intimate had built separate dwellings not far away. Moussa, Laila's father, was one of these.

Moussa lived in a big square mud-brick house at the end of the road that stretched in a straight line from the canal to the clearing around the mudhif. An excellent location, one would have thought, for here all the public activity of the settlement took place. Sheik Hamid's car, a four-year-old Oldsmobile, was driven into the clearing with a flourish when he returned from his parliamentary duties in Baghdad. All visitors disembarked here—tribesmen from outlying settlements, nomad Bedouin, parking their cars or tethering camels, horses or donkeys before going into the mudhif to do business. On religious holidays the villagers would gather in the clearing to greet the sheik ceremonially, to watch the hosas. Here the processions of Muharram, Shiite month of mourning, would terminate, after a march through the village. It was, in fact, the village green, the taxi stop and parking lot all rolled into one.

However, the occupants of Moussa's house had, apparently, no glimpse of the comings and goings around the mudhif, no view of the green palm groves beyond, for the front of the house was without windows. This, Laila told me proudly, was to insure complete privacy for the women, yet the ladies' pride in their privacy did not seem at all compromised by a succession of peepholes which had been carefully chipped out of the mud-brick wall at convenient eye levels.

There seemed to be no view through the public entrance, either—a side door facing the road—but here, too, I found peepholes. The ladies inside knew as soon as visitors had arrived in the clearing; the little girls told the neighbors in the rear, and if it was important, those neighbors also passed it on. Thus news traveled with lightning speed through the closed doors and windowless walls.

Whenever I came to visit Laila, I would pound on the heavy wooden side door with both fists to attract attention. I would hear the running of many feet, a whispered consultation behind the door, and would realize that two or three of the sisters were stationed along the wall, peering out to see who the visitor might be. For Moussa's house, consisting entirely of women except for Moussa himself, had no male guards near the entrance like Sheik Hamid's. The girls had to be sure of the identity of their visitors. After calling out and being satisfied by sight and sound that it was I, two heavy bolts would be drawn, the iron latch lifted, and the door opened a crack just wide enough for me to slip into the shadowy entrance passage. As many times as I visited the sisters, I never penetrated behind two mysterious closed doors giving on the passage; once one of the doors was ajar and I could see rugs and pillows and bolsters set out neatly along the walls, and in the center a smoking charcoal brazier. This was Moussa's private *diwan* or reception room; the other door led, Laila told me, to his bedroom.

I was always hurried along the passage to the end where it opened onto the court, a huge open space as big as an ordinary house, where most of the affairs of the household were conducted. Fatima or Sanaa or Nejla, Laila's older sisters, wending their way across the court with water or laundry or a broom, would see me and call out.

"*Ahlan*, Beeja, *ahlan, ahlan wusahlan*, Beeja!" Gradually women and girls (there were nine sisters, after all) would emerge from rooms opening on two sides of the court, or from the kitchen in the corner. Or they would raise themselves from their places along the far wall, where they would be squatting peeling vegetables, pounding spices or cleaning rice and flour. The older sisters came forward, adjusting the everyday black garments—chin scarf (*foota*), head scarf (*asha*) and abayah over a black dress—which flowed behind them gracefully as they walked; we would shake hands in the sunny court as though we had not met for years. Laila was always among them, but as a member of the younger generation, she no longer wore the traditional garments, only an abayah and veil when she left the house. Indoors she sported a house dress, of cotton print in summer, flannelette in winter; it always seemed a bit outgrown and short for her, and her hair was always escaping from the scarf she used to tie it back. She seemed shorter than she actually was because she was round-shouldered from stooping over a sewing machine day after day; her collars were stuck with pins and threaded needles. Only eighteen, she already had lines around her small, close-set eyes from squinting in the sun or in the bad light of the sewing room. But when she smiled in welcome, her face became a child's again, gay, mischievous, hopeful. She would take my arm and escort me into the sewing room. One of the little girls took my abayah and hung it on a nail, and I settled, cross-legged, on a rug-covered mat while the sisters and visitors gathered to chat and Laila, smiling still with pleasure, went on with her sewing.

Because Moussa was away almost all day, neighborhood women tended to drop by, for water, for gossip, for advice, perhaps to bring Laila sewing or embroidery. I joined this throng, knowing that I was not causing any extra problem by my presence. The house had a central water tap, one of five or six in the settlement which was connected to the village's chlorinated water system; Um Fatima had said that anyone might draw clean water from this tap, and the women flocked to take advantage of her offer. They always crossed the court to speak to Laila and greet the Amerikiya in passing, so I saw many women informally this way whom I might not have met otherwise. Sometimes they would set down their water jugs and their children and gossip.

Very seldom was this malicious gossip, for these women knew that idle conversation about a woman's reputation might have tragic results. Occasionally, I felt, they simply couldn't resist, and a village widow of nonexistent income was usually their target.

"Where does she get her money?" one would say. "She had a fine new abayah on the Iid and her children had new clothes too."

"Her relatives probably gave it to her," Fatima would suggest.

"Humph. She has no relatives in El Nahra. But she must get the money from somebody; she certainly doesn't dig it out of the canal."

The malicious laughter would be cut short by Fatima or Nejla and the conversation turned to other subjects: children, illness, the weather, the crops.

Moussa's family, with nine daughters and no sons, was something of a phenomenon in the settlement. Bob had told me that among other tribesmen Moussa was often the butt of jokes and an object of pity since he had no male heir. Yet, although the subject was never mentioned directly, Bob said he also sensed a grudging admiration and respect for the women of the household. What they could do—sew, cook, clean, make a man comfortable— they did better than anyone else. Certainly among the women this was the case. Women said, "It's because they have no men that they work so hard," but Um Fatima and her daughters were almost universally liked and admired.

The girls had long ago divided up the work, and in addition each girl had developed her own specialty by which she managed to earn extra money. Fatima made silk abayahs and Sanaa crocheted the heavy black tatting which edged the ashas. Nejla kept chickens and raised a pair of lambs every spring to sell for wool and meat. Basima and Laila embroidered bridal sheets and pillowcases; the three younger girls went to school.

Um Fatima herself knew a good deal about poultices and medicines. From the beams in her sitting room hung little bunches of dried herbs, twigs and leaves which she would pound up in a mortar and use to treat the eye infections, the carbuncles, the dysentery and fevers which plagued her and her neighbors' ailing children. In addition she was considered a pious woman, competent to give advice in religious matters. All religious holidays were observed scrupulously; the house was the site of many krayas each Ramadan and Muharram. Bob testified that male guests were treated to delicious food, and no visiting relative, male or female, had ever been turned away without bed and board.

The nine sisters found room in their hearts even for me, and one day, sitting in the sheik's house, I realized from a remark of Selma's that Laila had chosen me as her friend.

There it was; it had happened; I had been partially accepted and had not even been aware of it, though recently it had seemed to me I had not been as neglected as before. Mohammed had brought Sherifa to see me. Sheddir and her daughter Sahura paused and drank tea with me after cutting grass. But Laila was visiting me all the time. Her calls were never announced in advance and were often inconvenient, but I would put down whatever I was doing and sit and talk. At first Laila would bolt out of the house like a frightened rabbit as soon as she heard Bob's step outside the door; after a time she seemed to become less cautious, and even though Bob was working or typing in one room, she would sit with me in the other, cautioning me over and over and over again not to tell that she had been there while Bob was around as it was *ayb* (great shame). She did not mind Mohammed's presence, for some reason, and talked to him quite informally, although of course she wore her abayah whenever he was with us. Usually she came alone, but Basima or one of the younger girls sometimes accompanied her.

After a few weeks the family began to bring their female guests to view the village Amerikiya. I opened my clothes closets and food cabinets and one day I even delivered a short lecture in Arabic on the theory of electricity (a subject I had never understood in my own language) to a middle-aged cousin of Laila's who had ridden in four miles on horseback with her husband to discuss the forthcoming marriage of her son.

"My cousin doesn't believe you have a machine that

could make ice," said Basima, so we adjourned to the kitchen to look at the refrigerator.

The blank white front of the refrigerator and even the ice trays themselves elicited little response, but when the lady actually felt the ice (to make certain we weren't teasing her), her face changed; it was a hot day and the woman's face, bound round like a coif with the black foota and asha, was bathed in perspiration.

"How wonderful!" she said. "You must get one for Laila." She meant the ice tray, I think, but Laila apparently thought she meant the machine, and hurriedly announced that her father planned to buy one if the year's crop was good. Then she plunged into another topic to change the subject quickly and began to explain the process of ice making in such false minute detail that I was impelled to explain myself how the hot electricity made such a thing take place. We finished the afternoon with iced lemonade, but the visiting cousin refused ice, saying it was too cold and hurt her teeth—the three or four she had left, she said, opening her mouth to show me broken stumps in her old gums.

News of the novelties which the Amerikiya could provide for bored visitors must have spread throughout the settlement, for one afternoon Mohammed came rushing in to say that the sheik's oldest daughter Alwiyah and two lady guests were on their way to my house. "They'll be here any minute," announced Mohammed, depositing on my table cigarettes and pumpkin seeds in case we might not have a large enough supply. Then he dashed out, as quickly as Mohammed ever moved, for it wouldn't be fitting, he felt, for him to be present when the sheik's women arrived. I hadn't time to get nervous, so the ladies and I spent a pleasant hour smoking, drinking tea and eating seeds, splitting the husk with our teeth, removing the kernel and spitting the husk out, all in one motion. Laila's little sister Rajat crept in with the group of heavily veiled ladies and sat on my floor to watch the show. Laila herself arrived soon after, slightly flustered; she insisted on passing the seeds and cigarettes and tea and smiled the whole time, like a stage mother whose child has just been given a lead in a hit musical comedy.

When the women left, Laila stayed on.

"It's not often the sheik's women leave their house," she confided. "You should feel honored."

"But what about Selma?" I insisted. "Why doesn't she come?"

"She will, in time," said Laila, "but that's not important; someone from the sheik's house has visited you, and that's all that matters."

Mohammed brought water earlier than usual that evening; I suspected him of overweening curiosity about the party, and it is true he asked whether there were enough cigarettes left for Bob. I said no, it would be better to bring some more from the suq. When he saw the piles and piles of pumpkin-seed husks overflowing the ash trays and spilling on the floor, he said that the shopkeeper on the tribal side of the canal knew how to dry pumpkin seeds properly and we should always buy from him.

One morning Laila brought a gaunt old woman who grinned at me cheerfully, patted my cheek and sat down in my best armchair without being asked. Laila announced, "Qanda has business with you."

"*Ahlan wusahlan*," I replied, wondering what on earth her business could be. I offered candy, but the old woman refused.

"She wants a cigarette," prompted Laila.

Qanda took two, lighting one and depositing the other within the recesses of her black garments. I pressed the box of cigarettes on her, and after a minimally polite refusal she took two more. These also were stored away before she pushed her abayah aside and leaned forward.

"Now," she said, and began to speak very rapidly, gesturing floridly in all directions. I was having difficulty understanding and asked Laila to repeat for me in slower Arabic.

Qanda, it appeared, was the local beautician. She plucked eyebrows, removed unwanted body hair (with a string or with a sugar solution), pierced ears and noses, made up brides on their wedding days, and, most important of all, she was an accomplished tattooer. She stood up and yanked her black dress above her knees to show me two full-blown roses tattooed on the backs of her calves.

"Aren't they lovely things?" she asked, rolling her eyes. "I only charge a quarter of a pound for each." I agreed that the roses were very beautiful, but said I did not want to be tattooed.

She eyed me a moment, then started a new tack. "It seems expensive now, I know," she said, "but a tattoo lasts a lifetime, and by making you more attractive, it will help you keep your husband."

I smiled and said no, thank you.

Qanda muttered something to Laila, who giggled and repeated it.

"Qanda says you are young and newly married and don't know much. She says you are so thin your husband will soon grow tired of you, but if you will let her tattoo your backside for half a pound, perhaps that will amuse him." Qanda interrupted Laila, who added, "Qanda is sure it will amuse him, she can almost guarantee it, it works with all her customers." She broke down in uncontrollable laughter, and Qanda and I joined her.

I explained that it was not our custom to tattoo and therefore my husband would not find it attractive.

Qanda smiled sweetly. "You are just thinking of the money," she said calmly. "I can arrange for you to pay half now and half when your husband is satisfied. Remember, I am the best tattooer in El Nahra. I tattooed Abdulla's wife when she was a girl."

I assured her I believed her workmanship excellent, but I simply did not want to be tattooed. Qanda looked exasperated and began to glower, until Laila broke in to explain patiently that tattooing was considered old-fashioned nowadays, that none of the young girls wanted to have it done except perhaps one small tattoo "just for fun." And, she concluded triumphantly, the schoolteachers had told her that women in Baghdad had not been tatooed for many years.

Qanda grunted, but she subsided, accepted still another

cigarette, lit it and inhaled deeply. After a moment she leaned forward once more.

"At least you should have your ears pierced," she said. "I only charge 150 fils for that, and I will ask 125 from you as a special favor to Laila."

Actually I had been considering having my ears pierced, but much as I enjoyed Qanda, I was not sure I wanted her to undertake the operation. "All my earrings are from America and are different," I said, trying to demonstrate the difference between screws and clips and hooks, but Qanda shook her head in bewilderment.

"Show her," suggested Laila, so I opened my jewelry box, and at this Qanda leaned forward with real interest. I trotted out my collection of costume jewelry, false pearls, and my gold bracelet and gold earrings.

With the nose of a connoisseur, Qanda passed over the imitation items and seized on the bracelet and the gold hoops. Then she put them down.

"Is that all you have?" she asked.

I nodded.

She looked very puzzled indeed, glancing around the room with its radio, clock, books, electric light and other symbols of prosperity. She spoke to Laila, who said, "Qanda can't understand why you have all these things in your house and yet no gold. Not even Sheddir has as little as that."

I replied that I did have some gold in America which I had left behind for fear of losing it on the long trip to Iraq.

"Wear it, wear it, you silly girl," Qanda burst out. "What good does it do lying in a box far away?" Then she launched into a short, earnest sermon about the value of gold as ornament, but secondly and most important, the necessity of gold in every woman's life as insurance in case her husband should die or leave her or divorce her. I had not heard such an eloquent statement of the "diamonds are a girl's best friend" theory in a long time.

Finally Qanda stood up, peered at herself closely in my wall mirror, snorted, and announced that she must leave to prepare a bride for marriage. "Is there a wedding today?" I asked.

"No, it's tomorrow," she said, "and from now on I shall be very busy. This is the season, you know." She started out the door, turned and wagged her finger at me.

"You come with Laila to see the bride," she said, "and when you see what a good job I have done on her, you'll change your mind about tattoos and pierced ears. Maybe you'll even want to have your nose done, ha ha!"

I gasped out a sort of goodbye, and Laila, grinning and nodding, winked at me outrageously as she followed the skinny old woman, still laughing at her own joke, out of my garden.

My partial acceptance into the society of the women was a mysterious process, and I have often wondered what marked the turning point in our relations and what prompted Laila to single me out for friendship. Probably it was a combination of particular circumstances, many of which I remained unaware, plus the fact that people were just becoming used to our presence. Also, as my Arabic improved I was able to participate more fully in the half-joking, half-serious teasing with which the women entertained each other. Now occasionally I could reply to the sarcastic taunts that came my way, and this repartee succeeded brilliantly where my former bland and accommodating manner had not. Many months later Laila told a visiting Iraqi friend of mine that in the early stages of my residence in El Nahra the women had wondered whether I was deaf and dumb, or just not quite bright, because I smiled but often did not seem to hear what was said to me. Afterward, reported Laila, I had come to life and my company had improved immensely.

12

Weddings

Four weddings were to be held in the tribal settlement at the same time, and the families involved had pooled their meager finances to provide a more spectacular feast and entertainment.

"They are even bringing dancers from Diwaniya," said Laila. "You must ask Mr. Bob if you can come with me to see everything."

"Of course I can," I said. Laila looked exasperated.

"Ask him," she insisted, and when I looked puzzled she said, "It's at night, don't you understand? My father never lets us go out at night except to krayas during Ramadan and Muharram—no women do—but because of the weddings he might let us, especially if I tell him that Mr. Bob says you can go. Will you ask him?" So I agreed.

One of the prospective bridegrooms was Hassan, the son of Sheddir and Ali, the sheik's gardener. Bob reported that Ali had finally completed marriage arrangements with his brother. Ali's brother's son would come to El Nahra, bringing his sister who would marry Hassan. When the boy returned to his own village, he would take back as his bride Sahura, Hassan's sister, who would be dressed in her bridal finery in her father's house, but would not be married in El Nahra. There would be a token exchange of money, two marriage contracts would be signed, and the two couples would be united. So, said Laila, we would see both the traditional arrival and leave-taking of a bride. In addition we could visit the three other brides who were scheduled to be married the same night and compare their clothes, their jewelry and their beauty!

"You don't know how lucky you are," said Laila. "We haven't had four weddings together for a long time."

On the appointed day Laila and I went together after

lunch to Ali's house, where Sahura sat in state in her wedding finery, awaiting her bridegroom. The little court had been carefully cleaned for the occasion, and the scrawny chickens who usually scratched in the hard-packed earth were penned up in one corner. Women and children come to view the bride were passing in and out of the courtyard and pressing against the door of the one-room house. Qanda, filling a tray of glasses from a clay water jar by the door, looked up and smiled in welcome as we entered.

"*Ahlan wusahlan*," she said. "Come right in." She handed the tray of glasses to a young girl, and came running over to take me by the arm in a grasp of iron.

"Why didn't you come and see the bride I did the other day?"

I started to explain but she hurried on without listening. "That was a really good job, if I do say so myself. A fine tattoo between the breasts and rosebuds on both calves (I did them for her last year, when she became engaged). And the face of that girl—what plump cheeks, what eyes! I had some new kohl from Diwaniya and we hennaed her feet and hands—not too much, just enough. Ah, I wish you could have seen her," she sighed, as one whose masterpiece had just been destroyed by fire. "But now," she added in a changed tone, "come and see Sahura." She led us through the crowd around the door.

Sahura, all in white, sat against the far wall, cross-legged and very stiff-necked, on a small square of new matting covered with an embroidered sheet. Before I realized what was happening, Qanda had propelled us through the throng of women and children and we were plopped down on the ground, shoulder to shoulder with the old women of the family who had been given places of honor near the bride. Sahura stared straight ahead of her and did not turn her head as we entered. Laila whispered that the bride was not supposed to notice anything on her wedding day. Qanda had pressed through the crowd with us and knelt now at Sahura's side; she had picked up the girl's long braid of glossy brown hair and was balancing it in her hand.

"Look at that!" she shouted, in order to be heard above

the din in the tiny room. "A braid of hair as thick as an arm. Her husband will be glad to see that, I can tell you!"

For a moment I winced at Qanda's tone, weighing Sahura's hair like a commodity and then I realized that, good diplomat and saleswoman that she was, Qanda had selected Sahura's one good feature and was emphasizing it in order to encourage the poor girl and help her to relax during her day-long vigil before the wedding.

For Sahura was certainly no beauty. A big-boned girl with broad shoulders and heavy arms, she would be a good assistant to her husband in the fields. But she had tiny eyes set close together and a long, plain face which was usually redeemed by her cheerful expression. Now, however, her face was fixed in a tense look of waiting; the badly fitting white dress did nothing for her and the black kohl carefully painted around her eyes seemed to make them even smaller. Her hands and feet were hennaed, but there tradition ended; Qanda had used Western lipstick to redden the wide mouth, had powdered Sahura's skin a deadly white. I heard Qanda telling another newcomer how magnificent Sahura's hair was. "See how well it is oiled," she was saying, and I looked again at Sahura and hoped her husband would not be too hard on her when he lifted her veil for the first time and discovered he had not married a beauty.

Now the conversation turned to Sahura's jewelry, her own personal dowry bought with money given to the bride by her female relatives and female friends. She had silver ankle bracelets and heavy gold earrings and a pendant of silver into which had been set a large uneven turquoise.

The old women near us were discussing Sahura's faults and virtues, the chances of her husband's being handsome or at least kindhearted, her prospects in her future home. I gathered they did not think much of the latter, a small clan settlement hours away by horse, with no market, only a few houses and a small mudhif and a clump of palm trees in the middle of the sandy plain.

"It will be hard for the child," said the lady sitting nearest to Sahura. "The water is not good there, I hear.

She will be sick all the time until she becomes accustomed to it."

"I'm glad my daughter didn't have to go away when she married," put in another. "It's hard for a girl without her mother and it's hard for the mother, too."

"And then, of course, she doesn't know anything," added the second, leaning forward. "Sahura has been sheltered like a good girl. She has never even been to Diwaniya."

The two women clucked in sympathy and rocked back on their heels. Sahura, only inches away, must have heard this doleful interchange, but she made no sign, sitting up stiffly and looking straight ahead of her. We were drinking sherbet, a sticky sweet concoction with a base of ground-up oranges.

"Doesn't Sahura drink something?"

"Oh, no," said Laila. "She had breakfast early this morning before she was dressed, but she won't eat till after the wedding; then she and her husband will have a big meal together. If he is a good man, he will bring her fruit and sweets and sherbet."

Qanda was bustling around, distributing glasses of water and cigarettes and keeping the crowds of women and children moving in and out. She looked tired and her own make-up was streaked with sweat, but part of her job, it appeared, was to uphold Sahura and her terribly flustered mother Sheddir through this, their greatest and most difficult experience as mother and daughter.

"The groom has hired a taxi to take Sahura and her things to the wedding at his house," the old woman near me said. "It should be coming soon."

It was four-thirty. A little girl ran in and whispered to Qanda. The crowd of women stirred in anticipation. We heard a clatter of cans and a banging of drums, followed by a volley of rifle shots. The bridegroom was approaching to claim his bride. But he would not come directly to the house; Sahura would go out to him to show that she was to live with him in his father's house.

Qanda was shouting orders at Sheddir, who was distracted and did not seem to understand. She was staring at Sahura; finally she leaned over and kissed her daughter on both cheeks, and burst into tears. Sahura remained impassive. Qanda quickly leaned over the girl and covered her face, first with a white veil, then with a black. She motioned peremptorily to the weeping mother, who handed Qanda the new black silk bridal abayah; this was draped about Sahura's head and shoulders. Qanda put an arm around the girl to pull her to her feet and, supporting her, led her out of the house. As Sahura crossed the threshold, never to return again as a daughter, the women set up a keening wail of sorrow and farewell, and rose to follow the bride down the alley to the main road where the taxi was waiting. Crowds of young men and boys surrounded the car, and we could see the bridegroom sitting in the back seat. The couple's new household goods had been tied to the roof of the taxi: an iron bedstead, painted orange and blue, a chest, wrapped in bright woven blankets, a rolled up cotton mattress and several zinced-copper cooking pans. As Sahura approached on Qanda's arm, the boys beat their skin drums furiously and the men fired their rifles into the air.

At the door of the taxi Sahura turned, and Sheddir, screaming and crying with pain, ran up and threw her arms around her daughter. Qanda gently disentangled the sobbing Sheddir, pushed Sahura into the back seat of the taxi and shut the door. The taxi bounced in the ruts and the bedstead on top wobbled; the driver accelerated and the car raced off in a cloud of dust. Wailing, the women ran after the taxi, and we walked along with the crowd until the taxi was out of sight on the canal road; the men were firing a few final rifle shots, which were pop-popping in the hot still air. In the middle of the dusty road, Sheddir clung to Qanda and sobbed, but Sahura had gone.

The wedding drums began to beat before dark. We heard them as we were finishing our supper in the garden. The sound of the drummers mingled with the call of the mourning dove and the shrill cries of the giant black crows high in the date palms; we could hear the shuffle of many feet on the path outside. Bob left to meet Mohammed at the Sayids' mudhif, which was to be the scene of the festivities. By the time Laila came for me, the drums were louder and the road was thronged with people headed for the mudhif. Tribesmen in their robes walked in twos and threes, children ran shouting, and black-shrouded women walked close to the walls of the houses.

Laila had other ideas; she turned us off into an alley which led away from the mudhif. I protested, but she insisted that we should see the brides first; after that the party at the mudhif would be in full swing and there would be so many people milling about that no one would notice us.

All of the settlement lanterns had been commandeered to light the bridal houses and the mudhif, and we groped our way along in the dark, trying to avoid the center gutter, its trickle of slops and garbage dried to a muck by the day's hot sun. Soon the moon would come up, Laila said, guiding me over a rough spot, and I looked up to see the stars already filling the summer sky. Women brushed against us, giggling, and we joined a group on its way to view the first bride, who sat, like Sahura, on a white-covered mat in her house. There, however, the similarity ended.

This girl was relaxed and pretty; she arched her body in a pleased way under our gaze. An old woman pointed out the bridal bed, hung with white mosquito netting. She picked up the border for me to feel the heavily embroidered bottom sheet and pointed to Laila, who pursed her lips and admitted that she and her sister had embroidered it. I praised it at length and was rewarded with an exhibition of the top sheet and pillowcases, all embroidered with the same pattern of bright red flowers and green leaves, mottoes carefully traced in Arabic across the pillowcases. "Sleep here, and good health," said the mottoes, Laila informed me. The old woman patted the bed, cackled and looked at the bride, who actually chuckled and tossed her head.

The second bride sat in state in a large roomy house where the walls were freshly whitewashed and the date-palm logs supporting the roof were nearly new. I was surprised, and Laila explained that this girl was the daughter of a prosperous Sayid, who had a piece of good land near the sheik's holding.

"Who is the girl marrying?" I asked.

"Abdu, son of Abdul Hakim," answered Laila. "You know, he is a very religious young man from an old Sayid family."

Then I did remember Bob's mentioning Abdu as an unattractive but intense and ascetic young man, who was one of the religious enthusiasts of El Nahra. Abdu organized krayas during Ramadan, helped plan the yearly religious plays and was a leader of one of the *taaziyas*, a group of young men who performed ritual flagellations during Muharram.

I had difficulty reconciling my picture of the intense Abdu with the young girl in white before me. Lovely and dusky, she was loaded with gold: bracelets, earrings and two long necklaces, one of gold coins and one of cone-shaped beads. All were presents from her father, said Laila; he had given her two sheep besides. Her groom was a poor man, though of an ancient and pure lineage. Since the girl was a Sayid, she was bound to marry a Sayid, for Sayid girls were given only to men who carried the blood of the Prophet in their veins.

I praised the girl's wedding dress, which fitted her beautifully and seemed much better made than most of the clothes I had seen in the settlement. The women looked at each other but said nothing. I had made a mistake, but what? I turned to Laila for help, and was shocked at the invective which suddenly burst out of her. On and on she raved, criticizing the cut and the seams and the way the neck was finished, until I realized that one of her seamstress rivals had been employed. Laila stopped as suddenly as she had started, saying good-humoredly to me and the assembled women, "The material is excellent—it must have cost at least three pounds a meter—too good to be ruined by bad sewing." We rose and passed out into the alley again.

Laila rushed me along to the last house, murmuring that we would stay only a minute there. "I wouldn't go at all if it weren't for you," she said. "It's because I know this girl

so well and she is only fourteen, too young to marry;
everyone considers it great *ayb* [shame]. Her groom is
an old man."

But as we approached, I heard the beat of a kerosene-
can drum, and voices of women singing, "Samra, Samra,
how beautiful is my dusky maiden."

"Why are they singing, then?" I asked.

"Because they feel sorry for her and want to cheer her
up," said Laila.

The group of women and girls who sat in front of the
door of the bridal chamber urged us to sit down, but Laila
glanced into the poor room where the girl sat. In spite
of the voluminous folds of her white dress, she seemed thin
and small. She had been heavily made up to make her appear older; unfortunately the attempt had not been successful, and she looked like a child arrayed for a theatrical
entertainment. Staring straight ahead of her, like Sahura,
the girl did not seem to notice us, but she kept blinking
repeatedly, like a child with something in its eye.

"Let's go," hissed Laila, and we nodded at the old
women, refused politely their invitation to tea and although the girl beating the kerosene drum shouted at us to
stop, Laila plunged on silently back toward the main road.
Here, in the buzz of activity and noise, she regained her
good spirits. In the alley we almost collided with a black-
veiled figure who turned out to be the sheik's daughter
Samira. She and Laila dissolved in helpless laughter at the
comic coincidence of their meeting.

"Watch the slops," giggled Laila, pulling Samira out of
the center of the road.

Samira let out a mock scream and clung foolishly to the
side of the house nearest us. This brought on more laughter, until we were silenced by Laila.

"Shhh," she said sternly. "We must be quiet. The sheik
doesn't know Samira is out, but she says the guards are
looking the other way tonight so all the women can see
the dancing. Alwiyah is out too. They are the two bravest."

We took hands and moved along in the general direction of the Sayids' mudhif, heading toward a yellow glow
of light which was reflected in the sky above the flat roofs

of the houses. Somewhere a donkey raised his head and brayed fiercely; Samira clung to me and screamed; we all laughed again. There was much laughter in the crowds that moved along with us—high-pitched giggles of children, deep laughter from old women experiencing again, without the tension and pain, the excitement of their own wedding nights, long since past. The animals in the compounds we passed were moving restlessly, snuffling in the darkness; the sound of the drums was everywhere and even the dogs on the edge of the settlement had joined the crowds and were yipping wildly.

The square around the mudhif had been kept open as a stage for the entertainment and was glaringly lighted by scores of lanterns placed every few feet along the ground. At least a hundred men sat close together on the flat logs outlining the square, smoking and drinking tea, for the wedding feast was just over. Men were carrying out the empty food trays; everyone had taken advantage of the free meal of rice, mutton and flat bread in sheep broth provided by the grooms' fathers. I could see Bob sitting near the mudhif entrance, washing his hands over a copper basin, and Mohammed stood nearby conferring with a group of strangers.

"The dancers and musicians," whispered Laila.

"But when will it begin?" I asked. We had been wandering from house to house for two hours now; it was all very interesting, but my legs were beginning to give out.

"Soon, right now," said Laila, but she was wrong. A line of little boys moved out into the square, to perform as they had done during the Iid. One sympathetic drummer kept up a desultory beat for them, and the boys' mothers, anonymous among the crowds of women who stood, three and four deep on the edge of the square, clapped enthusiastically. We could see the children's lips move in the well-known songs, but the sound of their voices was lost in the clapping and drumming, the clink of tea glasses, the hiss of the Coleman lanterns, and the hubbub of many men moving back and forth across the square.

The drummer grew tired and stopped. The boys moved away, but nothing happened. Laila evidently sensed my impatience, and began to prod and push and elbow me forward and backward and sideways, until she had succeeded in pulling us both into a place among the women where we could see clearly the whole bright square.

"Now, now, see Beeja!" she said.

I looked and indeed the strangers and Mohammed had moved into the center of the square, followed by a drummer and two pipers who experimented with one tune, then another. After a long wait and some words between the musicians and the dancers, the three dancers linked arms closely and leaped into a *chobi*. The drums burst forth, five, six, then ten, the pipers joined in, and the men settled back to enjoy the long-awaited and expensive spectacle. But the dancers still were not satisfied, for they would leap and twirl gloriously for a moment, and stop to scratch their heads under their kaffiyehs and argue with one another. Mohammed, standing on the edge of the square and carrying a long staff to indicate his role as master of ceremonies, looked alternately perplexed and annoyed. Men began to murmur, and finally Ali, the father of Sahura and Hassan, leaped to his feet.

"*Yallah*," he shouted, "we are paying good money for this. Let's have the wedding dance and finish with this fooling around."

The dancers stopped, Mohammed move in to intervene, and Ali strode furiously into the square. This seemed to have the desired effect. Quickly one of the dancers dropped out, the second adjusted his kaffiyeh and the third shed his aba, pulled out and put on a woman's dress. A scarf was tied tightly about his hips, belly-dancer style. His kaffiyeh wrapped round his head like a turban, he was at last ready and moved toward his partner.

Pipes and drums clashed raggedly, found the desired tune, and the music swelled out, above the rhythmic clapping of the crowd and the high-pitched ululating wails of the women. The man held his arms up and concentrated on his footwork, not looking at the "woman," who undulated provocatively toward him, each body movement accented with gestures from "her" long, thin arms and hands. Lighted from above and below by the lanterns, the dancers cast vast shadows on the square, shadows which moved silently together and apart.

Closer and closer together the dancers came, and when the "bride" nearly touched her partner with her hips, the audience cried, "Ah," and a long wail tore through the air. One of the grooms leaped into the square and pinned a bank note on the dancer's dress. At this signal the man dropped out, and the drums and pipes began a new song for the bride's solo. This started slowly, a free-form undulating and wheeling across and around the dusty square. But in a prolonged whirl the kaffiyeh flew off the dancer's head, releasing an astonishing amount of long black hair which fell crazily about his head and shoulders. Faster he pivoted and leaped, the hair streaming and the long hands flung about in an agony of passion.

"He is good," I whispered. Laila's eyes were fixed on the man-woman figure twirling in the yellow glare of the lanterns, while the women screamed and the men counted the turns with "Ah," "Ah," "Yallah," and a spatter of coins and applause. How long could he keep this up? High above the maze of drums wove the thin melody of the pipes. The coins showered in, raising little spits of dust as they fell. The dancer, perspiring freely, clapped those long hands against his temples to keep the tangled hair out of his eyes as he whirled—dust, hair, hands, feet moving in the changing shadows and flickering lantern light. A group of men pushed through the crowd into the square, the dancer stopped and the drums ceased.

"The mullah has come; it is time for the weddings," whispered Laila. The bridegrooms and their close relatives rose. "First the men will go down to the canal to wash their faces and hands, and then each will go with the mullah to his bride's house, where he will say that he agrees and she will say that she agrees. After that he will go in to his bride."

The crowd rushed to follow the young men and their escorts toward the canal.

"We stay here," said Laila.

"Why?" I asked, wanting to see the washing ceremony at the bank.

"It's only for the men," she said, "we stay here," and she strengthened her grip on my abayah, so I turned back to the square, no longer a stage as the men hurried across it, oblivious of the exhausted dancer hunched against a log, drawing on a cigarette and pushing back his hair. His two companions were combing the dust for stray coins.

I gradually became aware that the drums had started up again, a low throbbing beat which continued insistently under all the noise. The beat was cut by volleys of rifle shots.

"They are coming back from the canal," said Laila.

I would have loved to follow one or another of the groups led by the mullah as they headed to one bridal house or another, signed the papers, the girl and man solemnly agreeing to take each other as man and wife, and then entering the bridal chamber together. But this was not to be. I stood with Laila and Sherifa and Medina and the sheik's daughter Samira, who could see nothing either but nevertheless were chattering with excitement.

"They're coming back, they're coming back," the murmur reached us from women closer to the alley, and we could hear the men approaching and entering a house near the mudhif.

"Come on, Laila," I pleaded. "It's just down the alley. No one will see us in the dark," and she agreed. When we reached the door, the groom, followed by the same insistent drum roll, was going in the gate. His mother and the bride's mother were already inside, said Sherifa, to bear witness to the fact that the consummation was a proper one.

The mullah came out.

"He has gone to his bride, I think," said Laila.

The drum roll continued and the crowd shifted uneasily, whispering and chattering to each other.

"It's taking him a long time," cackled one old lady. "What's the matter with him, is he sick?"

"Shh," said Sherifa sternly, "mind what you say," but the lady continued to cackle.

Minutes went by and the crowd grew quieter. The drum roll continued.

There was a loud cry within, and in a few moments the bridegroom emerged smiling. After a triumphant volley of rifle shots, the groom's friends and relatives pressed forward to shake his hand. The women surged into the compound to congratulate the bride, who would remain in her room, and to see the bloody sheet displayed by the bride's mother and the groom's mother, incontrovertible evidence that the girl was a virgin and a worthy bride. The drums ceased.

Sherifa sighed and Laila laughed with relief.

"It's all right, everything is fine," she said.

The groom's smiles meant that indeed everything was all right; the girl was a virgin, the man and his mother were satisfied. If they had not been, the groom had the right to demand that one of her relatives kill the bride on the spot. The right was not often exercised but it had happened within the memory of Laila. In that case the girl had not been killed, but sent home in disgrace. Her life was ruined; she might better have been dead, Laila told me.

The mullah was already at the next house, and we heard another volley of shots in the distance. Another wedding had been consummated. In a quarter of an hour, another. By this time, we had moved back to the square, where dancing had resumed. Tea was being passed around again and I could see Bob shaking hands with one of the grooms. The groom offered Bob a cigarette, Bob countered and offered him one, and the usual "after you, my dear Alphonse" shadow play began. Bob won, I noticed, by almost pushing his cigarette case in the poor groom's face. It wouldn't have been fitting for the groom, the guest of honor, to give a guest a cigarette. The groom accepted a light, then, magnanimous with the flush of his wedding night, threw a large coin to the dancers. I pressed forward, eager to see more, but Laila pulled at my abayah.

"It is very late," she said. "Samira and I must go." We bade goodbye to Sherifa and her mother and started home.

At the main road Samira turned into another alley so that she might slip unobserved through the sheik's back door. Laila said good night at my door. I latched the gate behind me and sat down in the garden to wait for Bob; the moon was high in the sky and the stars paled beside it. I could still hear the drums.

13

Salima

Laila and I were planning a formidable journey across the canal and around the suq to visit Salima, Laila's best friend from school, who had been married the year before and had a new baby. The visit, promised for many weeks, had been postponed again and again for reasons of etiquette.

First Salima's mother bore a son and Laila and her mother were unable to call because of sickness in their own house; then Laila's grandfather's sister died and Salima and her mother did not come to offer condolences. At this point the social omissions were equal, and either friend could make the first move. Salima had done so, and thus Laila felt secure in the knowledge that she had won the round and it was expected that she should return Salima's call.

Salima, according to Laila, was the most beautiful girl in El Nahra. She had a magnificent double bed in her house and many books and beautiful clothes. Her father was a cloth merchant, but Laila's family did not buy from him because his prices were too high. Salima's husband Khalil was the Arabic teacher in the boys' elementary school. Khalil's mother was the village wise woman. Bob had mentioned Khalil as an upstanding man possessing all the traditional virtues. He was intelligent and a good scholar, respected his elders, did not drink or spend money foolishly, and was saved from utter dreary respectability by a subtle and extremely sharp wit. I was looking forward to meeting his beautiful sixteen-year-old bride Salima.

It was five o'clock on a hot June afternoon when Laila knocked at my door. I adjusted my abayah and went down the path to meet her, still exhausted from two hours of steamy half-sleep in the 100-degree heat. Even Laila was complaining about the heat, and when we had been out less than ten minutes I could feel the sweat beginning to trickle down my neck and the backs of my legs. The sun was going down on our right, but no wind stirred the palms and cottonwoods along the canal. It would be a hot still night, I realized unhappily, for the lengthening shadows of the trees reflected in the water did not even shimmer. Empty when we started, the street was filling with people emerging from their afternoon naps. The coffee shop near the bridge was opening, and the yawning proprietor scratched his head and adjusted his agal and kaffiyeh as we passed. We cast down our eyes modestly as we walked, but when we mounted the bridge, the sight of a long camel caravan coming slowly toward the village on the opposite side of the canal made me temporarily lose all discretion and pause to stare.

"It is only the salt caravan from the south," Laila said, plucking at my abayah. "It comes every spring and every winter. The salt isn't as good as what we buy in Diwaniya; don't stop."

But I slowed my steps to watch as the score or more camels ambled along the road, setting down one padded foot and then another, jogging their heavy tasseled saddle-bags and striped trappings as they walked. Three drivers—Bedouin, I assumed, although they wore robes like the El Eshadda—walked beside them, tapping a bony camel with a stout stick when it looked as though it might turn aside, whopping the scrawny backsides of the beasts when they balked. An image of the camels in the gay trappings and the three robed men moving under the palms formed, broke and re-formed in the still bright water of the canal. Laila was plucking at my sleeve again, whispering, "Shame, don't stop, come on!" I dutifully dropped my eyes again and followed her.

Salima's house was near her father's cloth shop, only a few steps from the suq, but Laila would not have dreamed of walking through the market. Instead we made a wide detour around the suq, turning left into the maze of tiny alleys behind the main street where most of the merchant families in El Nahra lived. The blind fronts of the houses, with their tightly closed wooden shutters and mud-brick

walls plastered with mud and dry grass, were set close together along the alleys where we picked our way, avoiding
the gutter in the middle. Occasionally the doors would
open and women would emerge, carrying children on their
shoulders, on their heads a pile of pots, or laundry or a
water can, bound for the canal. They stopped and stared
at us, and Laila, who had discarded her face veil as soon
as we left the main street, answered their greetings, delighted to be out and delighted also, it seemed, to be seen
traveling with me, the village curiosity!

"Ah," they said, "so this is the Amerikiya," and Laila
smiled in a proprietary fashion as they surveyed me from
top to toe, not unkindly.

"*Ahlan wusahlan*," they said, and I responded, and if
the pots on their heads were not too heavy or the children
weren't wailing to be off, they would begin questioning.

Why does she cut off her hair in front like that (referring to my bangs) and does she have any children inside
her and why does she wear man's shoes (referring to my
heavy walking shoes) and did she get her abayah in America, and always, where are you going? Greetings to Laila's
mother followed, inquiries as to the health of her sisters,
and admonitions not to trip on the uneven cobble-
stones. Then the women would be off, clop-clopping down
the stones in their wooden clogs, children riding on their
mothers' shoulders and holding on to the black-covered
heads for support. So adroit were the children at clinging,
the cans, piles of laundry or pots on their mothers' heads
did not waver an inch.

By the time we had reached Salima's house, Laila was
beaming happily, and I realized that this roundabout journey was half the fun of the visit. We had chatted with
many women, whom she knew but seldom saw, and had
gathered enough village gossip to regale the harem for
the next three days.

A tiny girl with round black eyes and long dark braids,
dressed in a short cotton shift and wooden clogs, opened
the door of Salima's house, a door like all the others along
the alley, made of wood slats and set into the mud-brick
wall, closed with bolts and an old-fashioned iron latch.

"Salima's sister," whispered Laila.

The door swung to behind us and we were in a large, fairly neat courtyard, where a cow mooed in one corner and several chickens scratched. Reed matting had been laid along the shady side of the court from the door to the entrance of the house. Near the house stood a bedraggled tree, its leaves thick with dust, and under the tree, supported by pillows, an enormously fat woman sat, fanning herself desultorily with a broken reed fan. A mound of flesh, draped in black, her head wound in white, she did not indicate that she had heard us come in. The little sister escorted us across the court, and as we approached, the white-coifed head turned toward us, showing a lined face with pendulous cheeks, passive except for a pair of tiny piercing eyes. Laila bent down to kiss one of the woman's flabby hands and murmur a greeting; I, too, muttered something and the woman waved her hand that I might not kiss it, a mark of courtesy to me.

"How are you, Um Khalil?" asked Laila. The woman smiled, causing all the pouches and lines in her face to change position, but it was not a pleasant smile. She had stopped fanning herself for a moment to recognize us and now began to fan again, a signal for us to pass on. Salima, standing just inside the door of the narrow whitewashed room which was her home, embraced Laila as she entered. Then she remembered her manners and greeted me, reached for our abayahs (Laila stubbornly kept hers on) and indicated a sofa where we were to sit.

"*Ahlan wusahlan*," she kept repeating.

"How are you?" asked Laila, beaming.

"Well, thanks be to God."

"And your baby?"

"Well, thanks be to God. How is your mother?"

"Well, thanks be to God," replied Laila.

"And your sisters?"

"Very well, thanks be to God."

After a moment of silence the process would start all over again.

"How are you?" Laila would repeat delightedly.

Salima, sitting at our feet, would smile with pleasure,

"Well, thanks be to God. We have not seen you for so long."

"We are all well, thank God. But I am afraid," Laila would offer, "that our visit causes much difficulty for you."

"No, no, no, you honor us by coming and bringing your guest," all eyes turning to me.

Thus the friends, in the formal phrases of their mothers and grandmothers, re-established the social bond broken by long separations, before turning to conversation of personal interest.

Khalil's mother had been sick. As the village wise woman, she had dealings with many people, and the house had been filled with visitors day and night. This had meant much extra work for Salima, serving the guests with tea and coffee as well as preparing special dishes for her mother-in-law. To make matters more difficult, her baby girl, asleep in a wooden cradle, was cutting a tooth, and cried at night so Salima could not sleep. However, Khalil had brought her some perfume from Baghdad (it was produced and smelled all round) and had brought back many books for himself. Laila expressed astonishment at the amount of money spent on books.

"But Khalil is a scholar," said Salima, in tones of awe.

"Yes," nodded Laila, and paused politely before launching into an account of the wake for her grandfather's sister and the enormous boil which her little sister Amal had had on the back of her neck.

The bookcase standing against the opposite wall of the narrow whitewashed room did contain many books, the only books I had seen in El Nahra except in the mayor's house and the girls' school. The bookcase shared honors with the bed as the most impressive piece of furniture in the house, but where the bookcase was austere with its dark polished wood and glass-paned doors, the bed was a magnificent creation in pink satin; a canopy festooned with ruffles cascaded down in billows to the bedspread, which dusted the floor with more ruffles.

Looking at Salima herself, sitting on the floor cracking pumpkin seeds with her teeth, I had to agree with Laila: the girl was a beauty, the true nut-brown maiden of whose

loveliness balladeers in any country might sing. Her face
was almost perfect, sharply cut like a precious stone, with
elegant hollows and planes. In contrast, her slight body had
an unfinished look; she was full-breasted, yet had the thin
arms and knobby knees of a child. Even the face, despite
the full lips and deep-set black eyes framed by sooty
lashes and "eyebrows like swords," in the words of the
Arab poet, was quite empty of any expression other than
genuine childish enthusiasm at the presence of guests.
She and Laila giggled together over past school mischief
and busily spat out pumpkin seed husks onto the floor.
Salima was not completely unknowing, however. She wore
a tight-bodiced dress of wine-red velvet, rumpled and somewhat spotted, but the color gave luster to her long black
hair and warmed her dusky skin with a glow like a shine
on an apple. And though she wore no eye make-up, I noticed her hands and feet were dyed with henna and she
had stained her lips with brown-red bark juice, the favorite
lip rouge of the village coquettes.

Neighbor women came and endless numbers of small
children, to sit and stare and chatter awhile. A pail of gray
ice, in which nestled several bottles of Pepsi-Cola, was
handed in from the courtyard. Everyone exclaimed at Salima's extravagance, for ice was expensive in the heat of
June, but she laughed and said it was for her dear friend
Laila and her guest. Laila blushed and looked terribly
pleased. Little sister brought tea; the baby woke and Salima
nursed it. I looked to Laila for a sign of departure, but she
sat contentedly on the sofa as though she might never
move again. The talk circled and eddied around me, and
I looked from one face to another—a neighbor woman,
worn and drawn; little sister, big-eyed, with traces of Salima's beauty; the fat baby, drowsy with milk and warmth;
and Salima herself, the perfect face set on the half-grown
body. I remembered the story of Salima's marriage, which
had been the talk of El Nahra for more than a year.

Khalil was not related to Salima, and that was the first
surprising thing. Within the El Eshadda such a union
would have been unheard of, for tribesmen boasted with
pride that they never let their womenfolk marry outside

the kin group or the larger circle of the tribe. Among the merchants of the village the codes were less strict, but still the preferred marriage was that between first cousins on the father's side. The boy always had first claim to one of his father's brother's daughters (*bint-amm*), and if for some reason the girl was to marry another relative, the boy cousin (*ibn-amm*) first had to relinquish his claim.

Salima had been a beautiful child, and Khalil had noticed her playing near her father's shop and scurrying through the village on errands for her mother. One day she grew up and donned the abayah. Like many little girls in their first abayah, she went to extremes, covering her face with a fold of the abayah whenever she passed men or boys, keeping the garment tightly about her at all times. Yet the abayah did not cover the wide black eyes, and as Salima walked, the swishing folds of the garment would often part to reveal a slim ankle bound in silver, or a delicate arm as Salima reached for the hand of her younger sister. Khalil fell in love and waited, Laila said, for four years until Salima was fourteen. Then, fearful that her father would marry her to her cousin, he decided on a bold course of action. Without consulting his mother (another unusual circumstance which had, in the end, worked to his detriment, for the old woman was furious and took out her fury on the new bride), he went to Salima's father and formally requested her hand.

According to Laila, Salima's father had been confused and perplexed by Khalil's action. No daughter of his had ever married outside the family before. True, Salima's ibn-amm was an older man and already married, but he still had a claim on the girl, and even if he agreed to give her up, there were still many eligible young men in the family who would have been happy to pay a large bride price for his beautiful daughter. Also, Salima was very young. Her father, loving her as he did, felt she should not be married until she was seventeen at least. Yet he was honored by Khalil's request. As a schoolteacher, Khalil was a step above Salima's family of artisans and shopkeepers. In all of El Nahra there was not a young man of better prospects—a devout Moslem, a good son, a respected man in the community, serious, polite, advancing socially and, most importantly, assured of an income for the rest of his life.

He asked Khalil to wait until Salima was fifteen, but Khalil, wildly in love by this time, was afraid of a trick and refused. The negotiations were broken off. Through mutual friends, Salima's father was made to realize why Khalil was so eager. The father wrote to Salima's cousin asking him to renounce his claim, which he did. Khalil discovered what the old man had done, again through friends, and went once more, in his best suit, to Salima's house and asked her father for her hand. The father promised Salima to Khalil provided the young man would wait another year. Khalil agreed.

Although the negotiations were supposed to be secret, they leaked out through Salima's mother, and Salima had a delightful last year at school, the center of attention, surrounded by admiring friends who helped her plan her trousseau and sat with her constantly, giving advice and congratulating her on her good fortune in having such a handsome fiancé. Salima's father went all the way to Baghdad to buy brocade—wine-and-gold, blue-and-silver, white-and-gold—for her wedding clothes. Soon after Salima's fifteenth birthday the young people were married and went on a honeymoon (for Khalil was sophisticated by local standards) to Baghdad, where they made a pilgrimage to the tomb of the Imam at Kadhimain. Salima produced a photograph to show me, taken in Baghdad, of the two of them staring in astonishment at the camera. Salima wore a flower in her hair, Khalil had one in his buttonhole. Laila pronounced it very attractive. All of these exciting events had been recounted again and again to Laila, who had visited her friend constantly at first in her new home, then less and less as Salima became busier with her household, her child and her authoritarian and relentless mother-in-law.

Laila confided to me on the way home that it was wonderful for Salima to have made such a good marriage, but for her such a thing was impossible. Not only would her father not dream of marrying her to a man who was unrelated, but she, Laila, could not imagine a more horrible fate than being married to a stranger and sent to live away from her family. I mentioned one or two tribal girls who had done just this, and Laila explained they were from poorer families. "But nobody of the sheik's family could ever be given to a stranger," she said, "unless, like Sheik Hamid's sister, she married an even richer and more important sheik than Hamid himself."

"Who will you marry, then?" I asked. Laila hedged, saying she didn't want to marry, because Salima had told her marriage was nothing but work and not what it was cracked up to be at all. "But if you did want to, who would you marry?" I pressed her.

"Oh, my cousin," she said, "but there aren't enough to go around. My sister Basima and I have figured out that there are one hundred and eighty girls in our section of the El Eshadda and only a hundred and thirty-five boys."

"Would you want to marry your cousin?" I asked. "Would your older sister Sanaa want to marry her cousin?"

Laila looked shocked. "Of course," she said. "Sanaa is to marry Sheik Hamid's son Ahmar. She has always known she would marry him and she has been in love with him for years."

"But how can she be in love with him if she never sees him?" I asked. "Doesn't your father arrange the marriage, and doesn't she wait until the wedding night to be with him for the first time?"

"Yes, yes," said Laila impatiently, "but Sanaa has known Ahmar since she was a baby. They played together all the time till Sanaa put on the abayah and went to sit in the house. She watches for him when he goes by our house; we tease her about him." She looked at me oddly. "Naturally she wants to marry him; who else would she want to marry?"

"No one, I can see that," I put in hastily. It was nearly dark along the canal road where the water buffalo were being driven up the bank out of the water, toward their owners' lands to be milked. The sun had mercifully set and a vague breeze stirred the air, but Laila was walking with her head bent, absorbed in her thoughts.

"I will never marry, Beeja," she finally brought out.

"Why not?" I asked in surprise.

Laila explained, so quietly I could scarcely hear, that since she had no brothers, someone would have to care for her mother when her father died. "Last year my father told me that he had chosen me," said Laila, "because I can sew and can earn a living for both of us."

"But isn't there any man who would marry you and come to live in your house and help you take care of your mother?"

"Ye-es," said Laila, "there is a special marriage when the man agrees to come and live in his wife's house and the children inherit the land, but most men prefer to stay in their own house."

I decided to shift the conversation. "Who will your oldest sister Fatima marry?"

Laila sighed. "Well, she was supposed to marry Haji Hamid's son but he disobeyed his father and eloped with Selma's sister, so now Fatima has no one to marry."

"What about Basima?" I asked, thinking I was on safe ground, for Basima was still under sixteen.

Laila smiled. "She will marry Jalil, Sheik Hamid's brother's son."

"But—" I stopped. Several things that had been puzzling me for a long time were suddenly becoming clear. I had wondered why Moussa's beautiful daughters were unmarried, and also why three of the sheik's marriageable daughters were still sitting in the harem. There was no one for them to marry. Prohibited by the code of their tribe from marrying men other than first cousins or similar close relations, they were trapped by circumstance, by social forces within Iraq which they were powerless to change. One was an unusual case, an elopement. But the sheik's sons and his brother's sons were something else, something new. These young men had been sent to Baghdad to study in the new coeducational colleges there and they had emerged with Westernized ideas. They wanted to marry educated girls who could be companions as well as wives and mothers. The boys could find such girls, for Bob had told me that Jalil was hoping to marry a pretty schoolteacher in Diwaniya and the sheik's brother had reportedly quarreled with his two sons over the issue. The girls were the ones who suffered, destined to stay year after year, unmarried, in their fathers' houses, passed on finally in their old age to their married brothers to support. An empty and meaningless life, the reasons for which they would never be able to understand.

"I don't think I want to marry anyway," Laila was going on. We had reached my gate by this time, and neighbors, passing, greeted us, but Laila paid little attention. She was intent on finishing her train of thought. "In our house, we share the work. If I got married, I would have to do it all. My sisters feel the same way."

But I remembered her sister Sanaa's telling me that ten years ago everyone had said she was as beautiful as the sheik's bride Selma. "Look at me," she had said. "I've been sitting here, working and waiting for ten years, and my heart grows narrow and cramped and it begins to show in my face."

"The thing to do," continued Laila, "is to go to school and become a teacher. That is what Basima is going to do. My father says so. Perhaps he'll send me to school too."

"But what about your sisters Fatima and Sanaa and Nejla?" I asked.

"Yes, it is a pity," she agreed. "When they were little girls, it was considered great shame to go to school. Now it is not, and everyone goes, but it is too late for them."

14

One Wife or Four

Hussna, a woman who lived near the market, was noted for her bad temper, poor housekeeping, and unkempt children. During Ramadan Laila had pointed her out to me at one of the krayas. "Everyone feels sorry for her husband, Abad," said Laila. "He is a good man and deserves a better wife."

In early summer, when the rumor went round the settlement that Abad was considering taking a second wife, even the women I knew who usually vehemently criticized the man in such cases agreed that Abad was justified. Further, they approved of his choice, a recently widowed young woman with two small boys. By marrying the young widow, Laila explained to me, Abad would improve the situation in his own house and also provide a good home for the fatherless family. Or so he thought. When Hussna heard of the plan, she was reported to be thoroughly enraged. Without saying a word to her husband or her neighbors, she borrowed fifteen pounds from her mother and took the earliest taxi, leaving the village one morning at dawn. By noon, fascinated neighbors coaxed her mother into admitting that Hussna had gone to consult one of the powerful wise women in Samawa, some fifty miles away. Um Khalil, the village dignitary, could write charms to keep babies from harm and other such simple things, but the women in Samawa, I was told, could do anything: bring a baby boy, even twin boys, to a woman who had been barren for years; cure any sickness; even strike an enemy dead. But their charms and cures were expensive.

By late afternoon everyone in El Nahra knew where Hussna had gone, and her husband, sitting nonchalantly with friends in the coffee shop, was eyed curiously by acquaintances and passers-by. What would happen? Even I stared at the ordinary-looking man as Laila and I walked by on our way to visit the school. Abad's hand trembled a little, perhaps, as he raised his glass of tea to his lips, but that was all. The widow kept to her house. We were told that Hussna had returned late the same night, and that in the morning the widow's oldest boy was sick with fever and dysentery. The child recovered, but Abad abandoned his plan of taking another wife. Hussna reigned alone and triumphant in her slovenly house, and Abad was seen more and more often in coffee shops. Within a few months the widow and her children were forced by economic circumstances to leave the village and move in with relatives in Diwaniya.

When I asked Laila about this, she pooh-poohed the whole chain of events. "Once long, long ago, my grandmother's sister went to Samawa and paid ten pounds and when she came back, her husband never beat her again," she said. "But my sisters and I don't believe in these wise women, who have never been to school or studied with the mullahs and don't know a single verse of the Koran. Years ago, yes, but now, no!"

Bob told me the men joked about the charms of Um Khalil and scoffed at the mention of the wise women of Samawa, but visits to any of the wise women were always noticed, and served to draw attention to the household in question. This in itself may have had some effect on the men.

Few women went to the extremes of Hussna. However, Um Khalil had regular visitors, as did the woman mullahs of El Nahra. Medical services were relatively new to the village, and in case of barrenness or serious illness in themselves or their children the women had little recourse except their own experience, prayer, or a charm. They purchased charms to make cruel husbands kind, indifferent ones loving, to prevent divorce, to keep new babies safe from the Evil Eye. But more than any other single thing, they prayed, purchased charms, connived against being supplanted by a second wife.

This fear of the women seemed to me out of all proportion to the facts. In the tribal settlement of one hundred and four households, for example, only nine were or ever had been polygamous. There had been four divorces in the past year and a half. The Koran allows a man to take up to four wives, if he can provide for them equally and give them all the same amount of affection. But it is expensive to take more than one wife. Another bride price must be raised, ranging anywhere from 10 to 150 or even 500 pounds, depending on the economic and social status of the man and girl involved. (Selma, Sheik Hamid's wife, had commanded a bride price of 1500 English pounds.)

After the initial investment, the man must pay for food and clothing for the new wife and her prospective children. In case of divorce, the man must return a certain portion of the bride price to the woman or her family, and must continue to provide for the children of the marriage. And in addition to monetary considerations, there is the inevitable hullabaloo as the two or more women fight for supremacy in the household. Bob reported that the men mentioned the last problem most frequently; the quarreling among the women affected the man's peace and comfort, and most men confessed that, though they often desired another wife, they found it easier and cheaper to make do with one, even though one might not have the whitest skin, the darkest eyes or the longest hair of any damsel in the village.

But another wife was always a possibility which rose to trouble the hearts of the women, I noticed, when they were ill or out of sorts. They talked of it constantly, in a joking, indirect way most of the time, though there were times when the discussion became very serious. I, in my peculiar situation, was a favorite target for jokes on the subject.

"When," the women would ask, giggling, "is Mr. Bob going to take another wife?" We had been over this ground many times before, in Laila's house, in the sheik's house, in other households which I visited regularly, and my answer was always the same.

"He might like to," I would say, "but our religion and

the laws of our country permit him to have only one wife at a time."

"But," came the inevitable argument, "isn't our way better? Mr. Bob can divorce you and then you have no home. But if the sheik were to take another wife [sly dig at Selma, who always looked uncomfortable at this point] he would still have to take care of all his present wives and children. Which is better?"

And before I could reply they would chorus, "Our way is better," nodding their heads to each other in agreement.

Next someone would say, "Oh, by the way, I hear Mr. Bob is going to marry one of the sheik's daughters."

I was supposed to register shocked disbelief, which I always did, and the women would nudge each other and laugh at my mock consternation.

"*Ahlan wusahlan,*" I would say, "all of the sheik's daughters are my friends."

At this point the joke would cease being a joke, and one of the older women would intervene. Once Kulthum, the sheik's oldest wife, touched me considerably by adding, "Don't worry, Beeja, we would never let them do that to you because you are like our own daughter and we would not want to hurt you." If it had been her own son who was involved she might very well have been able to prevent such an eventuality, for I had been told by Bob that the men sometimes considered themselves victimized by their mothers, who always had the final say in choosing their sons' wives.

However, by the time a man had accumulated enough wealth to marry a second time, his mother was usually dead. The marriage of middle age tended to be a marriage of pleasure, the girl chosen by the man himself rather than by the women of his household. A man in comfortable circumstances who married again when his first wife was past the childbearing age was doing what was expected of him, although the occasional malcontent who wanted to divorce or remarry with every change of season was considered irresponsible. Bob found that the sheik, if he discovered that a poor tribesman was contemplating marrying a second time, would often try to dissuade him. For the sheik knew that, given a bad harvest, such a family would be an economic drain on the entire community.

In the time of the prophet Mohammed, polygamy was considered a great step forward. Mohammed wanted to discourage the pre-Islamic practice of female infanticide, and check the polygamous situation which seems to have bordered on licentiousness. To provide for the extra women he ruled that men could marry up to four wives. Today polygamy is disappearing in the cities of the Middle East, where it is rare and frowned upon. Some Koranic scholars have even gone so far as to insist that the Koran has been wrongly interpreted for centuries.

But in rural areas polygamy persists, partly out of tradition, partly because it still fills a social and economic need. In the cities women are now attending schools and colleges, taking jobs in the offices, factories and schools of a growing industrial society. Some are becoming financially independent, and though still tied closely to their families, they are beginning to weaken even these bonds by establishing separate households when they marry.

Yet in rural areas like El Nahra the extended family is still the basic social unit. There is no place for a woman outside the houses of her father, her husband, her brothers or her sons. Even as a second or third wife, a woman has a role and status and purpose. She has a respectable place to live and food to eat; her children, who will support her in her old age, have a chain of relatives to whom they may turn for marriage partners, for jobs, for bare subsistence if necessary. And the women of El Nahra, though they feared being replaced by other wives and insisted vehemently that two women were too many in any house, were well aware of the alternatives. I know of no woman in the village or tribe who would have chosen spinsterhood and isolation rather than marriage, whether as the first, second or third wife of a man.

In El Nahra, I found, polygamy was more or less palatable to a woman, depending on the personalities of the wives, the temperament of the husband and the demands of the particular household. Sheik Hamid's first wife had died giving birth to her third child. The sheik then married Kulthum and, fairly soon after, Bahiga, who cared for the motherless babies as well as bearing their own children. I did not hear much of the earlier history of the two women, but when I knew Bahiga and Kulthum they appeared friendly, though they did not visit each other in their private apartments. When Sheik Hamid was forty-five, he married for the fourth time, the beautiful Selma. Selma was married for her beauty and education (she had finished high school) as well as to cement a political alliance with a distant section of the tribe, but she did not sit in idle splendor on the pink satin bed, waited upon by servant girls with plumed fans. She had been married also because she was desperately needed as a working member of the household.

When he married Selma, Haji Hamid had recently succeeded his father as sheik, and thus was responsible for the traditional hospitality in the tribal mudhif. There were fifteen growing children in the compound, and Bahiga and Kulthum, aging now, could barely keep up with their duties. In addition to child care, laundry, tending the sick, keeping their own apartments and the compound in order, they had to cook three meals every day for approximately sixty people (fifteen children, two wives, the wife and four children of Sheik Hamid's eldest son Nour, the sheik himself, the aged wife of the sheik's father, two servants and from ten to thirty tribal retainers and guests who ate regularly in the mudhif). Even with Nour's wife, the two servants and teenaged daughters to help, this was an enormous task.

Selma lived in her own house for two years and bore her first child before moving into the compound with Kulthum and Bahiga. I knew, for I had been told by each wife in turn, that they were jealous of the sheik's affections and felt rejected when he favored one woman's child over another, or brought gifts to one and not to the other two. Yet the three women depended on each other, and knew that their work would be much more difficult without the help of the others. The basic jealousies and petty dislikes were there, but they were submerged and mitigated by the necessities of daily living.

Not all women accepted the situation with such good grace, however. I remember a young woman whom I met by chance in Selma's room one summer evening, a woman from an outlying clan settlement who had left her husband, fleeing to the sheik's harem, traditional respectable refuge of women in difficulties. She had arrived just before dark, Laila whispered to me, and had been telling her story over and over again to the crowds of women who came to see her.

It was not an unusual story, I gathered from the comments of the group. The second wife of a middle-aged tribesman, she had been married just a year. But from the day after her wedding, the first wife and the mother-in-law had joined forces to make her life miserable. They left the most unpleasant household tasks for her to do, insulted her before guests, and shouted at her from morning to night. When the husband came home, they complained that the girl was lazy and ill-bred.

Even while the girl was talking, one of Selma's little boys ran in to whisper loudly in his mother's ear that a man had just arrived in the mudhif and said he had come to take his wife home. When the girl heard this, her face changed expression; she looked at the ground and we waited for what was to come. After we had eaten a few more pumpkin seeds, Kulthum moved closer to the girl.

"Is your husband kind to you?" she asked gently, and the girl nodded, her eyes still cast down.

"Then you would be foolish not to return to him," Kulthum counseled.

The girl still kept silent. Selma spoke up.

"Tell your husband how mean the other women are," she said. "If he really loves you, he will beat them and they will understand that they cannot treat you so badly."

Several of the women disagreed loudly. Kulthum and Bahiga, the sheik's two older wives, looked at each other and looked away. What part of their past were they recalling? Kulthum spoke again.

"It will be better in the long run if you would try to make friends with them," she offered.

"Make friends with them!" The girl's head flew up and

she exploded in a frenzy. "They hate me, they hide the sugar and steal my cigarettes, they pour salt into the food I prepare for my husband, they gossip about me to the neighbors and they tell my husband I am mean and will not help with the housework. They want nothing except to get me out. How can I make friends with them?" She broke down and sobbed loudly into her abayah. Kulthum moved closer to the girl and touched her shoulder.

"You are still young and pretty," she said. "Remember that. They are old and ugly now and barren. You can still bear children who will be your comfort when you are old."

"I am five months along with child," hiccuped the girl through her sobs.

"Ah, then," said Bahiga, "you must go back."

Kulthum nodded and several other women voiced agreement.

Selma's servant Amina brought tea and we sipped it, talking of other things. Kulthum and Bahiga rose to leave, as did many others. Selma and the girl talked together in low tones. I realized that Selma had been unusually quiet during the evening, perhaps because of the presence of the two older wives, but perhaps also because the girl's troubles had revived memories of her own problems of adjustment when she had first married the sheik.

Laila and I rose to go, and Selma said, "Did you understand what we were saying this evening?"

I nodded.

She spoke to the girl, who was drying her eyes on a corner of her abayah. She looked at me hard.

"I am telling her," said Selma, "that in your country it is forbidden for a man to marry two wives at the same time, and if that were true here, she would not have been able to marry."

We all tried to laugh, and even the girl managed a smile.

"Well," said Laila, as she bade me good night at the door of her house, "I hope my father doesn't think of taking another wife, because she would be very unhappy. All of my sisters and I love our mother."

As I did not answer, she went on, "After all, that man

might never have married the girl if his first wife had been a better wife."

"How?" I asked, though I thought I knew what Laila would say.

"Served and respected her husband, worked hard, kept herself beautiful for him, made him laugh, and of course borne him sons."

What could I answer? I knew, as did Laila, that her mother had done a magnificent job on all counts except one: there were no sons.

"Of course I know my father wants a son," Laila half hissed, half whispered, "so Fatima and I have bought a charm from Um Khalil to put in my mother's bed so she can conceive a boy. It cost three pounds. She doesn't know, but just in case that doesn't work, we have bought another to put under my father's pillow to drive out all thoughts of a second wife."

A group of men were approaching on their way home from late evening tea at the mudhif, and Laila said good night hurriedly and stepped inside her door out of sight. I walked on down the path to my gate, thinking about Laila and her sisters, who appeared so happy and industrious and claimed to be above the magic of the ignorant. Yet they were silently helping their mother in every way they could to wrestle with the problem that faced all women, rich and poor, educated and uneducated: how to keep the love of one man and remain the only woman in a happy and respected household, surrounded by children who would provide for their mother in her old age. To achieve this end, they were prepared to do almost anything.

On the other hand, there were polygamous households in the settlement that were genuinely happy. The house of Abdulla, the sheik's older brother, was a shining example. Abdulla had married Bassoul, the young daughter of a Bedouin chieftain, after his first wife Khariya had been unwell for several years. She had rheumatism and various female complaints which made it difficult for her to complete the daily drudgery of the household. Some said that Khariya herself had urged Abdulla to take another wife

to help her out. Others discounted this. But wherever the
suggestion had originated, it had been a good one. From
the early days of the marriage, Bassoul had been Khariya's
friend, and now, when one saw them together, they seemed
devoted to each other. Bassoul was young and strong, with
bright eyes and rosy cheeks. She relieved Khariya of the
burdens of carrying water, washing and other tasks which
wearied the older woman. When Bassoul did not conceive,
Khariya took her to the local mullah, who wrote a sura
from the Koran for her. Khariya paid for this blessing.
Five years after her marriage, Bassoul finally conceived and
Khariya seemed as happy as though it were her own
daughter.

I had asked many women about the secret of this household's happiness, and the best answer came from Khariya
herself.

"You wonder why Bassoul and I are happier together
than the sheik's wives, don't you?" she said.

I nodded.

"Everyone says," she continued, "that it is because Bassoul is a good girl and helps me. This is true. But even if
she were the best-hearted girl in the village and worked
harder than any servant, we would not be happy together
if Abdulla were not the kind of man he is. He believes
the Koran and does what it says. When he goes to Baghdad, he brings back two presents: a gold bracelet for
Bassoul and one for me. When Bassoul gets money for a
new abayah, he always asks me whether I need one. And
he divides his nights equally between us. Women always
stand together before strangers and say they are happy together; they are ashamed to admit that they have not been
clever enough to remain the only wife, and so they pre-
tend that whatever they have is good. Don't believe them.
Women will always fight and quarrel and be discontented
if the man is not strong enough to give each of them what
she needs and wants from him."

PART III

15

Summer

Haji Hamid was preparing to leave for his summer vacation in Lebanon. Each year he spent the two hottest months in a small mountain hotel above Beirut, where he met sheiks from Iraq, Kuwait, Saudi Arabia and Syria, men distantly related to him by blood or by tribal affiliation. In the cool mountain air the men would talk away the summer, drinking tea and coffee, playing *trictrac* (backgammon) and occasionally driving into town to tour the fleshpots of Beirut. When September came they would head back to the deserts of the Arabian Peninsula, to towns and tribal settlements where many of them, like Haji Hamid, were still responsible for the welfare of many people.

Summer sojourns to fashionable watering places like Lebanon were a comparatively new thing among the sheiks of southern Iraq. Haji's father had been one of the first to go, and each summer he had taken one of his sons with him. When Haji had assumed the sheikship, he decided to be adventurous; scorning the little mountain hotel, he traveled to Cyprus one summer, accompanied by three retainers.

The men checked into a second-class hotel in Nicosia, and all might have been well if the hotel had not unexpectedly caught fire in the middle of the first night. Servants rushed up and down the hallways, pounding on doors and shouting "Fire! Fire!" alternately in Greek, Turkish and English. Haji put on his eyeglasses and opened the door of his room to see what the commotion was about, but of the clerk's screaming neither he nor his retainers understood a word. No smoke had yet penetrated the floor and the four Arab gentlemen stood looking at the frantic clerk in some perplexity. Finally in desperation the clerk pulled at the sleeve of Haji's white nightshirt; the three retainers stepped forward, but Haji apparently realized that it was no plot, the clerk simply wanted them to come with him, and they did so.

Hustled downstairs and out onto the lawn, the four Arabs were greeted by a sight which Haji told Bob he never forgot. All the hotel guests were assembled on the lawn, attired in odds and ends of clothes which they had been able to don quickly in their flight from the burning building. Some wore almost nothing. These half-clad men and women were talking and joking together, and Haji, coming from a society where strange men and women *never* talk together, and the women are always covered up to their eyes, found the scene very upsetting. Eventually the fire was put out, and little damage had been done. The guests returned to their rooms, but Haji had had enough. Next morning he packed his bags and returned to Lebanon.

The sheik was planning to drive to Baghdad and take the plane to Beirut. His car was being washed and waxed, and when I went to see Selma she was putting her husband's summer wardrobe in order for traveling: boiling the undershirts, dishdashas and long-legged drawers, and bleaching them in the sun to a dazzling whiteness. She was also cooking his favorite meals for him, "so he'll be anxious to come home," she explained. "Haji says the food in the hotel is very bad. You never know what they put in the stew."

I had wondered whether Selma might accompany him to Lebanon, because I knew she had gone to Baghdad with him at least twice and had stayed in the house of relatives.

"Yes, but I only had Feisal then," she said. "He was a baby and easy to take. I couldn't go now. It would be expensive to take all of us, and who would take care of my five children while I was gone?"

I nodded. "But it might be a pleasant change," I suggested tentatively.

Selma eyed me. "Pleasant? Why? To live in a strange

room all by myself, keep out of sight of strange men, eat I don't know what?"

"But don't you miss Haji?"

"Of course," answered Selma. She paused. "But I have a change when he's gone. Of course I miss him, but it is much less work for me. And then," she paused again, "he misses me, and he is much happier to see me when he comes home." She looked down at the row of gold necklaces about her throat and fingered one of lovely tapered cone-shaped gold beads. "See, Beeja," she laughed, "he brought me this last year. Lebanese goldwork is very good."

The night before Haji's departure, Bob brought him over from the mudhif to have tea with us in the garden. Haji sat down in one of our folding aluminum armchairs, took off his glasses and rubbed his eyes. He looked tired and complained that the heat seemed to affect him more every year.

"But it is very pleasant here," he amended. After the 110-degree heat of the day, the garden was cool and peaceful, and I realized how hospitable our host was. This was his only garden, he obviously enjoyed sitting in it on summer evenings, but now that he had offered it to us, he would not have dreamed of intruding.

A light breeze rustled the hot leaves on the orange and lemon trees, the dried banana stalks rasped against each other softly, and the stray cat we had adopted, who slept all day in the shade of a palm tree, was slithering about the yard, hunting for hedgehogs. I brought tea.

From the coffee shop on the canal we heard the announcer's voice from Radio Baghdad, giving the time and the station break. A pause, and the sound of a cello, round and full, of a violin and a piano swelled out of the tropical night. "It's Beethoven," said Bob, astounded. "The Archduke Trio." We waited for the coffee shop proprietor to turn it off, but he did not.

Bob roused himself to say to Haji that we found this music very beautiful. Did he?

"No," said Haji, "I don't. I have friends who say they

do, but I think they are just pretending to like it because the English and other foreigners do."

He sipped his tea and spoke of his weariness and his financial troubles and his feeling that he needed a change. The Beethoven went on, and Bob and I exchanged looks of pleased amazement at the sound of the music we loved and had not heard for so long. I went to get more tea.

With a click the station changed. Abdul Wahab, a well-known Arab vocalist, sang among the drums and pipes. When I returned with the tea, Bob and Haji were chuckling.

"Now this," said Haji, "is music."

I wished the sheik bon voyage and left the men to linger over their tea glasses.

Two days after Haji left, Selma's oldest son Feisal was in bed with an unidentifiable illness. I went up to the house, where the boy lay on a cot in the *sirdab*, or summer cellar, a room much cooler because it was set in at least two feet below the surface of the ground. Feisal's mother and aunts, his brothers and sisters and cousins all sat on the floor around his bed, clucking in anxiety. A glass of water stood on a little bedside table. From time to time one of the children would take a sip from the glass, only to flee screaming in mock terror at a reprimand from the women. The noise and the crowds and the bright electric light in the sirdab had no effect on Feisal; he lay in a stupor and did not move.

Selma's eyes were red from crying. "He is so sick, Beeja," she said, "and he won't eat and he won't drink, since yesterday afternoon. Feel him."

I put my hand on his forehead; the child was burning up with fever.

"He vomits," said Selma, "but he won't drink at all and he gets hotter and hotter and I don't know what to do."

I didn't know either, but it was obvious that the child was seriously ill. The temperature outside was at least 110, and if Feisal would not drink and the fever continued, he was in danger of dehydration.

"Has the doctor come?" I asked.

Selma said that Nour and Abdulla had gone to get
the village doctor. I sat for a few moments before excus-
ing myself. Selma had her hands full and another guest
was the last thing in the world she needed.

After lunch Bob brought bad news from the mudhif;
the doctor had diagnosed Feisal's illness as typhoid fever.
This panicked us. We ordinarily did not meddle in community affairs, even if asked, but typhoid in midsummer
was something we did not like to contemplate. Bob had
suggested to Nour that the people living in the compound
should be inoculated, but Nour had replied that only Haji
Hamid himself could authorize such drastic action.

"I think I'll call Haji myself," said Bob. "He's probably
still in Baghdad. It would be terrible to have a typhoid
epidemic break out."

Haji, as we expected, thought inoculation an excellent
idea. When Bob reached him, he had just received news
of Feisal's illness and was wondering whether to return to
El Nahra. Instead he called Nour and talked to Abdulla,
giving instructions that everyone in his house and Abdulla's house was to be inoculated.

Soon another crisis developed: Dr. Ibrahim had no
serum. Abdulla and Nour and Bob got the postmaster out
of bed to open up the telephone exchange and place another call to Baghdad. Haji promised he would buy the
medicine as soon as the pharmacies opened in the morning and put it on the first taxi bound for El Nahra, tip-
ping the driver well to deliver the serum directly to the
doctor.

In the morning I could see the boy was worse. Even
more women and children had gathered round his bed.
They moaned when Feisal moaned, cried out when he
cried out. The presence of so many people in the small
sirdab had warmed the usually cool air, and Selma was
perspiring freely, wiping her face with her foota and trying hard not to cry. She fell on me as I entered, something
she had never done before, and demanded what she should
do. I could think of nothing new, and merely said that the
boy should be bathed and that somehow she must get
water into him.

"But Beeja, I can't," she said desperately. "He knocks the water out of my hand. He's my first-born and I've spoiled him and his father has spoiled him. But he gets worse and worse and I'm afraid—I'm afraid he will die." She broke down and sobbed.

I put my arm around her shoulder, which seemed little comfort, and several of the older women got up and told her not to worry.

"No, he won't die, no, Selma he won't die," I kept repeating over and over again while she sobbed, talking for lack of anything more concrete to offer. "No, he won't die," I said again, but not out of conviction, for the boy looked dreadful.

Nour spoke through the screen to Selma.

"We must all leave—the doctor is coming," she said, drying her eyes on her foota again, and we all adjourned to Selma's room where the women loudly debated Feisal's chances of recovery.

The boy cried out in anguish from the sirdab, and the women shook their heads, silenced for the moment, and whispered in sympathy. At another cry Selma half rose, realized she could not enter her son's room while the strange doctor was present, and sat down again. We all knew the doctor was not doing anything awful to Feisal, but his cries were piercing. Selma sobbed again, and Kulthum patted her knee. The screaming gradually subsided and a knock sounded on the door. Selma put on her abayah, talked for a few moments with Nour outside the door, and came back into the room.

"The doctor says Feisal will get w-worse tonight," she announced, her voice trembling, "and tomorrow he may be better. And the doctor says he must stay in the room alone, with only me to watch. And the door must be shut."

This was greeted with cries of protest.

"He'll be frightened."

"He can't stay alone."

"No, no, Selma, we must keep watch."

"Nour says so," interrupted Selma firmly, "and he also says the doctor is going to give everyone in the house injections against the fever."

Shock, disbelief, fear and displeasure registered in rapid succession on the faces of the women as the force of this statement penetrated to them. The barrage of objections was almost too much for Selma and she appealed to me.

"Beeja will have the injection too," she said.

I replied that I had already had it, and the injection did not leave a scar, baring my upper arm to show it unmarked. They crowded to look, distracted momentarily, and I showed them my smallpox-vaccination scar—"very small and it didn't hurt"—lying blithely and babbling on about how many different kinds of injections I had had for how many different kinds of diseases.

"The doctor is coming after supper," pronounced Selma.

By late evening Bob reported the doctor had inoculated more than thirty men, women and children. Feisal was approaching the crisis, and the doctor felt he would reach it, and the fever would probably break, before morning. He was right. I went visiting in midmorning and found the crowd of women in the sirdab again, but now Feisal was conscious, and crying, in his usual wheedling way, for sweets, for toys, for a bird to play with. He struck his mother's hand when she came near him. Yes, the spoiled son was getting well.

The summer wore on and each day was a little hotter than the day before. We found we were accomplishing less and less. An hour's cooking tired me. Bob made the effort every morning to visit the mudhif or the irrigation office, but found almost no one to talk to. People were hoarding their stores of energy to last through the two months of heat yet to come. About this time we both had bad bouts of dysentery, which sapped our strength even more. After this experience we decided to boil the drinking water, and each night before bed we would pour boiling-hot water into two huge porous clay jars to cool during the night. For despite our relative inactivity, we were drinking between us over a gallon of water a day.

At night we slept outside, on camp beds and under mosquito nets. Each morning the bedclothes had to be carried inside or they would have been so hot and dusty by nightfall that we would not have enjoyed lying on them. We found that an afternoon nap had become a necessity, and this grew longer every day. By mid-July we were eating our lunch at noon and immediately afterward retiring to the living room to try to sleep. But even protected by our foot-thick mud walls and by window screens of woven camel-thorn dampened by a bucket of water several times a day, it was so hot that sleep came with difficulty. We lay on the camp beds and read mysteries and waited for sundown. Fortunately we had a little fan and, more important, electricity to run it, for Abu Saad, the mayor, had a fan too and liked to keep it running while he napped. When the mayor ordered it, naturally the town generator was turned on. Even so, in that one summer we perspired so much during the long hot afternoons that we rotted through the canvas of both brand-new camp beds.

At five we would get up, take a cold sponge bath and dress, and as the sun dropped to the horizon, we would hear other people on the paths outside. By seven o'clock dusk had settled over the countryside and the settlement was alive again.

"In Iraq in summer the days are very hot, but the nights are very beautiful," ran one of the phrases we had learned in our colloquial Arabic course at Georgetown University.

I have often wondered about the homesick Iraqi who was the author of the phrase, writing about the marvelous summer nights of Iraq from his desk in the steaming humidity of a Washington, D.C., summer. For I shall never forget the sense of release we felt when night had descended after the fierce heat of the day. The birds woke and added their voices to the buzz of the noise as families cooked their dinners and went shopping in the reopened suq. The children played a game with sheeps' knuckles, shouting, in the road. We sat in our garden, eating supper from a big tin tray and tasting the coolness of the air. We stayed up late, for it was too wonderful to go to bed. Bob would go to the mudhif and I would head for Laila's house or Selma's or Sherifa's.

The women gathered in the courts under the stars. One

by one, children would come home and fall asleep in their mothers' laps or on the summer beds of split reed mats which ranged round the court; the women sat on and on, smoking, chewing pumpkin seeds, talking and relishing the breeze that frequently came up after sundown. It was on these evenings that I felt closest to the women, as we relaxed together after sharing the day's heat and talked and exchanged confidences as friends.

"What do you dream about, Beeja?" asked Laila one evening. We sat in an irregular circle in the court of her house. Fatima was passing around a tray of khubuz laham which she had just made, and we nibbled the bread contentedly, washing it down with cooled water from the clay jug in the center of the circle.

"What's the matter, are you *afraid* of us?" Nejla, the family jokester, opened her eyes very wide and looked melodramatically into mine. Everyone laughed.

"How could I be, Nejla? You are so funny," I answered.

Nejla was delighted. "Yes, I am, aren't I?" she asked the group.

"Well, what do you dream about?" persisted Basima.

"Many things," I said. "My mother, Mr. Bob, things that have happened in the past. What about you?"

"I dream about my cousin," said Basima. "I always dream of him, and the day we shall marry."

Fatima said slowly, "I have one dream again and again. I go out in the morning to get water and the canal has gone dry. Soon everyone is standing by the bank, waiting for the water to come."

"And does it come?"

"I don't know. I always wake up."

We sat quietly together. A finger of the new moon was visible in the sky above us.

"When you see the new moon," said Basima, "my father says you must look at something beautiful or someone you love and then make a wish."

"What if there isn't anything beautiful nearby?" I inquired.

"Then you look at water," she replied.

"Has the canal ever dried up?" I went on.

"I don't think so," said Laila, "but my father says that once the British cut off the water because Haji was fighting them and winning."

"Haji Abdul Emir, our grandfather, you mean," said Basima.

"Sometimes I dream about Haji Abdul Emir," Fatima put in unexpectedly.

The girls exclaimed at this. "Really, Fatima?" "How do you dream about him?"

"I dream he is on horseback," she answered. "You girls are too young to remember, but before Haji Abdul Emir got sick, he had a beautiful horse—it cost nearly a thousand pounds. He would gallop up the road to the mudhif very fast and all of us children would run after him. Once he even rode a racing camel up the road, a milk-white camel."

"Well," said Laila primly, "I dream about my friend Salima, and when you leave us, Beeja, we will dream about you and what good times we had together."

"But I'm not leaving yet," I pointed out.

"You will, and you will forget us," they said.

"No, no," I protested.

Fatima smiled and winked at Laila. "Let's buy a charm from Um Khalil so Beeja won't forget us."

"Or look in the Book of Stars and see what it says," suggested Basima.

"What's the Book of Stars?" I asked.

"Selma has one, that she keeps hidden from Haji, and it tells you about everything," said Laila. "I've looked in it many times to see whether I am going to marry and it always says no."

"I want to marry a fat man, a fat man," chanted Nejla, "a man as big as a bar-rel." She laughed at her own joke, but no one joined in; they were too interested in what they are saying.

"We don't believe in the Book of Stars, Beeja," said Fatima, "we're just joking. This kind of magic is against the Koran."

"But Fatima," Laila put in, "the Book of Stars must be worth something because look what Selma did with it!"

"What did she do?" I asked.

Fatima looked disapproving, but Laila plunged ahead. "When Selma first moved into the compound, Haji would sleep one night with her, the next night with Bahiga and the night after that with Kulthum. But Selma didn't like that at all. She wanted Haji all to herself."

"Laila—" cautioned Fatima.

"Well, she did, and you know it, and so she got this Book of Stars from her sister in Diwaniya and after a while Haji stopped sleeping with Bahiga and Kulthum and only came to Selma."

"Yes, but—"

"She did it with her Book," finished Laila triumphantly and looked around her for confirmation. The other girls nodded.

"That is against the Koran," repeated Fatima angrily, "and you should know better, Laila. You know what the mullah says."

"Is the *hiriz* against the Koran too?" I asked, trying to turn the conversation. I had seen these charms everywhere in Iraq, small silver or tin amulets containing a few seeds and a roll of paper on which some Koranic verses had been written by a mullah. The amulet was pinned to a child's clothing to ward off the Evil Eye, or it was suspended from the mirror of a taxi to bring good luck. Something blue was usually a part of it, a blue glass bead or a fine turquoise set into the silver of the more costly amulets.

"Well, no," admitted Fatima. "Everyone buys a hiriz for his children. Rajat was so sick when she was a baby that my mother bought three for her from Um Khalil."

"If children are afraid at night, they hold on to the hiriz and then they are all right," Laila added.

"And a hiriz can do a lot of good," put in Basima. "Remember Um Farid?" They nodded.

"Tell me," I pleaded.

"Um Farid was once asleep in her house. Her husband was away and only her mother and her baby were there. A wind came in the night and blew out the lantern, and a burglar came afterward and Um Farid got such a fright she could no longer speak. After a while her mother went to Um Khalil and bought a big hiriz and Um Farid got better. She was at Sherifa's house the other day and said quite a few things."

"I think Um Khalil must be very rich from this work," said Laila. "Once Salima opened a big black box which belonged to her mother-in-law and it was filled with five- and ten-pound notes."

"That is bad," said Fatima, "very bad. Um Khalil takes money for doing good and for doing evil too. One of the wives of Haji Abdul Emir used to claim that all magic, the Book of Stars and even the hiriz, were *haram*, a sin against God. But when she was very old she said that what you do for the good of your family is all right, *halal*, but if you try to use magic and charms for a bad reason, then it is haram."

"It's better to pray at the tomb of Hussein and forget all this," said Sanaa, who had been quiet throughout the conversation. "Or pray for something and promise to fast in Ramadan if you get your wish. Then one is sure one is not committing haram."

Sometimes Nejla would entertain us with imitations. She loved to dress up in her father's clothes and play the irate man, scolding wives, daughters, or sons. Her instinct for gesture and gait was excellent, and we could always guess who her target of the evening happened to be. Her *pièce de résistance* of that summer, requested again and again, was the scene after the kraya, when the mullah had set upon the girls who were pulling at me. Nejla did us all, the rowdy crowd of little girls, myself shrinking timidly away trying not to show my distaste (how had she seen that?), the erect mullah shouting and striking fiercely out in all directions.

In Sherifa's little court the neighbor women gathered also, and Laila, Basima and I would often walk up to spend part of our evening there. Once a woman, distantly related to Sherifa, began to query me about the intricacies of child-bearing in America.

"What I can't understand," she said, "is how American women stop having babies. Do they refuse to sleep with their husbands?"

"No, no," chorused the group. "How could they? They don't, do they, Beeja?"

"No, they don't," I started.

"They have operations by men doctors," offered Basima, "so they don't get pregnant."

"But what if they do get pregnant?" insisted the woman.

"American women want children too," I began again.

The woman burst out, "So do I, but I have ten, *ten*, and the doctor says I will die if I have one of those operations, but I don't care. If I have another baby, I will die anyway. I'm pregnant again, and I've eaten lots of pumpkin seeds, but nothing has happened. So now what do I do?"

"Never mind, Um Ali," cautioned Sherifa. "Go to the midwife. She knows how to get rid of babies. And don't worry. God knows best."

The woman gestured impatiently and sighed, a long, tearing sigh.

"Really," counseled Sherifa, "the midwife is very good. And not expensive either."

Talk turned away from the woman's insoluble problem. Laila blurted out that she had always considered Christians unclean because she had been told that they did not shave any of their body hair.

"And is it true," asked Basima, "that in America they put all the old women in houses by themselves, away from their families?"

I admitted that this was sometimes true and tried to explain, but my words were drowned in the general murmur of disapproval.

"What a terrible place that must be!"

"How awful!"

"And their children let them go?"

"Thank God we live in El Nahra, where the men are not so cruel!"

It had never occurred to me before, but the idea of old people's homes must have been particularly reprehensible to these women whose world lay within the family unit and whose whole lives of toil and childbearing were rewarded in old age, when they enjoyed repose and respect as members of their children's households.

For months the women had begged me to tell their fortunes with coffee cups. This I could not do, but finally I admitted I could read palms, and soon the palm reading became part of the summer evening's entertainment. I had to change my approach, for one could hardly say, in this culture, that a woman would have four or five flirtations and then a marriage, but rather that she would have many offers before marrying. Travel for these women meant religious pilgrimages or visits to the doctor; a long travel line indicated a possibility of visiting Mecca. Everyone wanted to know whether she was jealous, whether she was passionate. The passion was important; the married women would giggle and tell the unmarried ones that they had yet to learn how much fun it could be to sleep with one's husband.

"Always?" I asked.

"Of course," they would reply. "If we did not enjoy sleeping with them, how could we love them?"

I thought to myself, truly how else, for they seldom saw their husbands except to serve them at meals, and at bedtime.

On the night of the prophet Mohammed's birthday a fine full moon rose over the canal. For the occasion, the main street of El Nahra and the suq as well had been hung with paper streamers and colored lights. Bob left after supper to attend the festivities, a skit to be held in the suq, followed by refreshments. Laila and Sherifa and Fatima and Basima and I could not stay indoors that night. We were not daring enough to cross the canal, but sat in a row by our wall, wrapped in our abayahs, watching the reflections of the colored lights and the moonlight in the water and listening to the sounds of merriment from the opposite bank.

Fatima and Laila tried to persuade little Rajat to go across and watch the skit and come back and tell us about it. Although Rajat wore the abayah, she was only eleven and could easily have passed unnoticed, but she grew shy and stubborn and refused to go alone. Fatima, to make up, entertained us with accounts of the skits she had seen when she was a girl and had hovered around the suq on the night of the Prophet's birthday.

"I wasn't afraid of life the way this one is," she said with a contemptuous glance at the shrinking Rajat. "Abdul Latif, the *mukhtar* of the suq, always played the stupid pilgrim on his way to Mecca," she began, "and the foreigner was always played by—" and she went on, describing the skit in detail, complete with gestures, until we all laughed at her cleverness.

The moon was high in the sky and we sat close together, loath to leave, when Rajat, the shy rabbit, sprang up as if shot, hissed that she could hear Nour and her father coming along the road, and that we had better hurry home.

We rose quickly and almost ran toward our respective houses, still in good spirits. As I closed my gate behind me, I heard the men's voices on the path and knew the women would be safely home before them.

When Bob came, he presented me with two pieces of imitation toffee and a Jordan almond, the "favor" of the evening.

"It was very interesting," he recounted. "Abdul Latif, the mukhtar, played a stupid pilgrim on his way to Mecca. He meets a foreigner on the road, and this was very well done, I thought, by a man named—"

"Yes," I smiled. "I know."

He looked a bit surprised. "What do you mean? Were you there?"

"No, but it was just as good," I answered and went on to explain about my evening with the girls by the banks of the canal.

16

Hussein

During the summer we also acquired an armed guard, or rather Abdulla, Sheik Hamid's brother, acquired him for us. Abdulla told Bob that Haji felt we should have a guard, and had instructed Abdulla to find us the right man. So we took on Hussein, more to please Abdulla than out of any felt need for a man with a loaded rifle to stand outside our door every night. Hussein belonged to another clan of the tribe, a somewhat impoverished group which lived down the canal about half a mile. Hussein's wife Sajjida, accompanied by two thin daughters, came to visit me, and I returned the call.

Their house was poorer and smaller than any in our settlement. The single room was hardly more than a hovel, with a ceiling so low one could not stand upright, but the floor was swept neatly and the one reed mat was clean. We had Coca-Cola, all of us, sitting together knee to knee in the tiny room—Hussein, Sajjida, an aged woman cousin who lived with them, and the two little girls.

After that Sajjida and I visited each other several times, but though we both tried, the relationship never ripened into friendship, for the odds were too uneven. I had so much and Sajjida so little. I was the one who was at fault, for I felt uncomfortable, but Sajjida felt no constraint at all and would ask me constant and unanswerable questions.

"Can't you give me something to keep boy babies alive?" she said once, looking around the room as though the answer might be found in the closet or the bookcase or behind the radio.

I must have looked perplexed for she explained that she had had two boys, but both had died, one after four

months. Hussein had told her that in America boy babies
did not die.

"What do you use?" she wanted to know.

While we were in El Nahra she had another boy, born
dead, and when I went to see her she merely looked at
me out of huge sunken eyes. I felt ashamed, thinking of
the vitamin pills and orange juice and incubators and
oxygen tents in the maternity hospitals at home. That
whole world might have been on another planet, so far was
it from the hovel where Sajjida lay on a worn reed mat
and delivered one dead baby after another.

"Is it true that you eat meat every day?" she said another time. I think the question was purely one of curiosity
but I wasn't sure and again I felt ashamed. For the first
time since coming to El Nahra, I had become distinctly
aware of hunger. Although I had read of famine and seen
films and photos, I realized I had never personally known
anyone who went to bed hungry. Sajjida and her little girls
often did, or at least they had before Hussein had found
work. Even with a steady income, their average daily diet
consisted of bread and tea, rice and dried dates occasionally, meat rarely.

Hussein was lucky to have a job in El Nahra, but many
other members of the clan had turned to migrant labor.
They traveled to Baghdad in early spring to hire out as
workmen in the building trades; in Baghdad they could
sleep in the streets on the warm summer nights, and thus
save almost all their earnings to take back to El Nahra
and support their family during the winter. The clan had
been hit hardest by the soil salination which was creeping
slowly over most of the farmland. Forced by one bad season after another into near bankruptcy, the members of
the clan had either sold most of their land, bit by bit, to
Haji or one of his uncles, or simply abandoned it.

Yet, Hussein told us proudly, his clan was the oldest
clan of all, and the sheik of his clan had once been the
sheik of the entire El Eshadda. He did not seem to feel
any resentment against Haji Hamid for being the current
leader and landowner, though he may have kept silent
since it was to Haji that he owed his present job. Bob

believed that Haji felt some responsibility for the fate of
Hussein's clan, for it was reported that he gave rice and
flour regularly to the poorest families. We thought his
insistence on an armed guard for us simply a way of providing income for still another poor family, but we were
wrong. Hussein, it turned out, had had a good job with
the irrigation department, but when Abdulla approached
him as a representative of his clan, Hussein dutifully gave
up his job and came to us. We wondered then whether
Hussein's undue praise of Haji might not have been a bit
forced, because the irrigation department job would have
been permanent, whereas we were temporary guests at
best.

There was no doubt, however, as to Hussein's pride in
his lineage and his clan. He could give us, from memory,
his entire family tree going back five generations, when
one Jassim and his brother Shebib had settled in the
valley. This was what it meant to have a sense of the past,
for Jassim's and Shebib's eight daughters and sons, their
husbands and wives and children and *their* husbands and
wives and children were as real to Hussein as though they
were alive today, although they had been dead for more
than a hundred years. As a boy, Hussein had spent the
long summer evenings and the long winter evenings sitting
in the tribal mudhif with the men; he had heard his
father talk of the family and the clan and the tribe and,
hearing it again and again, stored it in his memory as
evidence of his own identity, his place in the world, such
evidence to be passed on to his children after him. This
was what kept Hussein and Sajjida alive, I think, for certainly nothing in their physical environment augured toward hope or pleasure, but they felt themselves part of
the chain, passing on Jassim's and Shebib's ancient blood
to their thin daughters, who would marry cousins within
the clan and so continue the lineage. Then Hussein and
Sajjida could die in peace, assured that they had done their
duty and that something of themselves lived on.

Each night at sundown Hussein reported for work, his
rifle over his shoulder. He slept outside our gate. The
nights were warm and he insisted that he did not need a

mattress or a sheet. I don't know that the consciousness of his presence ever gave us any greater feeling of security, but it did touch off two incidents which were the talk of El Nahra for days afterward.

One night we had as a guest an Iraqi woman school-teacher, a friend of mine from Baghdad. She had come to visit because she was interested in the area, she said (she had never been outside Baghdad in her life), but after she had arrived, she seemed very nervous and kept asking us questions about the friendliness of our neighbors. We had convinced her finally, I think, of the tribe's good will and hospitality, and had just settled her for the night in our best bed when we were nearly startled out of our shirts by a volley of rifle shots, very loud in the still summer night, which thudded directly into our garden wall. My friend leaped out of bed with a cry of fright and came running to me in her nightgown, then turned back in sudden modesty to look for her robe. Bob shouted that he was going out to investigate and at this my friend clung to me and began to tremble all over.

"Don't let him go out there, B.J.," she pleaded. "Please!"

I pointed out that he had already gone and I was sure there was some simple explanation, but my friend would not be comforted.

She wrung her hands and kept repeating, "Oh, you don't understand, you just don't understand," until Bob finally reappeared.

Although he had only been gone a few minutes, it seemed much longer. He appeared unconcerned, and explained that Hussein was considering buying a gun from one of the sheik's guards and they had been trying it out by shooting it into the mud wall of our garden.

My friend looked at him suspiciously. "You are hiding the truth from me," she said accusingly.

"No, honestly, that is what he said," Bob replied.

"And you believe it?" she insisted.

"Of course," said Bob. She was still not convinced, so I made some tea and we sat in the kitchen, talking of other things, until my friend was calm enough to go back to bed.

The next day, when we went to visit the women, they

had all heard the story and went out of their way to tell my friend how rude they considered such behavior, especially to a guest as distinguished as herself. I think she was mollified, but she never saw us again without reminding us of the "Experience with the Tribe," as she called it.

The second incident proved to be not so easily forgotten. One night I was raising the mosquito net to climb into my bed, which had been set outside in the garden, when I was struck a furious blow on the head. I screamed, loudly and involuntarily, and screamed twice more in rapid succession before I recovered enough to pull myself together and look around to see what had happened. Then I felt rather silly and embarrassed, for on the ground by the bed lay a mourning dove, fluttering and trying to rise. Later Bob and I decided that a hawk must have dropped down on the dove, which in turn plunged to escape capture and hit my head accidentally on its downward flight. But that was later.

The doorbell now began to ring furiously. Bob had been in the toilet when the incident occurred; as I ran around the house, I saw him coming from the garden and he motioned me back as he headed for the door. A shot was fired just before he reached the gate.

In five minutes Bob was back, looking very puzzled, and I am sure I did not help matters by flinging myself on him and sobbing. I was trying to explain what had happened, but I was nearly incoherent.

"Hussein insists you were screaming, but I told him no," Bob said.

"But I *was* screaming," I replied.

"I didn't hear you," he insisted.

As the story gradually emerged, he began to laugh. "Now I see why Hussein was acting the way he did."

"Why?" I asked.

"He obviously thought I was giving you a good beating," Bob explained, "and when I said you hadn't screamed, he nudged and winked so I would know he understood."

He laughed again and looked at me. "You'll have some explaining to do tomorrow in the harems," he said.

Bob was right. For some reason the women found this

story extremely funny, whether because they believed it *was* a bird or because they thought I had concocted an ingenious tale to hide my wifely punishment, I don't know. But whenever conversation languished during the rest of the time I spent in El Nahra, Laila or Fatima would say, "Tell us the story of the bird that hit you in the head," and when I obliged, everyone would dissolve into hysterical laughter. It became one of my most successful social anecdotes.

17

Muharram

That year the Islamic month of Muharram came in August, when the heat had reached its peak, and no breeze came after sundown. The hot close nights were filled with the sound of religious chanting and breast beating, for krayas were being held everywhere, in the suq and in the mudhif for the men and in private homes for the women. Attendance was greater than at the krayas of Ramadan, for El Nahra is in a Shiite area and the month of Muharram is of special significance to all Shiite Moslems. It was during Muharram, in the seventh century, that Hussein, grandson of the prophet Mohammed, and the *imam* or religious leader at that time, went to Kufa to press his claim to the caliphate and was slain in battle on the plains of Karbala. Hussein's death contributed to the split into Shiite and Sunni sects which persists in Islam to this day.

Each year during Muharram the pious Shiite communities in Iraq and Iran and in India commemorate Imam Hussein's martyrdom, through daily krayas and through mourning processions and passion plays which dramatize each important occasion in the last days of the martyr.

"You will see them all, Beeja," promised Laila. She, like the other women, was very excited about the coming events, which marked an annual period of color and drama in the village.

First of the major occasions was the wedding procession, in memory of Hussein's daughter's marriage, which had taken place just before his departure for Kufa.

"In the wedding procession my little sisters will carry candles. All the small children do," said Laila.

"The burying is also very good," she added, "but very sad. We will go to the mosque that day and you can come with us."

Go to the mosque? "Yes, I would love to," I answered. No one had even suggested I go near the mosque before. But Laila was already onto something else, the re-enactment of the battle between Hussein and his foes, which, it appeared, would not be presented in El Nahra.

I asked, "Why not? I should think it would be exciting to watch."

"Oh it is," she replied.

"Then why isn't it going to be presented?"

Laila was vague. "Ask Mr. Bob," was all she would say.

Bob asked several of the tribesmen, who were also vague about the reasons, and finally he turned to Jabbar, the irrigation engineer.

"It's very simple. The sheik and the mayor won't put up the money," explained Jabbar. "The government asked for 2000 English pounds this year."

Bob was puzzled and said so. "You mean the government charges the village for putting on the battle scene?"

No, Jabbar answered. In the past the battles had sometimes led to bloodshed when feuding families had used the general confusion and excitement as a cover for settling old scores. First the government had tried to prevent the performances. Failing in this, they required the village to pledge a large amount of money which would be forfeited in case of trouble.

"Why are you so curious to see this sort of thing?" Jabbar then asked Bob.

"Why not?" Bob retorted. "All the tribesmen seem to find it interesting."

"Oh yes, of course, the ignorant people, yes, they enjoy it," Jabbar replied, "but it really has nothing to do with us. I cannot see why you should bother."

His manner was so odd that Bob pressed him until Jabbar finally burst out that he was certain that Bob would find the ceremonies, especially those of flagellation, primitive and uncivilized.

"And then you will go home to America and lecture and tell everyone that all Iraqis are backward, uneducated, superstitious people."

Bob was quite disturbed. "Jabbar," he asked, "do you really believe I would say that?"

"Well, why shouldn't you?" Jabbar replied. "I myself find these ceremonies primitive."

Bob tried to reassure him, told him of the processions of the Western churches, of the self-mortification practiced by the early Christian martyrs and by some contemporary religious orders. Jabbar nodded, but seemed unimpressed.

"I used to walk in the processions myself when I was a child," said Jabbar. "I do not think such things are peculiar to us. That is not the whole point. The point is also a political one."

"Political? How?"

"The British encourage these productions just to exaggerate the differences between Sunni and Shiite Moslems, and thus keep the Arabs from uniting as one people," he said. "But when the revolution comes, all this will change."

"Perhaps," Bob replied, and they finished the evening by drinking together nearly a whole bottle of arak, the strong local liquor brewed of dates which, when mixed with water, tastes and looks like Pernod.

Every woman who could afford to give an appropriate gift to the mullah held a kraya in her home. I listened to the mullah's sermons and the women's chanting in the house of Laila, in the apartments of Kulthum and Selma, in the house of Sherifa, and in the house of Abdulla's wife Khariya. But I was beginning to shrink from the evening sessions, for one of the mullahs had apparently decided that I had been an observer long enough. She would stand beside me during the kraya, exhorting me to beat my breast and shouting the responses in my ear so I would join in. I found I was reluctant to do so, partly out of shyness, partly because I suspected the mullah had other things in mind for my religious education after Muharram was over. Laila and Sherifa made excuses for me on these occasions, but even they suggested I might participate. It was becoming a difficult situation and neither Bob nor I could think of a quick and easy solution.

Fortunately I was saved from the necessity of facing this

particular issue by an emergency call from the Davenports, our missionary friends in Hilla. Joyce, just beginning her third pregnancy, had been ordered to bed by the doctor. Would I come and help with the household and the two small boys while she was out of commission? I was doubly glad to say yes, for the Davenport house had been a haven for us on many occasions. When Bob was first scouting for a village in which to settle, the Davenports had offered him their spare room whenever he should be near Hilla. Months later, when he fell ill on our way back to El Nahra from Baghdad, we had stayed with the Davenports until he was able to travel again. And I found that when I needed a break from the village round and the eternal struggle with Arabic, my energy and optimism were restored in two or three days spent speaking English with Joyce and playing with the children.

Joyce was ill and terribly tired, so I stayed with her almost until the end of Muharram. My last night in Hilla was the night of the wedding procession, and that day Rosa, the Davenports' servant girl (a Christian), and Um Hussein, the gatekeeper's wife (a Moslem), talked of nothing else. Um Hussein came to the back door several times to hold whispered conferences with Rosa, who would then manage to say loudly, in Joyce's hearing, that it was really a shame that we couldn't all go to see this beautiful thing. But Joyce and Harold were a bit doubtful, wondering if it was wise for Christians to wander out on such a night. By suppertime we could hear the crowds gathering in the streets, and even the boys felt the excitement.

"Hussein is going to the procession with his mama," said Stevey accusingly. He was nearly five, and Hussein, the gatekeeper's son, was only four.

"Go, go," said Timmy, pounding the table with his spoon.

Rosa brought in a bowl of rice pudding. "Let me take the children, madame," she pleaded. "It will be very pretty and everyone is going." Joyce looked at Harold.

"I'll go along," I offered. "If I wear my abayah no one will notice me, and the children are so small no one will notice them either."

At that moment Um Hussein arrived at the door again, bearing paper flowers and candles for the little boys, and at this overture Joyce and Harold gave in.

All of the people of Hilla seemed to be out that night. Hundreds of children, dressed in their best, walked with their parents, carrying candles and paper flowers or fresh-leafed branches of laurel. After a time several policemen marched by in a group—a signal, according to a woman standing near Um Hussein, that the procession was about to begin. The children lit their candles and joined together in a long, uneven queue, chanting as they moved along the street. The parents walked beside them, and one father carried his infant daughter in his arms, holding her candle and laurel branch and singing as he walked. Then came flags—green, Hussein's color, black and scarlet, and standards of colored lights. Finally the wedding float appeared, borne aloft by eight young men, an elaborate glass-sided palanquin in which a married couple could easily be carried through the streets by bearers. This one, however, was empty. Mounted in a gaily painted and carved wooden frame, the palanquin was decorated with tiny glass lamps and gilded globes.

"What is it?" asked Timmy.

"See how beautiful it is?" hissed Rosa. She had only one eye but that one was sparkling with enjoyment.

"Yes, but what is it?" Timmy insisted.

I was not quite sure how to reply, but Stevey, the five-year-old, solved my problem, for as the palanquin passed us, the eight bearers shouted in unison and all of the colored globes suddenly blazed with electric light.

"It's a Christmas tree!" shouted Stevey in ecstasy.

"Christmas tree!" echoed Timmy.

"Shhh," said Rosa, but no one had heard. They were all looking in admiration at the glittering palanquin, with its red and blue and green lights brightening the night.

Without warning, the generator failed and the lights went out. The bearers cursed, lowered the palanquin, fussed with the mechanism until the lights flashed on again, lifted it once more and the float continued down the street.

We turned toward home, for it was now long past the

children's bedtime, but the chants echoed after us, and the loudspeakers in the coffee shops blared far into the night the refrain of the marchers:

"Hussein, ya Hussein."

"Hussein, he dies tomorrow."

After the wedding procession begins the period of deepest mourning during Muharram. My train arrived in Diwaniya, the railroad junction, after the ceremonies were finished, but Bob told me about them as we drove, in the familiar old taxi, over the road to El Nahra.

This night, in Diwaniya, the flags and the standards of colored lights were only a prelude to the taaziya, or mourning procession of men. Wearing only black, their shirts cut out at the shoulders, they marched in groups of twelve or eighteen, chanting in unison and flagellating themselves with chains and swords.

"How do they flagellate themselves?" I asked.

"Well, they beat themselves with the chains mostly," said Bob. "The chains are bound together in bunches, like a cat-o'-nine-tails. A few men cut themselves lightly with the swords, too. They had several male nurses walking with the group, and once they stopped a man and bandaged up his head before he continued walking. Also there was an ambulance."

"It sounds frenzied," I said.

"Oddly enough, it wasn't," Bob answered. "I was really struck by how orderly the whole thing was. And it was quite moving."

He added, "Jabbar says there'll be an even bigger one tomorrow, which is Ashur, the tenth of Muharram. That's the day Hussein was killed."

"Even in El Nahra?"

"Yes," he said. "Jabbar says taaziyas are organized in every Shiite village in southern Iraq. They practice in advance and the village takes up a collection so that its taaziya can be represented in the big mourning procession which takes place every year, forty days after Ashur, in Karbala. That," he put in, "I'd really like to see."

"Why don't you go?"

"Jabbar says better not, but anyway we'll see the one tomorrow."

Early next morning Laila arrived to welcome me back. "You must come right now so we can get a good place to watch the procession."

I started out the door in my abayah, but Laila held back.

"What is the matter?"

"Well," said Laila, "my sisters told me not to ask you, but we are friends and I thought you would like to see it and so—"

"And so what?"

"I—we—Beeja, you do want to see the play of the big battle when Hussein was killed, don't you?"

"Yes, of course, but Bob says it is not going to be held in El Nahra."

"It isn't, I know," said Laila, stepping close to me, "but it is being held in Suffra, just down the canal. Why don't you ask Mr. Bob to take you in a taxi, and then I can ask my father if I could go too."

I smiled to myself, wondering how many days and nights of plotting had gone on among Laila and her sisters before they had formulated this plan. I promised Laila I would try.

Bob had left earlier for the mudhif, and Laila and I joined a group of women who stood at the corner of Laila's house, commanding a view of both the road and the clearing around the mudhif. The women were visibly perspiring in the hot sun, but they were in a holiday mood. We could hear shouting and chanting from the other side of the canal.

"How is the American lady in Hilla?" asked Fadhila. "Did you see the wedding procession there?"

"Yes," I said. "It was lovely."

"Wait until you see the taaziya *here*, Beeja," said Sherifa. "It is always very good."

"There's Mr. Bob standing with Haji Hamid and Abdulla," Laila interrupted. "See, right by the door of the mudhif," and I, squinting against the sun, could just make out Bob's white shirt and khakis among the abas and kaffiyehs.

"Every year the taaziya comes to the mudhif," explained Sherifa. "Afterward the people from the market and from the rest of the village sit down and have coffee as the guests of the El Eshadda."

The shouting was coming closer and several women peered down the empty road.

"Look, look Beeja," hissed Laila.

A few children had turned the corner by the canal and were running toward us up the path, which was now lined with women pressed close together, their abayahs drawn over their faces. In the crowd of villagers which followed the children, we could see the green and black flags heralding the appearance of the taaziya.

"*Ya, Hussay-in!*" The men in black or white moved within the crowd, but remained together as a group, in the form of an uneven circle. A few were stripped to the waist. Their heads were bound in black kerchiefs, they stared straight ahead of them as they walked, and their right hands, holding bunches of chains, swung up in answer to the cry, and came down with a thump on the bare shoulders.

"*Ya Hussay-in,*" they cried again in unison, moving ahead in formation, and the chains thudded on their shoulders again.

An anonymous wail came from one of the women lining the path, and the ululation was taken up by the women clustered against the wall of the sheik's house and standing around the edges of the mudhif clearing.

"Hussein!" the men cried, so close to us in the bright sunlight I could see their shoulders bruised blue from the blows of the chains. The rest of the refrain was lost in the general hubbub, women wailing and children crying. In the hitching area near the mudhif the horses whinnied.

Several groups of taaziyas were moving into the clearing, chanting together, then apart, and in the syncopation of the chant and the stamp of bare feet in the dust we could hear, as regular as a metronome, the chains jingling, free in the air, and the dull thud as they struck flesh. The flags wavered on the outskirts of the clearing where the tribesmen had gathered, and the taaziyas moved in formation toward the door of the mudhif. The sheik moved forward to greet the participants, and the tribesmen and townsmen went with the taaziyas into the mudhif to drink tea. An old Sayid in a green turban circulated among the bystanders, collecting contributions for the performers' coming trip to Karbala.

"Beautiful, wasn't it?" the women said to each other and several reached up under their veils to mop their sweaty faces.

"Did you see Ali's son, Beeja?" asked Laila. "He was in the second group."

"He has been doing it since he was eighteen," Fadhila pointed out, "because his mother promised him, you know."

"Why?"

"Well, Sheddir had two stillborn babies, and she went on pilgrimage to Karbala and at the tomb of Hussein in the mosque she prayed and promised that if she had a healthy son, she would dedicate him to the taaziya during Muharram."

"And he does it?"

"Of course. He is proud to do it, it is a great honor," Fadhila said. "A great honor for anyone," she added with a look at me, "but even better if your mother had promised you, because then you are fulfilling a holy vow."

Laila interrupted. "Beeja, if Mr. Bob gets a taxi to go to Suffra, who else will go? Will there be room for Basima?"

Several women turned at these words and looked at me expectantly.

"Well," I temporized, "I don't even know if he has gotten a taxi, but if he has, then anyone can come who wants to, provided there is room."

When we saw the size of the crowd which had gathered outside our gate to go to Suffra, Bob decided to let the driver decide when the taxi was full. He was certain, I think, that this would cut down on the load, but women piled into the back seat and children crawled in and sat on the floor. Mohammed and Bob and the driver were in front, and the driver seemed quite unconcerned despite the fact the car was so tail-heavy we hit bottom whenever we went over a rut. The windows were wide open, otherwise I felt we might have come close to suffocation from the heat and the pressure of the crowd. Also, it appeared, some of the women were unaccustomed to motor travel, and they retched quietly and constantly into their handkerchiefs. Nausea and discomfort did not seem to detract from the delights of the day's excursion, however, and I noticed that even the carsick ladies managed to smile when, at each bump in the dirt road, the women in the back seat clung together and dissolved into whoops of muffled laughter.

I had seen the square of Suffra only once before, when we had driven through with Jabbar on our way to visit Sheik Hamza. It had been the day of the weekly sheep market, and the square had been crowded with lambs and full-grown sheep, bleating loudly and pressed so tightly together Jabbar had had difficulty getting his Land-Rover through.

Now, completely cleared, the square looked like a playing field, and this impression was strengthened by the sight of a small reviewing stand, four or five tiers of seats behind a bunting-draped wall which had been erected along one side of the arena. To this canopied stand Mohammed and the taxi driver led Bob, pushing ahead of him through the crowds of villagers and tribesmen who had come to town to see the annual enactment of their *shabih*, or passion play.

With the women I trooped down to the far end of the playing field, where a group of eucalyptus trees offered shade. As we walked, four costumed men on horseback cantered by, wheeled and cantered toward the center of the playing field again. Completely covered with yellow trappings, the horses could have been the mounts of medieval knights waiting for the jousting to begin. Their yellow covers were bound and decorated in black, and from the black-rimmed eyeholes, the horses looked out, their eyes seeming bigger than life, as though they wore eye make-up. The men's costumes were green and red, of some silky material which shone in the sun and billowed out from their shoulders as they swept by. They wore sashes and high cardboard hats, cut like war helmets of some indeterminate historical period. Swords, curved and painted, were brandished high.

In front of the reviewing stand a small group of horsemen waited; green and black flags, like the flags of the taaziya, were held up and outward. All that was needed, I felt, was a brass band or at least a trumpeter to herald the opening of the drama.

"When does it begin?" I whispered to Laila.

"It has begun," she replied, and the four costumed horsemen trotted by us, stopped near the tree, and waited.

"Oh," I said lamely. What was going on? I looked at the horsemen, but their costumes told me little.

"The swords aren't real," Fadhila confided in me.

"Of course they are real," replied Laila.

"They are not real," retorted Fadhila. "Mohammed says the government has forbidden it."

"Well, when we had the play in El Nahra, we had real swords," Laila returned, in some contempt, and this began a spirited argument between Laila, Fadhila and some women from Suffra, near whom we had found a seat on a hard, sandy hummock under one of the eucalyptus trees.

"What is happening now?" I asked.

Laila turned, abstracted, from her conversation. "What?"

I repeated my question.

"Oh, well, the battle is beginning."

The horsemen near us spurred their mounts and galloped to the center, thundered back, wheeled and rode into the center of the arena again, where they were met by other horsemen, in different costumes. The flag-bearers moved toward the center and moved away again, and both sets of horsemen returned to their corners.

I turned to Hathaya, the weaver's daughter. "Now what is going on?" I asked.

"Now?" she said, looking briefly at the arena. "The battle has started," and she moved closer to one of the women and they resumed their conversation.

Rebuffed, I sat back on my hummock and peered across the square. I could barely make out the figure of Bob in the reviewing stand and at that particular moment I wished mightily I were with him. I could not see him clearly, but I was sure that, as an honored guest, he was sitting on a chair drinking Pepsi-Cola and having the play explained to him in detail by the village elders. It's hardly fair, I thought peevishly; I've come all this way too and I can't even find out what I'm supposed to be seeing. My friends were no help at all. And besides, I was thirsty.

Laila introduced me to several of the women, who were relatives or friends of friends, but they did not offer any explanation of the play either. They were far more interested in family news from down the canal. I shifted around, trying to find a more comfortable place on the hummock. There was none.

"Isn't it wonderful?" said Laila.

"Yes," I said, noting the crowds of colorful horsemen in the square.

"It's a war, Beeja," explained Laila, "between the good men of Hussein's family and the evil men of Muawiya."

I nodded.

"The costumes are very beautiful, don't you think?"

I nodded again.

"What's the matter, Beeja? Are you sick?"

"No," I said, "I'm very very thirsty. Let us find a man selling Pepsi-Cola."

Laila demurred. "Don't waste your money, Beeja. Why, today I am sure the Pepsi-Cola will cost four fils instead of two."

"I don't care. I—"

"Soon the play will be over and then we will go to the house of Hathaya's aunt. She brought up Hathaya after her mother died and Hathaya loves her very much. This is the first time she has seen her in four years."

I looked at Hathaya, her puny baby asleep in her lap, deep in conversation with her aunt, and suddenly felt a little ashamed of myself for my pique. If I had not been an outsider, I would have enjoyed the social aspect of the occasion as much as they, and, I realized, I would have appreciated the play too, for I would have seen it so many times I would not have needed an explanation. But I was still very thirsty and found myself thinking longingly of water and Coca-Cola and iced lemonade and a whole succession of cool drinks, despite the colorful and ancient drama being enacted in front of me.

The forces of good, on green-caparisoned horses, and wearing cardboard helmets, fought with the forces of evil in turbans and on yellow-caparisoned horses. Neutral elements, represented by the flag-bearers, tried to make peace and failed. Everyone knew what the outcome would be, but the battle was still worth the seeing. By this time fifty or sixty horsemen filled the square, and the two groups of warriors galloped toward each other, met briefly in the center in a clash of wooden swords, then regrouped at each end in preparation for another assault. In between rounds, several small boys would run into the arena and rescue from the dust objects which Bob later told me were papier-mâché arms and legs carried by the horsemen and thrown up into the air after each assault to give an air of reality to the proceedings. With shouts and cries the women and men urged on the forces of Hussein and hissed the forces of Muawiya. I wanted to cry out too, but what I felt like shouting at the top of my lungs was, "I'm so thirsty."

Then came rifles, passed up to the horsemen from the audience, and the battle started anew. The knowledge that the bullets the men fired over each other's heads were real bullets added danger and a certain awe to the affair. Even the gossiping women were silent.

My view was less superb than Bob's, I was sure, but at least I had a sense of participation, for as the battle raged faster, the horsemen drew up closer and closer, until I could taste in my parched throat the dust raised by the panting horses, who were brought up short only a few feet from us and then turned to gallop back into battle. The legs of the horses ran with sweat, the cardboard helmets were wilting, and the silken tunics stuck to the backs of the horsemen. But the riders, at full gallop, continued to fire their rifles, and the smell of gunpowder was added to the odors of sweat and manure that drifted toward us from the arena. I tried to moisten my lips, but

my tongue was dry too. I tried to forget my thirst by con-
centrating on the spectacle. I found that half closing my
eyes filtered the spectacle quite effectively, reducing the
glare of the sun and the density of the dust clouds until
the ancient play became a fine kaleidoscopic whirl of odor
and shining blurs and flying sand.

Without any particular concluding action that I could
see, the battle ceased. I looked at my watch. We had been
onlookers in the hot sun for more than three hours. No
wonder I was thirsty. In a few minutes the crowds filled
the square, and the horses, still in their brilliant trappings, were led off to the canal to drink. The costumes
and horses' coverings would be saved for next year's performance, Laila told me. The reviewing stand was hidden
in the throngs of people who pushed on, back to houses
or shops or to the long road home to their clan settlements
on the plain. Where was Bob? I saw a pail of Coca-Cola
pass by, carried by a man, and I rushed after it, but Laila
pulled me back so fiercely that I turned to her, and saw
Bob and Mohammed and the taxi driver walking near us,
but not with us. We headed up a narrow street leading
off the square to a wooden door in a mud-brick wall. Once
inside the door, we separated again. The men disappeared
into one room and we were led into another, where in coolness and darkness (such a relief from the dust and heat
outside) several women were seated in a circle on reed
mats. We sank down also, and loosened our abayahs.

"*Ahlan wusahlan*," said a large, square woman seated
near the door.

"*Shlonich* [how are you]?" asked Fadhila, and we repeated her greeting.

"I am afraid we cause trouble by our presence," said
Fadhila.

"On the contrary, you honor us."

Using the phrases traditional between host and guest,
the square-faced woman and Fadhila set about building a
polite relationship for the short period of time we would
be together. Could I interrupt the dialogue to ask for
water? In a moment they were discussing mutual friends

and near-relatives in El Nahra, and after this, Fadhila felt the moment had arrived when she might appropriately make a request.

"Good aunt, may we trouble you for some water? We are so parched from the heat."

At a word from the square-faced woman, a young girl slipped out and came back with a tray of glasses.

"Water is a gift from God," said Fadhila fervently, setting her empty glass on a tray.

"The Koran says that water is the source of all life," quoted the square-faced woman.

If, at that moment, I could have remembered any proverbs about water, I would have quoted them, that water tasted so good to me. It had obviously been drawn from the depths of a porous clay jar, for chips of the clay were visible in the bottom of the glass. But in my great thirst, the flat earthy taste of the clay seemed only to give flavor and sweetness to the water. I drank slowly, savoring each mouthful, until I looked up to see the girl waiting for me to finish and replace my glass on her tray.

"Thank you very much," I said.

"By the Prophet, good aunt, may we trouble you for more water?" Fadhila asked.

"*Ahlan wusahlan,*" the square-faced woman replied, and more water was brought.

I thanked the woman again. There was a pause. Then she said to Fadhila, "Why doesn't your new friend talk very much?" Fadhila replied that I was American and didn't speak Arabic well.

"Don't they speak Arabic in America?" piped up another woman.

"No, of course not," Fadhila said.

"Then what do they speak?"

"They speak English," answered Fadhila.

The woman said, "Say something for us in English so we can hear what it sounds like."

I smiled, remembering my American friends who had made the same request in reverse, and recited:

"Under a spreading chestnut-tree
The village smithy stands;
The smith, a mighty man is he,
With large and sinewy hands;
And the muscles of his brawny arms
Are strong as iron bands."

A spurt of laughter followed my effort. "How funny it sounds," said the young woman, but she stopped talking at a look from the square-faced woman.

"Why did you come to El Nahra?" asked our hostess.

"I came with my husband."

"Her husband is an effendi; his name is Mr. Bob," announced Laila, as though that explained everything.

The girl had returned and set down in front of us a brass tray containing several spoons and a large soup plate full of what appeared to be porridge centered with a well of slightly congealing oil. While we watched, the square-faced woman rose and sprinkled sugar over the porridge.

"Eat," she urged. "It is *hareesa*, a special dish for the tenth of Muharram."

We began to spoon it up, mixing the oil and sugar together. I found it not unpleasant, but the plate was enormous and after five minutes we all stopped eating. The square-faced woman urged us on. We protested. She urged again. She was so insistent one might have almost believed that not to eat more would incur her lifelong displeasure, but I had been around long enough now to know that this was not necessarily so. Several other people would eat from what we had left.

"It is simply delicious, good aunt, but we have had enough," said Fadhila, and Laila and I echoed her.

The girl took away the tray and brought us a basin of water and a towel. The damp towel and the tea which followed revived us enough so that we could converse with enthusiasm about the spectacular performance we had just witnessed.

"The horses were very beautiful," I offered.

"Always in Suffra the shabih is performed very well," said our hostess.

"Majid rode very well today," the weaver's daughter Hathaya said.

The square-faced woman nodded and smiled and the young woman who had asked about my English looked gratified.

"Majid is her son," explained Hathaya, "and is married to her" (pointing to the younger woman).

"A good boy," said the proud mother. "He does not forget me even though he has his own children now. He gives me a pound every month."

"Sons should always care well for their mothers," murmured the young wife deferentially, and cast her eyes down.

The weaver's child was thrust forward. "Good aunt, what can I do about this?" asked Hathaya, pointing to the baby's horrid scabrous rash.

Our hostess took the child in her lap and examined the sores gently. "A poultice, I think," she suggested, and described the ingredients which should go into it.

"You have no children?" she asked, turning to me.

I shook my head and then the women asked if I had any inside me and where my mother was and how much gold my husband had given to my father as my bride price.

I explained, or tried to explain, that our customs were different, and that no bride price was given.

"No bride price?"

"Then what do you furnish your house with?"

"Who pays for your trousseau?"

"Don't you have *any* gold jewelry?"

I said that the families of the bride and the groom gave presents to the couple to furnish the house, and that the bride's family bought her trousseau and the groom offered gifts of gold jewelry. Anyway, some did.

"Where is your gold?" they asked eagerly.

"I have left it in America, so it will be safe," I replied.

This dodge was greeted with a snort from the young wife, but Fadhila came to my rescue and said that I did have some small gold earrings and one gold bracelet which was worth, she thought, about twenty Iraqi pounds. My wedding ring was also said to be gold, she said, though she personally thought it was silver.

In all fairness, she added that the schoolteachers had said my ring was made of white gold, but how much that was worth she did not know.

"Let's see," the women clamored. I took off my ring and passed it around.

"Gold, that's not gold," asserted the young wife.

"That's what I feel," agreed Fadhila, "but the school-teachers said—"

"Let me see it," said the square-faced woman. She examined it carefully while we awaited her verdict. She weighed it in her hand.

"Well," she said, "I don't know. It's not very heavy. If it *is* white gold, which I doubt, then it's not very *much* white gold. But," she added kindly, returning it to me, "it's quite pretty."

I was both annoyed and amused.

A knock on the door was the signal that the men were going. We rose, exchanged numerous elaborate farewells and trooped down the narrow street to the taxi.

"Tomorrow," Laila said in my ear as we neared El Nahra, "is the *dafna*, the burying ceremony. My sister and I will come and get you after lunch."

A single costumed horseman circled quietly around the open area near the taxi stand. Laila was pushing through the watching crowds of tribesmen and townsmen so that we might have a better view. But when we finally stood near the front, there was nothing to see except the horse, in green trappings, the color of Hussein, walking slowly around and around.

Still, there was something strange about the rider in his medieval dress and sash and headdress, trailing a long white handkerchief in one hand. And then the horse turned toward us and we could see the rider's face, swathed in heavy white bandages like a mummy or a victim of the horrors of war. Only his eyes were visible. He continued to walk the horse, in its trappings, around and around. The crowd was silent.

A young boy in black, carrying a green flag, pushed through and began to follow the horseman around the ring. We were still quiet. What were we waiting for?

I was pushed violently from behind and stumbled against Laila. Amid cries and shouts, the crowd parted to let the taaziya in their black cut-out shirts and black head scarves pass. The chains rustled against my shoulder as Laila whispered, "Here, Beeja," and pulled me out of the way.

Behind the taaziya, carried by eight men in abas and kaffiyehs, came the funeral bier, on which a headless body lay, draped in black velvet.

"It's not real, Beeja," hissed Laila at my side. "It's made of straw."

Straw or not, the body had a macabre realism about it, for the butcher (according to Laila) had supplied a freshly slaughtered neck of a cow for the occasion and this protruded, still bloody, from the black velvet.

At the bier's appearance the crowd wailed, the horseman began to wipe his eyes with his long white handkerchief, and the procession, led by the horseman, the taaziya and the boy with the green flag, headed down the main street of El Nahra.

"Beeja, we'll go with them," said Laila.

The procession moved quickly, and from every alley and side street along the way women and children and more men streamed, swelling the crowd following the bier out of town. Groups of women would stop in the middle of the street and spontaneously began beating their breasts and chanting the way I had seen them do in the krayas. Little girls stood near their mothers, imitating the breast beating and trying to keep on the beat.

We passed the mayor's house, the jail and the school, and in a moment were out of the village limits, onto the dusty road that led to Diwaniya. Where were we going?

"Not far," said Laila. Her sister Fatima, who had appeared from nowhere, greeted me, then turned away, pulled her abayah over her face and emitted a piercing wail.

The horseman turned off the road toward an abandoned brick kiln. Here, around a slightly raised platform, eight black flags had been placed at regular intervals. The boy with the green flag moved until he stood at the head of the platform, and the bier was set down in front of him.

Reining in his horse, the rider halted at the foot of the platform. The crowd—so large now that people surrounded the platform and filled the road we had just left—surged around him. A few old men circulated among us, distributing handfuls of straw over the heads of the multitude. One man had a container of mud which the women took and smeared over their faces, hands and abayahs.

"No, Rajat, no," Fatima spoke sharply to her little sister, who was vigorously applying the mud all over her clean cotton dress.

"Ya, Hussein, beloved," shouted a woman in face veil, and in a frenzy plucked dust and stones from the ground and threw them over herself. "Hussein. Do you not mourn for Hussein?" She came closer. "Laila. Beeja." She stopped in the act of throwing more dust and raised her veil briefly to smile at us. It was Amina, Selma's servant. She quickly let her veil fall and resumed the dust throwing.

A ceremony was in progress on the platform but we could hear nothing above the noise of the crowd, which thronged around, still tossing straw and mud and beating themselves intermittently. The horseman turned his swathed face to us, raised the hand with the long handkerchief and spoke. He sobbed and mopped his eyes, exhorting us, it seemed, and the people responded with cries and wails. The taaziyas swung their chains. Laila and I were talking to the sheik's daughter Samira and consequently hardly noticed what was happening before the bier was lifted off the platform and the procession started out of the burial area and back to town.

"They are taking it to the mosque," said Laila, and we fell into line with the crowd behind the sobbing horseman, the boy with the green flag, and the eight pallbearers bearing the velvet-draped bier with its grotesque, bloody burden.

But this time we moved slowly, for every few steps the

bearers would let down the bier and the horseman would stop, wheel and deliver to the crowd another short sermon punctuated by his own sobs and echoed by the wails of the women.

At the mosque the whole town seemed to have gathered, and the noise and confusion were overpowering. People fought for positions near the door in order to see the ceremony inside, and we were jostled back and forth until we had difficulty keeping our balance.

"What is this? Have you no manners? We are near the mosque," shouted Fatima in cutting tones.

No one listened.

"Fatima," Laila cried to her sister. "We must see. Beeja must see. I will try to get near a window and you see if you can get someone inside to open it."

"All right," said Fatima. She departed, and Laila took my hand and dragged me until we were against one of the shuttered windows of the mosque.

In a moment we could see Fatima again at the edge of the crowd, red-faced but triumphant.

"Don't move," she called over the heads of the people who separated us. "Stay where you are."

As she elbowed her way back, the shutters of the window suddenly banged open outward, and an old woman grinned at us. "*Ahlan wusahlan*," she said.

At this coup, the people behind pushed us even harder, mashing us against the wooden bars of the window. Although we were uncomfortable, we had an excellent view of the ceremony inside. The sobbing, bandage-faced rider had spurred his horse into the mosque; still mounted, he stood in the center of the mosque, alternately exhorting the crowd and muffling his sobs in the long white handkerchief. By the niche, which I assumed to be the *minbar* of the mosque, another man stood, and whenever the horseman paused, this man raised his arms and spoke.

Other windows were being opened and the people pushed toward them.

"Stop shoving—stop it!" Fatima cried, but it was no use. We were jammed so tightly against the window bars I felt I could stand it no longer.

"Let's go, Fatima; it's almost finished," suggested Laila. She was having difficulty holding her abayah on, the crowds were pulling and pushing at us so hard.

"Yes," said Fatima, "and these impious people are rude. It's shame, shame, shame!" she shouted, her voice rising with each repetition of the word, elbowing her way out with dark looks at the indifferent, roistering people.

"This is a funeral for the martyr Hussein, not a party," was her final shot before we hit the open street.

"It's late," said Laila. We had crossed the bridge and walked now along the tribal side of the canal, where the road was calm and almost empty. On the other bank, the crowd still milled and shouted around the mosque.

My clothes under my abayah were soaking with perspiration; we had walked and pushed and been pushed during the hottest part of the day. Although it was near sundown, the heat still shimmered, a felt and observed presence in the air. The water in the canal was at low level in this season, and the sides of the mudbanks were dried and cracking in the heat.

"Will you come and have tea with us?" said Laila.

I felt exhausted, and I was certain they must be too.

"No, thank you," I replied. "I should fix supper for my husband."

They left me at my gate and I watched my friends go, two black-robed figures, one tall and proud, one shorter and slightly stooped, walking gracefully home through the hot powdery dust.

18

Pilgrimage to Karbala

After the burial ceremony, the village seemed visibly to relax. The krayas were over, the yearly cycle of religious drama successfully complete. People set about their chores in order to be ready for the pilgrimage to Karbala.

Summer crops were harvested. The sheep were sheared and the women washed the wool in the canal, piling the damp fleeces in the courtyards of their houses to dry before beginning the carding and spinning. Okra was threaded on long strings and hung from the roof beams to dry for winter. Soon it would be time to harvest the dates. In spare hours the women returned to the everlasting task of cleaning rice and flour, tossing it expertly on woven plates to rid it of chaff and then laboriously picking out, one by one, the stones and hulls and bits of dirt and straw.

Clothes were washed and mended for the coming journey. The hajj, or pilgrimage, is one of the five basic obligations of Islam and every Moslem hopes to visit Mecca before he dies. But the Shiite Moslem has a further duty, to visit the shrines of the twelve imams of the Shiite sect.

In El Nahra, the sheik and one or two rich merchants were the only people who had been to Mecca, but even the poorest fellahin and their wives had been several times to the three nearest Shiite shrines, at Najaf, Karbala and Khadhimain.

The most propitious period to visit Karbala was the time now approaching, the fortieth day after the death of the martyr Hussein. This year Laila had invited me to make the pilgrimage with her, her mother and her older sister Fatima. I had accepted immediately, or rather Bob accepted for me after talking to Laila's father, Moussa. Moussa had first apologized to Bob for not inviting him, and explained that it might not be the best time to see Karbala, when it was crowded with pilgrims. But we guessed that the real reason lay in Bob's appearance. With his crew cut and light skin, he was too obviously foreign and Karbala, during the ceremonies on the fortieth day after Hussein's death, was particularly sensitive to the presence of unbelievers. I, on the other hand, could easily pass unnoticed in abayah and face veil. I had been wearing the abayah for several months and was accustomed to it by now. My Arabic was good enough so that even if I had to speak, I might be mistaken for a Persian pilgrim whose native tongue was Farsi; my light skin, should the face veil slip, could also be attributed to Persian origins.

Moussa added that Bob need not worry about accommodations in the crowded city, for we would stay at the home of his cousin Yehia, a doctor in Karbala.

As the time of our journey grew near, Laila visited me several times a day to discuss the presents we would take to Sitt Najat, Cousin Yehia's wife, to talk about the glories of the golden mosque, and to plan what we would do when we got to Karbala. Laila was very anxious to go this year. She hoped, she said, that if her pilgrimage and prayers were worthy, her father might send her with her sister Basima to the secondary school in Diwaniya.

The other women too spoke of nothing but the coming pilgrimage; Medina, Mohammed's mother, and Sherifa, his sister, were determined to go, although there was scarcely enough money in their house to buy food for the coming month.

Nearly three quarters of a million Shiites actually made the pilgrimage that year, 1957, filling the little town of Karbala (normal population 30,000) far beyond capacity. Pilgrims came from Pakistan, Iran and Iraq. Many were poor and illiterate but many were men and women of education and wealth, come to find solace together at the tomb of Hussein.

For the essential character of the pilgrimage has not changed much in a thousand years. In the past, pilgrims had brought spices, rugs, copper and silver to exchange for food and lodging; they also brought new ideas and communicable diseases. In 1957 the pilgrims brought hashish, spices, copper and rugs to trade in Karbala; they managed also to bring smallpox and cholera, and agents disguised as pilgrims brought in Marxist leaflets. The mosques were lighted by neon instead of by candlelight, the wealthy pilgrims came by airplane rather than by palanquin, but the ritual was approximately the same as it has always been. The trade in goods and ideas and the mixing of people from all parts of the Shiite Moslem world were marginal to the principal purpose of a good pilgrimage, spiritual renewal through penitence and prayer.

But before we started, I did not know all this. I guessed at the vital place the pilgrimage held in the lives of all my friends, and was therefore startled and surprised when Laila came the day before we were scheduled to leave and announced that she was not going. She cut short my expressions of sympathy. Her father had ruled that it was too expensive for so many to go. Fatima was to represent the family, accompanied by Rajat (who could travel for half fare) and I would accompany them.

"It is good that Fatima should go," Laila said. "She works hardest at home and she is the most religious girl in the family."

"Now," she said, changing the subject, "let me see what you are taking to Sitt Najat."

I brought out two freshly baked cakes and a basket of fruit to be inspected, and Laila pronounced them adequate. The bus left at six the next morning; I must not be late, she said.

Bob and I rose at five. The sun was just up and we breakfasted in the garden, hearing already a babble of excited voices near our gate, where the bus was loading.

Bob had earlier felt a little uncertain about the wisdom of my pilgrimage. Now, on the last morning, he repeated his fears.

"Are you sure you want to go?"

"I'm sure."

"It will be hard, probably."

"Yes, but it's only five days."

"Well, be careful," he said. "I really think everything will go well, especially since you're staying with Moussa's relatives. I'll telephone you tonight to make sure you arrived safely."

"What will you do if I haven't?" I was only half joking.

"Come myself, notify the Karbala police—I'll think of something."

I nodded, thinking that in spite of all the perils I had imagined and Bob had imagined, I really wanted very much to go. The excited voices outside infected me with a great new sense of freedom and possible adventure.

At five-thirty Mohammed arrived with a jug of water, and told us his brothers were going, and would look out for me if I should need anything. Then Laila came, smiling and gay as though she were leading the pilgrimage personally; she and her sister Fatima had saved me a place in the bus near the back window and I was not to hurry over my breakfast. "After all," she said, "you will be away from home for five whole days; it's a very long time."

"Goodbye dear." I kissed Bob and clung to him for a moment. The pilgrim city with its golden mosque was a long way from our little mud house. What would I find there?

At the bus my arrival, with a hand satchel and a basket containing the fruit and cakes, increased the commotion.

"Look, look, the Amerikiya is making the pilgrimage!"

"What is she taking with her?"

"See, she wears the veil!"

"Where will she sit?"

The latter question signaled the opening of a pitched battle of words between Moussa's daughters and a neighbor woman who had managed to pile her bedroll, a basket of food and two small children in the space Laila had presumably reserved for me. Laila appealed to the woman's honor, to her sense of hospitality, the honor of her family and the honor of her as yet unborn children; the woman remained unmoved. Laila looked defeated and things appeared to have reached an impasse when the woman suddenly rose, dragged the children onto her lap and passed her luggage out the window to be placed on the roof. I felt myself pushed forward and down into a place which might have been comfortable for an emaciated eight-year-old. Then Rajat clambered in on top of me and curled up on the floor at my feet.

The bus was actually a covered wooden truck which had been converted to the passenger trade by the addition of a few wretchedly narrow wooden benches, placed so close together that one was forced to turn one's legs sideways if the seat opposite was occupied. The seating capacity was about twenty, but I counted forty-five men, women and children inside that morning, not to mention babes in arms. Even as I counted, more young boys were clambering up onto the roof.

The driver was haggling with a man who wanted to carry four sheep on top of the lorry. A two-year-old began to wail and was handed out the window to do his business. I waved at Bob, but he did not respond. He later told me he could hardly distinguish me from the other women. Not having been brought up with women who wore the costume, he was unable to detect the subtle details—the way the head is turned, the gesture with which the abayah is adjusted—by which men recognized their mothers, their sisters and their wives in a large crowd of identically attired and veiled women.

Finally the driver climbed up into his seat and slammed the decrepit wooden door. The crowd which had gathered to watch us leave shouted last-minute instructions and farewells; a chorus of traditional blessings—"Allah go with you," "*Maasalaama*," "*Fiimaanila*"—followed us as the truck, full of people hanging out the glassless windows and waving handkerchiefs as though they would never again see their beloved families and friends, rounded the corner on two wheels and we were off.

It was seven-thirty and already hot. The road followed the canal, where women washing their breakfast pots or doing the morning's laundry looked up at us as we rattled by. The date palms on the opposite bank were gray with the accumulated dust of the desert summer and the fields we passed were brown and dry. Only the stubble of the small summer crop remained. On each side of the road the flat, dun-colored land stretched away for miles, broken only by the cuts of small waterways carrying water to the fields and the dips of old canals, their dry hollows green with a little shrubbery nourished by some dampness remaining in the soil. Here and there a single fellah was visible against the horizon; his dishdasha tied up around his waist to allow freedom of movement, he broke the dry ground with a hand hoe, preparing the land for autumn planting. Clusters of green date palms marked the clan settlements, each with its mudhif, the high round arches of bound reeds dried to sand color. We passed one mudhif which was leaning sharply and which looked ready to collapse. My sullen neighbor roused herself to point it out as an abandoned settlement where the land was too salty to produce a crop. We could see the white patches of salt, like glistening early snow, on the land.

The road was dirt, dried to a fine powder in the summer sun which was now rising in the sky and beating down on the wooden roof of the truck. Even though we seemed to be moving unbelievably slowly, the truck's speed was just enough to raise the dust which poured in the windows, depositing a gray film on our black abayahs, settling on the children's hair and faces, and even penetrating the fine black mesh of my face veil. The young men and boys sang for joy at the prospect of five days' holiday. "Ya Hussein, ya Hussein," they cried; the women responded with ululating cries and the children who could move in the crowded truck clapped in time.

My nose and throat were soon clogged with the dust and I made an effort to find my thermos bottle, somewhere under the seat. This operation forced Rajat to get up off the floor and flatten herself against the wall of the truck, my neighbor to lift up her children, and the entire row of women to shift position, which they did with a subdued moan. At first the thermos was refused politely by everyone, but I insisted, and soon we were all sipping lukewarm water. My neighbor pulled out her breast for her year-old boy to suckle, and he nursed away contentedly while we settled back into our cramped postures on the benches. I looked at my watch. It was nine o'clock.

We were slowing down and the men were hanging out

the windows to see what the obstruction was when the truck swerved sharply to pass a Bedouin caravan. We came so close the side of the truck nearly grazed one of the camels, and as we passed I looked up into the face of a withered old woman, who in turn stared down at me from the nest of bright rugs in which she sat on her camel, steadying two small children in front of her. Copper pots and pans swung from the saddle on ropes braided of variegated wool. We passed four more camels, bearing women and children and bundles of belongings, then donkeys carrying fuel and sacks of grain. The caravan was moving slowly and we left them behind in the dust. As we passed I saw one of the men in front on horseback choking and shaking his rifle at us furiously. The boys in the truck gleefully laughed and shouted back at him.

By 1958 the road to Hilla, on the way to Karbala, was a straight paved highway, but at this time it was only a cart track winding along the canal between stands of date palms which appeared, because of the lowland, to be growing out of the water. Rice was grown here near the canal's edge, my neighbor volunteered, and pointed out the families of migrant workers. The men stand all day in mud and water that have a harmful chemical reaction on the flesh, and thus the workers are reputed to suffer from an incurable rotting disease. I had been told that fires are kept burning all night in the swampy country to keep away the wild jackals who smell decaying human flesh and come in packs to investigate. I remembered the stories and looked curiously at the peaceful scene we were passing—the rows of men, dishdashas tied around their waists, bent over patches of gleaming mud to pick the lush green plants into reed baskets. My neighbor was looking too. She clucked sympathetically. "A difficult life," she said.

Each hardship that the pilgrim experiences on his way brings him added grace in the eyes of God. I began to feel that all forty-five of us, including my infidel self, must be storing up many indulgences as the morning grew hotter. The dust continued to pour in, my limbs grew cramped and aching, and the truck creaked and rolled from side to side, giving me a good whack in the back of the head with a bare bolt in the woodwork every time the wheels hit a pothole. The company's spirits had wilted in direct proportion to its discomfort, but when we climbed up out of a rut and onto the paved part of the road, the boys burst into song again. We roared along the straight pavement at an incredible speed of twenty miles an hour, and there was no dust. We were hot, hungry and dusty but we were going to Karbala!

Excitement mounted when we reached the Karbala-Baghdad crossroads, which had been transformed by the pilgrim traffic from a quiet truck and taxi stop into a thronging metropolis. Buses, trucks, private cars, donkey carts and walking pilgrims were pausing here for lunch and rest on their way to the holy city.

Our truck had not even stopped before the sherbet sellers and the sweets peddlers crowded up to the doors and windows.

"*Sammoon, sammoon haar!*" A little boy bore on his head a tray of the fish-shaped loaves of white bread.

"*Khubuz, khubuz laham,*" croaked an old man.

A clatter of castanets announced the cold drink seller, a glass barrel of iced liquid strapped to his shoulder, who called, "*Tamurhindi! Tamurhindi!*" and banged his round brass castanets once more.

The smell of lamb roasting over charcoal braziers reminded me that I had not eaten since five that morning. With Fatima and Rajat I made a tour of the stalls which had been hurriedly set up to handle the pilgrims. We ordered kebab and squatted down by the roadside, as scores of other women were doing, to watch our meat wrapped around skewers and put on the fire, for Fatima, good housewife that she was, would not have dreamed of eating kebab that was already cooked, that had been handled by many people and visited by families of flies. We bought some hot khubuz to hold the kebab and its traditional accompaniments: tomatoes, onions and young celery leaves chosen from big blue enamel bowls on the counter and washed ceremoniously before our eyes by the hands of the proprietor himself. As a final noble gesture he threw in a few turnip pickles at no extra charge, and we settled back by the roadside to enjoy our meal.

After devouring our lunch we bought tea, and Fatima tried to persuade Rajat to go across the road and down the street to the public market to buy us a watermelon for dessert. But Rajat had never been out of El Nahra before and was afraid to leave us. Fatima cajoled, pleaded, ordered; Rajat remained stubborn. So, rather than make a public scene, Fatima gathered her abayah around her, threw a particularly scornful look at Rajat, and marched across the road where, in an empty field under some dusty palms, a few of the women from our truck were taking their ease. We sat beside them and finished my thermos of lukewarm water.

It was pleasant in the shade. We were secluded under the trees and yet had an excellent view of the comings and goings at the crossroads. Every few minutes a truckload of young men and boys would career around the intersection and head out the Karbala road. The trucks bore hand-lettered banners which swelled in the wind as they rounded the corner. Bareheaded and white-shirted, the boys were standing in the backs of the trucks. "Ya Hussein, ya Hussein," they shouted, clapping, as they rolled by.

"The taaziyas," murmured Fatima. "I don't see a banner from El Nahra."

"It must be there," said Rajat.

I remembered the collection taken for the taaziya after its march to the mudhif on the tenth of Muharram. This was what it was for, to bring the taaziya or mourning procession to Karbala for this holiday so that it might, together with all of the taaziyas from the other southern towns, perform in the great mosque and in processions through the streets the ceremonies which the occasion demanded.

Our truck honked its horn warningly, and we repaired to a canal to wash before resuming the journey. Now every vehicle we saw on the road was full of pilgrims bound for Karbala. The men and boys shouted back and forth as the trucks passed and repassed each other. Someone in front took up the chant and refrain again, and the women joined in with piercing cries. Even my neighbor, inspired, drew her veil modestly over her face and let out a cry that shook us all. Rajat, still on the floor, got the full force of this shriek but only looked up at the woman admiringly.

At Twaireej, the last town before Karbala, many pilgrims had stopped to rest and were washing their feet and hands in the canal, crowding the old pontoon bridge and its long stairways leading down to the river. From Twaireej the road followed the canal, and on both banks we could see pilgrims on foot, on horse or donkey, heading for Karbala. A party of five men in the snow-white coats and trousers of Pakistan strode along under the palms with knapsacks and heavy walking sticks. The long-suffering women jammed into the rear benches with me noticed the Pakistanis, and one old lady pounded me on the knee to tell me they were Shiites from India come thousands of miles to pray at the shrine of Hussein, the great Hussein who was so treacherously betrayed and murdered. She shed a few noisy tears, dried her eyes on the corner of her abayah and then smiled at me. I nodded in return and muttered some inane platitude through my veil; she laughed delightedly and announced in a loud voice to the truck in general that even the Amerikiya appreciated Hussein's sacrifice. As the men in front turned around to look, I shrank back shyly and whanged my head on the screw again.

Suddenly we rounded a bend, had a glimpse of throngs of people and colored flags flying and came to a jolting halt in a narrow street. We had arrived in Karbala, and I could have wept for joy at the thought of stretching my cramped limbs, washing my face, discarding the abayah briefly and perhaps sitting in a cool, quiet place. But other forces were at work, which fortunately I could not anticipate or I might have abandoned my adventures then and there and hired a taxi to take me back to El Nahra.

Everyone crawled out wearily, the old women groaning, the children wailing, and we stood around in the hot sun, collecting luggage as it was dragged from under the benches and tossed through the windows of the truck. The sheep, bleating in protest, were handed down from the roof, and a little boy with a stick was commissioned to keep them from running off crazily in all directions. I assumed that Fatima, Rajat and I would start out for Uncle Yehia's house, but instead we headed with three other women into a dilapidated mud-brick house almost opposite where the truck had stopped. Here we climbed a dark, steep stairway into an upstairs room where we sat down on the only furniture, a length of none-too-clean reed matting.

Through a broken wood screen we could see into a court below, where a few scraggy trees provided a minute amount of shade from the noonday sun. I recognized Abdul Karim and Abad, Mohammed's brothers, among the men and boys who had congregated in the court and were arguing with the man of the house. We took advantage of the privacy to remove our veils and wipe some of the dust from our faces. Presently the mistress of the house appeared, a sloppy fat woman in run-over clogs and a cheap black shift, spotted by many greasy lunches. She looked us over and Fatima asked politely for water. The woman turned her head and shouted to someone, and a pale young girl, also in a soiled black shift, slunk into the room with a battered tin bowl which she presented to me. I drank a little of the water, which was not too clean, and passed the bowl along. Fatima was conferring with our companions and did not trouble to conceal her distaste. The woman of the house kept interrupting and her voice, rising, became an angry shout. At this Fatima frowned and stood up, adjusting her abayah and motioning to me to do likewise. We put on our face veils and trooped down the dank stairway and out into the street again. It appeared that we had considered taking a room in the house, but it was dirty as well as expensive and the woman's personality had not appealed to Fatima. Rajat took my basket and I picked up my satchel.

Surely now, I thought, we will head for Uncle's house, but Fatima said no, first we would go to the mosque and pay our respects to the martyr Hussein. I fell back into line, temporarily resigned to my fate, and we set off single file into the heart of the city, crowding the cordons marking the area restricted to pedestrians only, passing khaki-uniformed policemen holding back the trucks, buses, donkey carts and horse-drawn carriages.

As we neared the center of town we had difficulty keeping together in the crowd. For the first time I realized in consternation that I was totally dependent on Fatima for my welfare during the days of the pilgrimage. I could not go back now, as I had no idea where to go. I found myself reluctant to use my Arabic among the throngs of strangers. My only alternative was to follow the line of black-veiled women in front of me carrying their bedrolls on their heads.

But my feelings of dismay receded before the sights and sounds around me, the city decked out in all its finery for the yearly festival and the thousands of people pushing forth to the golden mosque.

We were passing an elaborate diwan, a tent which had been erected just off the main street, carpeted in fine Persian rugs and hung with tapestries. A few obviously rich male pilgrims had settled into overstuffed gilt chairs. Undisturbed by the crowds milling by, they were sipping coffee in comfort while they fingered their worry beads and listened to readings from the Koran piped in through a radio loudspeaker.

The town was a sea of splendid colored flags and strings of colored lights. Every shop, from the shabbiest kiosk offering cigarettes, shoelaces and chewing gum to the larger "magasins" displaying Western clothing in the window, had some illumination and flew a green flag for Hussein, a black one for mourning, and often others of pink and purple, scarlet or sky blue. Some were mere token flags, a twist of cloth suspended from a stick and propped up among the wares, but others were elaborately embroidered with mottoes and hung from carved gilt standards. Long bright bars of pink-and-white neon illuminated with a garish light the mourning finery which decorated the major coffee shops and hotels: black silk banners lettered in white; fringed tapestries portraying in vivid colors the important events in the lives of Hussein or the Prophet, black-framed portraits. The smaller mosques had erected black canopies at their entrances; clusters of flags marked the doors and from each mosque now we could hear the chant of the muezzins, high and shrill from the many minarets of the town, summoning the crowds of faithful to their noon prayers.

We walked and walked in the blazing sun, probably not as far as I thought, for I had to struggle constantly to keep up with my companions, elbowing and prodding my way, even pushing with my satchel to get through the tightly jammed masses of people. Occasionally the crowd would separate me for a moment from the figures of Fatima and the other women from El Nahra and I would panic and push ahead fiercely, hardly caring whom I shoved, until I could again see, among the hundreds of black-clad women with bedrolls on their heads, the bright familiar bundles on the heads of the women I knew.

Where to step was another problem. The sidewalks were fast being transformed into *byut*, temporary households set up for the duration of the pilgrimage by families who could not afford lodging elsewhere. This was the great holiday of the poor, to come by truck, donkey, horse or camel or even on foot from all parts of the Shiite Moslem world, and camp out on the sidewalk as close to the great mosque as possible, so that they might go many times each day to pray at the tomb of the martyr. Even as we walked, people were unrolling mats, setting down squares of carpet and claiming a strip of sidewalk as their own. The old people sat on the strip to hold the space while the wife or son went to buy fuel for the Primus stove, to fill a battered teakettle with water, or bring bread and a measure of sugar. Turning to look back at a woman in face veil and abayah sweeping her square of sidewalk with part of a broken broom, I was elbowed into a blazing Primus stove on which someone was preparing lunch. I felt a stab of pain as the flame seared into the side of my shin, but there was no time to stop and look down to see how bad the burn was. I had to fight to catch up with Fatima again.

Finally, after half an hour of tortuous walking, we turned into the main street. My leg was throbbing steadily by this time and my shoulders and arms ached from the effort of keeping my abayah modestly around me and holding onto my satchel at the same time. My face veil, which I had been so worried about losing, was pasted to my face with sweat, and sweat dripped down my arms and legs and into my shoes. I tried to jerk my abayah up and pull it around me more securely. What would I do if it were to slip down and I were revealed, uncovered and foreign, in the middle of this crowd? Why had I ever come anyway? Then suddenly, in a break in the crowd, I saw at the end of the street the three golden domes and the slender minarets of Hussein's shrine shimmering in the dusty sunlight like the fantastic mirages seen by the faithful in the desert. Crowds milled below the minarets, which reached their shining peaks up into the fierce blue sky. A little boy pushed past, shouting in my ear, "Sammoon! Sammoon haar!" and Rajat pulled me by the hand. The moment passed, but it had crystallized everything about this strange day for me: the golden mosque, the flutter of bright flags, the small boy shouting in my ear, the sibilant sounds of Koranic verses sung from the loudspeakers, and the smells of sewage, strongly brewed family tea, and perfumed Arab gentlemen hurrying by.

The crowds were pushing us forward with them to the mosque. As we tried to step aside and let the strongest go past, we were knocked against old ladies selling eggs packed in grass-lined woven baskets, against the itinerant peddlers loudly hawking the tinware and painted enamel bowls that the poor bring back as keepsakes from the pilgrimage. In the huge circular open area surrounding the shrine, the earliest-arrived pilgrims had camped, and these households bore signs of longer habitation—an old man sleeping on a mat, a girl washing a cooking pot in a cupful of water. Trays of food were offered for sale: chickens, roast fish still clamped in iron grills, bowls of stew, but few could afford to buy. Fatima looked longingly at the fish.

"I think I'll ask how much it is," she said.

The other women laughed. "You wouldn't."

"I will too," insisted Fatima and marched up to the peddler. "How much?" she repeated, and snorted derisively at his reply. "Who do you think will buy your fish?" she asked. "Is it made of gold?"

Just when I thought we could not go further, we stopped, at the entrance to a side street leading away from the shrine and here, unexpectedly, ran into some other women from El Nahra. Fatima was overjoyed; the women embraced each other like long-lost sisters and we promptly deposited our luggage in the shade of a house, sat down on our bags, and began to exchange experiences. In a few minutes Sherifa and Medina, who had come the day before, wandered up, and we embraced again. Medina dug out a handful of pumpkin seeds from an inside pocket and handed them around. The holiday had begun.

While the women talked, I looked about me. A flashing neon sign to our left announced the presence of a first-class hotel, and above the sign on the hotel's spacious balcony I could see a group of wealthy Pakistani pilgrims, the men in snowy white, the women in brilliantly colored saris, drinking lemonade and watching the crowds below them in front of the mosque. On a mat near us four children and an old woman huddled together, watching the mother trying to make tea on a Primus stove which alternately smoked and belched forth yellow flame. A few feet away a small boy lay rigid on a rug, his head supported by a pillow, while two women and an old man took turns fanning him. The younger of the women was trying to force a few spoonfuls of hot tea between the boy's clenched lips. The man removed his kaffiyeh briefly, mopped his forehead and passed his hand over his face. Then, while I watched, the adults moved the boy's pallet into a larger patch of shade, away from the traffic, and I got a closer look at the child, who was emaciated, his eyes glazed and sunken from fever, the skin of his face tight over the bones, the mouth slack. He looked very near death. The father now began to fan and the two women straightened out the boy's thin dishdasha and arranged his feet more comfortably. At first I wondered why on earth they had brought this sick child to Karbala in such heat, but the obvious answer came. Dying on pilgrimage assures the soul immediate entrance into heaven.

Fatima leaned over to tell me that we were going to a house just down the street, where some of the women we knew had stayed in past years. Through a large central courtyard full of women and children, we were ushered into a small room where the dirt floor was covered with part of a mat. A painted and locked wooden box stood in a corner. That was all. Before I could summon up my scattered bits of Arabic to ask Fatima about Uncle Yehia, she had disappeared, and Rajat with her. I was left in the room with our luggage and Um Ali, an older woman from El Nahra whom I knew only slightly.

"Where have the girls gone?" I asked.

Um Ali grunted. She did not know. Perhaps they had gone to the mosque.

We sat in silence for a few moments. I was tired, dead tired. And I was thoroughly annoyed with Fatima for leaving me behind without explanation, as though I were a sack of potatoes or at best a poor relative of whose reactions one could not be certain. Surely Fatima was old enough and experienced enough—but there I stopped. Fatima was certainly old enough, past twenty-five, but she was hardly experienced enough to handle any out-of-the-ordinary situation. That situation, apparently, was myself. She hadn't wanted to take me to the mosque, perhaps. All right. I understood that. But was I then to be dumped thus, unceremoniously, in a corner whenever they went off to participate in anything on this five-day holiday? If that were the case, why had I come? But it seemed there was nothing I could do about it, because I was totally dependent on her. Or was I?

A crippled boy whom I had seen occasionally in the settlement limped into the room, sat down and looked up at me. Um Ali grumbled to herself, produced a few coins from the knotted corner of a handkerchief and gave them to the boy with instructions to buy her some sugar. Aha! An emissary to the outside world. I produced a few coins of my own for the boy and asked him to bring me a Pepsi-Cola.

The Pepsi-Cola, which was quite cold, raised my spirits considerably. I loosened my abayah, wiped my arms and

face with a handkerchief and examined my burn which
had now developed a puffy white blister but did not
hurt any more. Um Ali drank her tea and dozed in a
corner. Flies buzzed about over her empty tea glass. I
waited.

Sherifa came in to whisper that she thought we were
to stay at Fatima's uncle's house.

"Why don't you go there?" she asked.

I replied truthfully that I did not know.

"If you don't stay there, you may not find any place, it
is so late," warned Sherifa. "Tell Fatima. Even this place is
full. The room you are sitting in now has been reserved
for tonight."

I will, I thought grimly, if I ever see her again.

When Rajat appeared after nearly an hour, I pounced
on her.

"Why," I said, "don't we go to Uncle Yehia's?"

"Oh, we can't possibly go to my uncle's," she answered. "It would be great shame [ayb] because we didn't
bring any big presents, like chickens or butter."

I pointed out that I had two cakes and a bag of fruit
which she herself had carried the whole length of Karbala
for that very purpose.

She merely stared.

"Are we to stay here?" I asked.

"No, it is full."

"Then where will we sleep tonight?"

"After lunch," said Rajat patiently, in the manner
one uses with a recalcitrant child, "we will look for a
place. Fatima says so."

"Where?"

"Near the mosque," she answered.

That was all I could find out.

At that point I decided I could not face the possibility,
which was now very real, of sleeping on the street. It was
past three o'clock, the ceremonies were scheduled to begin
at sundown, and as Sherifa had pointed out, most of the
available space was filled by now. Sleeping on the sidewalk did not bother me so much as the prospect of keeping myself wrapped up in abayah and veil for five days and

nights, with no private place in which to wash or go to the toilet. All the apocryphal stories of Shiite fanaticism rose before me, and I had a few bad moments imagining a Grade B extravaganza in which I was unveiled as an infidel and an impostor in the middle of the night by excited crowds and borne aloft to the mosque where I was presented to the mullah to do with as he wished. I knew I was being silly, that my friends were with me, and that even sleeping in the street would not be a catastrophe, but by now I felt panicky. I was tired and hot and hungry and my leg hurt. But what could I do about it? First, I had no bedding, as Laila had told me I would be staying with her uncle and hence would need none. Second, I had the cakes and fruit, and thirdly, Bob was supposed to telephone me that evening at Uncle Yehia's. These all seemed points in my favor, and I decided to confront Fatima with my case and ask if we might at least go to Uncle Yehia's house and say hello; I had no idea where he lived or even what his full name was. Then I would have an address at least in case of trouble, and perhaps Sitt Najat, the wife (who I had heard was a trained nurse) would be sophisticated enough to perceive my dilemma and invite me to stay there. It was worth a try.

When Fatima returned, I outlined the plan: we could visit Uncle Yehia and give him greetings from the family. I would leave the cakes and fruit as presents, and we would tell Sitt Najat that Bob was to call, and she could tell him I was all right, in fact having a fine time. Otherwise, I pointed out boldly, Bob might get in touch with her father if he did not hear from me. The latter seemed the clinching argument, and Fatima agreed we might go after lunch. I offered to help prepare the meal, but the women urged me to wash and rest. I had been steeling myself for an appearance in the courtyard full of strange women and this seemed the time, so I wrapped my abayah around me, made a quick trip to the muddy filthy enclosure which served as the toilet and then stood at the common tap to wash my hands and face. It was quite a trick to get everything clean, and still keep the abayah out of the mud and covering one decently. I developed new respect for the many skills which my friends took for granted.

Suddenly all conversation stopped, and I heard a horrible inhuman barking sound. It came from the throat of an adolescent girl who was hopping and jerking her head as she came forward, her insanity so obvious that a woman near me involuntarily murmured, "*Mashallah.*" The girl pursued another woman who was teasing her. Someone snickered, and then a small child snatched an object from the woman's hand and returned it to the insane girl; she subsided, coughing and hiccuping, in a corner. I stumbled back to our room where Um Ali was saying her prayers. Fatima unpacked her bag and produced a couple of cold chickens and some hard-boiled eggs. After two glasses of hot tea, I asked if we might go to see Uncle Yehia. To my great relief, Fatima said yes. We would leave our baggage with Um Ali and go for a very brief visit.

We started back the way we had come, past the family of children, where the old woman had curled up to sleep on the mat, past the fever-ridden boy whose old father still fanned him. We turned into a small street and knocked on a narrow wooden door, set up three short steps from the street. Someone looked out and said Uncle Yehia was not home. Then another woman came and she and Fatima argued for a while about whether we would go in and have tea. For one terrible moment it looked as though the door would shut in our faces, but finally someone's charity for poor relations prevailed and we straggled in, past some visitors sitting cross-legged in the central court, into the sirdab, or summer cellar room. We sat on a clean mat and drank strong tea. I offered my cakes and oranges. Sitt Najat, a short stocky woman with very white skin and short shining straight black hair looked at the cakes, looked at me and smiled in welcome. I felt my plan had worked and I was right. I was presented with a *fait accompli.* Fatima said I *must* stay with Sitt Najat (courteous weak protest from me, fortunately overruled) and she would come for me in the morning. She would have a definite place to stay then.

We made another trip to the house of the insane girl to

bring my bag (we had not brought it the first time, of course, as it would have looked as though we were asking for hospitality). Night was coming as I plodded down the street of the shrine for the third time that day, and the neon lights cast a weird phosphorescent glow on the flags and banners. When I sank down for the second time in Sitt Najat's sirdab, I felt that the pilgrimage might not have been in vain as far as my spiritual education was concerned. I had endured bumping and banging, jostling and burning already; now I was being given the absolution of privacy and a good meal in this charitable Moslem house, and later, oh joy unbelievable, a bed on the roof under the stars. Sitt Najat's understanding was profound, I thought, as she led me up to the roof, past the cots of her four children, her husband and herself, and the beds which had been set up for her five visiting relatives, to a cot strategically placed in a corner, away from the multitude. I could hear the Koran still blaring from the loudspeakers, mingling with the chants of the taaziyas, whose performances had begun. From the roof I could see part of the mosque, the very top of the main golden dome and the spires of the minarets, but tonight I was too tired to appreciate the view, too tired to begin to digest the impressions of the long day. I lay down on the iron cot, its cotton mattress covered with a spotless white sheet. "Sleep here and good health," the familiar adage, was embroidered on my pillowcase, in a pattern of vines and flowers.

Bob never did phone. I realized why, after a quarter of an hour in Sitt Najat's house. There was no telephone. Bob later told me that he had, desperately, called the hospital and asked for Uncle Yehia, only to be told that there was no doctor by that name on the house staff. This was correct. Yehia was only a dresser in the hospital, a sort of male nurse, but his devoted relatives in El Nahra had promoted him to the status of a full-fledged physician and he probably did not deny it. Finally Bob had turned to the sheik and to Jabbar, asking what he should do. They both had told him that if I was staying with Moussa's relatives, I would be all right.

This, too, was correct. Najat's house was my home and my refuge during the five days I spent in Karbala. Fatima and Rajat came every day and took me out to walk and watch the taaziyas and see the sights of the town, but they always brought me back before dark. Fatima could now pray at the shrine and gossip with her friends without worrying about me. I was very content. It was an ideal solution for all of us, except perhaps Najat, but even she insisted it was a pleasure.

However, I know that as a guest I presented problems to Sitt Najat. She later told me that she had known personally only two Western women, Englishwomen who had been her instructors in the nursing college she had attended in her native Mosul. Neither had ever been a guest in her house. I could tell she was uncertain that first morning when I came down. First she jumped up and ran to the bathroom, where she noisily rattled the water can (to let me know it was full of clean water) and then emerged to greet me, leaving the door ajar in order to leave no doubt in my mind about the location of the facilities in case I did not know the necessary Arabic words. When I had finished, she jumped up again, ushered me past the relatives drinking tea in the court and into the sirdab. A breakfast tray followed, and Najat sat by me as I ate the flat bread and goat cheese, drank the *leban* (watered yogurt) and the tea, watching me anxiously and asking every few minutes whether this was like American breakfasts. Lunch was the same: I ate in lonely splendor in the sirdab, my only company a child who had wandered away from the cheerful group eating from a big tray in the court to take a look at the strange Amerikiya eating.

I decided this special attention was ridiculous and a needless burden on my harried hostess. Najat had offered the hospitality of her house to me, a complete stranger. And now she was giving me choice bits of food in addition to personal service when she already had six other guests.

When suppertime came, I sat down firmly on the mat in the center court and made a valiant effort at bright conversation with the relatives. By the time Najat had dished up the meal—rice, stew, pickles, a jointed chicken in tomato sauce, flat wheat bread for everyone—I was firmly ensconced between two of the stout older relatives, and declined to leave.

Najat laughed. "You see, she can eat like us. Don't be afraid of her," she told the old ladies.

I pretended not to hear, and from then on we always ate together, spooning rice and stew from the common bowls, sharing the basin of leban, finishing off with a glass of tea.

We sat in two groups—the four lady relatives and I, Sitt Najat and her niece and her five children at one tray, the two young male relatives, resplendent in their snow-white dishdashas, at another tray in a far corner of the court. The men came to the house merely to sleep and eat, and it was only on the last day, when we were exchanging addresses, that I discovered the oldest boy spoke fairly good English and could have simplified my life immeasurably during the five days I had been there.

But in retrospect I am glad I didn't know he spoke English or I might, in my laziness, have depended on him for most of my communication, and thus have missed many of the stories and confidences of my hostess and her guests.

The four ladies from Mosul, Najat's relatives, would occasionally venture out to pray or to watch the taaziya processions passing by, but they spent most of their time sitting on mats in the court, eating, drinking tea and gossiping endlessly. Their gray hair was long and loose, kept in place by white or black head scarves tied like caps over the tops of their heads; they covered their big, shapeless bodies with ankle-length cotton dresses yoked and smocked at the neck like nightgowns. They were pleasant, passive old ladies who, after a lifetime of serving husbands, in-laws and children, had retired to a comfortable old age in which their sons' wives and their other younger female relatives waited on them. During the entire time they were in Karbala they made no attempt to help Najat as she scrubbed the house and prepared the meals for fifteen people, and she did not expect it.

Fortunately Najat was a strong, wiry woman and could carry the burdens which a household, an influx of seven guests and a full-time job outside her house placed on her shoulders. She had five children, and also served as chief nurse in Karbala's free, government-run maternity and child welfare clinic. An adolescent niece of Yehia's lived with them, theoretically to look after the children while Najat was at the clinic, but the niece was much more interested in doing nothing, and spent most of her time in the house next door while the nine-year-old daughter watched the children. Najat told me she kept her job, in spite of the heavy home schedule, because it got her out of the house and in touch with people. Otherwise she would have been as secluded as a village woman. She missed her relatives and friends in faraway Mosul; she missed the simple escape of the movies, for Karbala, being a holy city, boasted no cinema. But she enjoyed life and obviously felt lucky to have found an approved public outlet for her talents, even in the holy city. Her neighbors, whom I visited while I was there, spoke admiringly and respectfully of her, not, I found, because of her emancipated status as a nurse and wage earner, but because of her large healthy family, her tireless industry, and her great store of cheerful good will.

Najat wore no face veil, and only donned the abayah when she left the house. She had laughed at my veil when I arrived, and urged me to discard it. "People think that Karbala is a fanatic city just because it is Shiite," she said. "It is not true at all. Everyone is friendly here; you don't need to wear the veil. Take it off."

How much of what she said was traditional Arab courtesy (she could see how uncomfortable I was in the veil) and how much she really believed herself, I do not know even now. But the only occasion I followed her advice and went without the veil was the evening, at the height of the festival, when she took me into the city to watch the taaziyas performing near the mosque. That night she was frightened considerably, I know. Perhaps until that time she had really believed it was all right for me, an unbeliever, to go without the veil. Perhaps she got a new insight into her own countrymen that night, but whatever she felt, the events silenced her. She never mentioned the veil to me again.

We set out that evening ostensibly to buy her two daughters new shoes for school, for the term began just after the ceremonies ended. I knew perfectly well that we were going to see the taaziyas and so did the girls, but a good woman Najat's age does not go wandering outside her house at night even during religious festivals unless she has a cast-iron excuse for her husband, should he object, and for her neighbors, should they feel like gossiping.

I was told later that there were nearly a million people in Karbala that night—Karbala, which normally has a population of 30,000. I believe it. Before we even left Najat's house we could hear the muted roar of the crowds, and by the time we reached the main street leading to the imam the noise was deafening.

"Walk near the shops," shouted Najat, "or we'll never make it. Don't lose sight of me."

It was almost impossible to move at all unless we let the crowd carry us along, but Najat was determined. Single file, holding onto the little girls, we plunged into the dense mass of people and pushed our way through until we could walk beside the shuttered shop fronts. Occasionally we fanned out to dodge the counter of an open kiosk or avoid stepping on someone lying prone on a mat. But most of the mats were rolled up that evening. This was the climactic night of the spectacle of the taaziyas; no one who was able to walk upright was asleep.

"Mama, we can't see anything," complained one of the little girls.

"Can't see," whimpered her younger sister.

They were quite right.

We could hear the hoarse cries of the taaziya processions, but a mass of spectators ten and twenty deep blocked our view completely except for occasional glimpses of flags and smoking torches held high.

"Never mind, we'll go up to the mosque and watch the taaziyas coming out," promised their mother. "That will be much better."

So we resumed our struggle forward against the stream

of traffic. Holding tight to the hand of Najat's daughter, I kept my eyes fixed on the resplendent mosque at the end of the street and surrendered to the general air of excitement and tension that I felt in Najat, in her daughters, and in the hundreds of thousands of people who pressed around me. Night had heightened the holy day sounds and sights of Karbala. The radio loudspeakers blared, turned up full volume to compete with the cries of the taaziyas and the roar of the crowds. Neon blazed white and pink and gold all along the street, casting a weird glow on the flags and banners; on the faces turned upward—white, black and brown; picking out the jumble of costumes worn by the group of believers: the black-and-white kaffiyehs of the southern Iraqi tribes, green turbans of Sayids, white coats of Pakistanis, navy-blue and wine-red abayahs of Persian women. Garlands of electric lights festooned the slender minarets of the mosque, and the broad golden dome, illuminated by thousands of bulbs, shone like a sun set in the black night sky. There was no wind, but the crowd moved ceaselessly back and forth, while the colored flags and banners hung limp above in the artificially bright air.

We had almost reached the imam when Sitt Najat motioned me into a shoe store. There were no customers, but the proprietor, a distant relation of Najat's husband, had opened his shop so he might watch the processions. He expressed amazement at the size of the crowds; usually, he said, he had a very good view of the parades, but tonight he had to stand on a chair or on his counter to see over the people's heads.

I was introduced, murmured traditional greetings, and the shoe-store proprietor asked Najat, to my everlasting delight, if I was a Persian pilgrim visiting the family.

Sitt Najat smiled and said that I was an American.

The proprietor's eyes widened in surprise. He recovered enough, however, to say to me, in careful English, "I see you wear the beautiful mantle of my countrywomen. Is it not a graceful robe, the abayah?"

I replied that I had found it so, and useful as well;

this gave him the opening for a sad little speech, phrased in the same stilted English.

"If even a foreigner, such as yourself," he said, "finds the abayah beautiful, why then do our young women begin to despise it so? I have heard from reliable persons that in Baghdad young girls now walk about without the abayah, exposing themselves on the streets to men they do not even know. Is this true?"

I said yes.

"And they laugh at the abayah and call it ugly," he added, shaking his head.

Then, remembering his manners, he ordered Coca-Cola for us to drink while the girls tried on shoes.

When we left, he took my hand gravely, with a mournful "what is the world coming to?" sigh, and pointed out a place near his shop where we might stand on a raised step to get a good view of the taaziyas.

We thanked him and inched our way into the spot he had indicated. He was right; there were two high steps leading to the closed door of a shop, and from the top one we could just see over the crowd. Najat and I took turns lifting the children.

Each taaziya group performed the prescribed ceremony before the tomb of the martyr and then marched out of the main entrance of the mosque to proceed down the street, repeating the ritual, in religious ecstasy, before the thousands of pilgrims. By the time we finally had settled ourselves, one taaziya had just passed down the street. We could hear the chant of the group next in line, echoing and re-echoing within the great courtyard around the tomb. Then the new group emerged; a green banner and a black, lit by flickering torches held high, were borne forward by the hands of very old men and boys who were not of the age to perform the ritual of flagellation. Then a score of young men, bare to the waist, wearing only black or white trousers and white head cloths, surged out, marching in strict rows of fours. I do not know what I had expected, from the torches and the noises and the sounds of the chant and chains, from the small procession I had seen in El Nahra. An orgy? An exhibition of sensationalism? Whatever I had expected, this was completely different, different in scope and quality from the taaziya I had seen in El Nahra.

The torches and weirdly lit banners, the bunch of black chains in the right hand of every man, the black garments, the glazed and exhausted eyes of the performers, and their drenched, sweating bodies signified a religious experience with which I was totally unfamiliar. Intense yet deliberate, the rhythm of the slow, liturgical chant never varied, its tempo ruled by the downward sweep of the chains, by the long, sustained cries of the leaders, by the thud of metal on flesh. In ancient and dignified figures, these young men were spelling out once more for a million pilgrims the renunciation, the humility and penitence which lie at the heart of Shiite Islam. Mourning for the lost martyr was exalted into a great drama of sorrow and became the individual sorrow of every pilgrim.

"Ohhhhh—— Hussein, most great, most honored, we grieve for thee," called the leader, walking backward, step after measured step down the cleared aisle of the street. At this signal the chains were swung like incense burners, across the body, out to the side; a silent half beat, marked by the thump of bare feet marching in unison, passed before the score of chains swung back to thud on the bared shoulders.

"Yaaaa—— Hussein," responded the young men.

"Ohhhhh—— Hussein, most betrayed, we mourn for thee," cried the leader, shaking the sweat out of his eyes. Click went the chains across the body, out, and then the unbearable silent half beat. The crowd held its breath, letting it out in a concerted sigh as the chains struck the bare shoulders.

"Yaaaa—— Hussein," answered the young men. Their shoulders were bruised blue from the ritual beatings, the kerchiefs around their heads blotched from perspiration. Still they kept up the sustained note, the measured beat, and the chains swung again like censers. The chains thudded and the chant swelled higher from a score of throats, from a hundred, as the taaziyas awaiting their turn inside the mosque were heard in the distance, in the silent half beats of the continuing ritual.

"Ohhhhhhh—— Hussein, our beloved martyr, we grieve for thee," cried the leader.

Tears streamed down the faces of sobbing men standing near me, and the piercing wailing cries of the women spoke of loss and pain and grief and lamentation.

The taaziya procession passed us, chanting and marching, striking their shoulders. The cry of the leader receded into the distance, but already another group was poised at the mosque entrance, eager to take part in the yearly ceremony. Another black banner and a green; gold tassels, flaring torches, a bare-chested leader; the group fanned out into a circle, varying the figures and beats accordingly. A careful circle, they moved together down the street, swinging their chains, chanting in sadness and yet in exultation.

Now a third group waited impatiently for the circle to pass out of earshot. The men, their tempers taut from the heat and the heightened emotions of their ritual exertions inside the shrine, were clamoring to start. Their leader and the mullah at the entrance tried to hold them back, but in a total break with the dignity and restraint of their mission they pushed forward, almost on top of the circle of men who chanted and swung the chains in front of them. A green banner toppled and fell, breaking the thin line between frenzy and disciplined ritual. Men from rival groups tussled briefly and bitterly. The crowd fell back, gasping at this breach of conduct, and the police intervened. The leader of the unruly group pushed his fellow villagers back into line and began desperately to mark the slow, strong beat.

"Ohhhhhh Hussein, oh betrayed one!" he cried. The men shuffled into place and the chains clicked, almost in unison again. Farther down the street the green banner was raised once more and the perfect figures, the circle and the square, reasserted themselves.

But now four or five taaziyas were backed up at the entrance to the shrine, their appearance delayed by the melee. The leaders had started the litany already, apparently to keep the groups in line, and they could be heard alternately chanting and shouting in strange cacophony.

"At the next break we must cross the street, or we'll be here all night," Sitt Najat shouted in my ear.

She took my hand, and I took the hand of her daughters. We started forward and had pushed ourselves nearly to the front edge of the crowd at the door of the shrine when we were forced backward again by the banners and torches of a new group. I heard an oath behind me and turned to see angry faces thrust next to mine, a woman gesturing in my face and a man with his arm raised to strike me. I looked down, to discover in horror that I was standing on someone's tiny prayer rug! How anyone came to be praying in that crowd I will never know, but I had stepped on the woman's hands with my heavy shoes and had almost stepped on the disc of clay used by Shiites to rest their foreheads while bowing in prayer.

At the shouting and angry words, people stood back and turned around to look. I opened my mouth to apologize, but Sitt Najat had already taken my hand again and was pulling me away. I felt myself propelled through protesting crowds that nudged and prodded and elbowed me as I was dragged forcibly along; I felt the daughter's hand slip from mine, but I was powerless to turn and find her again.

"Hold on!" shouted Najat, covering her face with her abayah and motioning to me to do likewise. I held my abayah in front of my face with one hand, and felt the other nearly being pulled out of its socket as Sitt Najat, now in obvious panic, jerked me through the crowd, away from the incident and the growing number of shouting people who stood at the door of the shrine.

We might have spent only a quarter of an hour pushing our way through that crowd, we might have been much longer, but I was ready to drop when we reached a side street and were suddenly lost in an unlighted alley. Let us stop, I thought silently, oh, let us stop, but Najat did not pause. She pulled me on and on, and I stumbled through the dark, tripping over unknown objects and stepping into puddles, my foot squishing in my shoe as I ran. Najat continued to drag me on.

Finally she slowed down, and I asked her where the children were.

"Oh, they'll find their way back," she answered.

We plodded along in silence.

"You must be tired," she finally said. "Let's have some tea when we get home." When we sat at last on the mat in her own courtyard, drinking hot tea, she spoke. She did not refer to the incident, nor to the furious pace at which we had traveled.

"It was much better to come home that way, don't you think?" she asked. "Not so many people." That was all she ever said.

I never saw the tomb of the martyr Hussein. No one suggested that I go, and after the evening incident with the taaziyas I lost my interest in going into the mosque altogether.

In the days that followed I went out again each morning and afternoon with Fatima and the other women from El Nahra, who came to Sitt Najat's to call for me. We would watch the taaziyas, still performing, though their fervor was somewhat spent, or we would stroll toward the outskirts of the city, away from the crowds. We would stop at some strange house, Fatima would ask the women politely for water, and, after satisfying our thirst, we would sit under a tree and talk. We went to the maternity clinic where Najat worked. We walked to the hospital where Yehia was stationed. He came out, in his white coat, and talked to us as we sat in the garden, like hundreds of other relatives and patients waiting for a doctor or a nurse or simply resting from the heat and the crowds. One day I insisted that we ride in a horse-drawn carriage. The women were shy about getting into it, and insisted that the driver would not let us off where we wanted to go and would then overcharge us, but I insisted and promised to pay if we were overcharged. Once we got into the carriage and jostled along the dusty streets behind the old horse, the women were enchanted. They laughed and sang and did not want to get out when the ride ended.

I asked them if we might go to the bazaar, for before

leaving Bob had suggested I look around and see what treasures might have been brought in by pilgrims to sell in exchange for food, lodging or travel home. The days passed, and we did not go. Finally I insisted that I must go to the bazaar, because it would be great shame not to bring a present to Bob. This seemed to impress Fatima, and on the last day she came to call for me in the morning accompanied by Ibrahim, her young cousin, who she said would take us to the bazaar. So I hurriedly donned my abayah, reminding Fatima again that I wanted to go to the old bazaar, where we could find copper and silver and rugs. She nodded and said that Ibrahim knew where everything was and would take us wherever we wanted to go.

Ibrahim was fifteen. Fatima treated him like a brother (he was more than ten years younger than she and hence not a possible marriage partner for her) and I did the same. In his striped dishdasha he stood nearly a head taller than everyone on the street, and was easy to follow as he led us along a circuitous route, up one small street and down another, "to escape the crowds," he explained. It was a bright clear day with a cool breeze. Many of the peddlers were packing up their wares, workmen were beginning to remove the strings of colored lights from store fronts and, as we turned onto the main street, families were rolling up their mats and bedding, preparing to leave for home.

Fatima chattered gaily all the way, though I noticed dark circles under her eyes and asked if she were ill.

"No, just tired," she replied. "But I can sleep in El Nahra. I won't be in Karbala for another year and maybe not then, for it's Sanaa's turn to come next time."

We were close to the shrine, walking along the outer court where a row of fancy shops displayed Western goods to attract the rich pilgrims. I knew the old bazaar was on the other side of the court, and was just then thinking smugly how much more beautiful the indigenous copper and silver work was than these cheap, flashy Western imports, when suddenly Ibrahim stopped, announced grandly that this was the place and ushered us into the largest and shiniest of the shops.

My face must have shown my dismay, for Ibrahim hastened to explain that he knew Bob would not want any of the old things in the native bazaar. These were the places where rich foreigners shopped, and he assured me that the one we were in was the very best. My heart sank. I looked around at the colored nylon blouses, the Ronson lighters and printed scarves and perfumes and had a fleeting vision of gleaming old copper and brass. Fatima was wandering happily about, looking carefully at everything and commenting on the beauty of the merchandise. Rajat stood at the door, her eyes very large and round above the abayah which she was shyly holding over the lower half of her face. At the end of the counter Ibrahim lounged, obviously quite pleased with himself, waiting for my approval.

I pulled myself together, trying to see the humor of the situation, and said yes, it was a fine shop.

"It's a wonderful shop," answered Fatima, touching the cut-glass stoppers of the French perfume bottles and looking at the transparent, lace-edged nylon blouses. There was nothing like this in El Nahra or Diwaniya.

Fatima bought a small scarf for her mother. I realized somehow as she was buying it that she had not counted on the price being so high, but she would not have dreamed of saying so, and thus she now had no more money to spend.

But I plunged on anyway. First some Evening in Paris cologne for Laila, and for Fatima herself. A black elasticized belt for Rajat. Handkerchiefs for Ibrahim. A large painted tin box of toffee for Sitt Najat. Elizabeth Arden night cream in gold-lettered jars for Sanaa and Nejla. A ball-point pen for Mohammed. And for Bob, after much discussion and bargaining among Ibrahim, the proprietor and myself, a polka-dotted maroon wool tie; the label said Regent Street, London. The proprietor felt that a small music box which held cigarettes and also played the Blue Danube would have been more fitting. I held my ground. Finally the tie was wrapped and all the other packages as well, except for the belt, which Rajat insisted on wearing.

When we left the shop, it was noon and very hot. Ibrahim bought Coca-Cola at a kiosk and we sat on the curb near the shrine to drink it, watching the thinning stream of people passing in and out to pray. Pilgrims with bright bedrolls were heading out of the city.

"I hope my mother is all right," said Fatima suddenly, and I found myself wondering about Bob and our mud house. The pilgrimage was over. We were already thinking of home.

PART IV

19

Autumn

The date palms in our garden, like all the date palms in El Nahra, were heavy with ripe fruit. For the past three days we had seen above our wall the neighbor boys high in their trees, and heard their shouts as they called to the men and women below that dates were cut and coming down. Like enormous bunches of heavy yellow grapes, the dates would break through the crackling palm fronds and fall with a thud to the ground. One morning Bob opened the gate to a group of strangers—two men, three women and several children—who identified themselves as the part owners of our date trees, and said they had come to harvest their crop. "Haji owns the land," explained one of the men to Bob, "but the trees are owned partly by him and partly by the descendants of one of Haji's uncles. My wife is one of the descendants, and we collect the dates every fall and give Haji part of them."

They began to work, and by midmorning the garden was covered with mounds of golden dates and with dried stalks and fronds pruned off by the boys after cutting down the fruit. The women and girls plucked the dates from their stalks and sorted them into piles. The dead fronds and empty stalks were also sorted to be stored for eventual use as fuel.

In the afternoon the women paused to rest, and I invited them in for tea. "I have heard about you," the oldest one said, "and we wanted to come and see what you looked like, but we live on the other side of the canal, near the suq, and it is a long way to come."

"You're related to Haji, but you live on the other side of the canal?" I had not met anyone with tribal affiliation who lived with the market people.

"Yes, Haji's great-grandfather was my great-grandfather," said the woman. "But my husband was from another clan of the tribe, and he took up sheep trading when his land salted up. So we live near the suq, where he works." Then she hastened to explain, "But we are not really of the ahl-es-suq [market people] because we still own our tribal land."

The tribe, Bob had said to me only yesterday, considered itself superior to the market people. He had found, he said, that the social divisions in the village were clear: the tribal people living in the clan settlements, the people of the market who lived near the market, and the government servants or *muwadhifin*, who lived in the government houses. Each of these groups kept apart from the others, seldom intermarried, and each considered itself superior. The woman's quick explanation that she was not of the market people only verified Bob's observations; though she had lived near the market all her life, she was still of the tribe and proud of it.

I invited her and her sister to drink tea with me every afternoon while they were harvesting, and during those afternoons I learned how thoroughly useful the date was to the local housewife. Dates of the best quality were sold to a date merchant in Diwaniya. Damaged dates were fed to livestock. Dates were eaten with bread and watered yogurt, as a nutritious and filling meal. They were boiled up into a heavy syrup, almost like sorghum, which was a substitute for jam (we had discovered it was excellent on pancakes) and good for cooking purposes. My friend also made her yearly supply of vinegar from dates. "But I never have enough bottles for the vinegar," she said, casting her eye around the room. I followed her train of thought easily enough, and that day when the little girls filed out of the garden, each carried an armload of empty bottles from my kitchen.

The mounds of dates grew higher and higher in the garden; the children tied the stalks into bundles and the men came with sacks to carry away the fruit. The harvesters departed and we saw no more of them until a child appeared at the gate one morning with two bottles of date vinegar, a gift from the old woman. I peered at the murky gray liquid, and the child advised, "Let it settle and then it will be all right."

I thanked her, but she did not go.

"Grandma says if you have any more bottles, she can give you more vinegar." I produced some more bottles but told her the vinegar she had brought would be enough.

The beginning of the new school term brought earth-shaking news. Sitt Aliyah, principal of the girls' school for thirteen years, had been transferred. She had been given a teaching job in Diwaniya and had settled down with her mother in a comfortable modern house. Selma, Laila and her sisters, Um Saad, Jabbar's sister Khadija, all the women were stunned. Sitt Aliyah had become so much a part of the community that it did not seem possible that school could continue without her.

Although the women rejoiced in Sitt Aliyah's promotion, they could not quite believe that she had gone from El Nahra forever. So many people had depended on her for so many things; she educated their girls, of course, but she also knew how to make excellent mosquito nets that fitted exactly over one's bed and kept out the myriads of insects that plagued one's summer sleep. Her mother made sherbet from fresh lemons and knew how to store it for months so that it would not spoil. Sitt Aliyah was never too busy to write a letter if one wanted. She would even advise about tonics for thin children and eyewashes for the infected trachoma eyes. She would read the Koran for a woman in trouble.

Hind, her younger sister, was to become principal of the school; the women said, "Hind is a good girl, but she is young and wants to get away and go to Baghdad. Aliyah was like us."

New rumors flew: Aliyah would stay, Hind would go, Um Saad would be principal, a new schoolteacher was to arrive. A new schoolteacher, it turned out, was really going to arrive, any day, to fill the vacancy left by Aliyah's departure. And now the speculation turned to the new teacher. Her arrival was breathlessly anticipated, not only by the tribal women and girls, to whom she was a symbol of the world outside the village, but also by the middle-class women to whose tiny social horizons she would be an important addition. If the new teacher were gay and enthusiastic, it would mean a good year for the school and a pleasant winter of afternoon teas for the middle-class wives. If she were dull—the women sighed and hoped she would not be dull.

Aziza, when she finally came, made an excellent first impression, for she was pretty, well-dressed, poised, educated, and her family background satisfied all camps. She was of tribal background but her father was a teacher in Diwaniya, so she had status with the middle-class ladies. This was her first job after graduating from the teachers' training college in Baghdad, and she was eager to please and ready to work hard. She was not above sitting cross-legged with the tribal women and chewing pumpkin seeds, and she dutifully visited all the civil servants' wives and brought them the customary present of sweets. Yet I sensed something different about this girl, and the townspeople must have, too, for although in the beginning she was liked and entertained, she did not develop any close friendships, and she was never taken to heart the way Aliyah and even Hind had been. Perhaps Aziza was too serious and found herself unable to respond to the ironic teasing which went on among the women. Perhaps it was the curious reserve in which she seemed to hold herself.

She begged me to help her improve her English, and I found her an apt pupil. Then Hind insisted that I must teach her too. Hind was clever, but she had no patience and seldom finished anything. The lesson hour with Hind usually degenerated into gossip and fortunetelling, whereas Aziza would drill on English plurals. The two girls began to vie with each other about who was to teach me Arabic in exchange for the English lessons. The competition became unpleasant and I finally had to suggest a compromise. I would come twice a week to the school after four o'clock. One day I would study the Arabic primer with Hind and give her a lesson in reading English; on the other day Aziza would help me with spoken Arabic and I would reciprocate by instructing her in conversational English.

Gradually my days with Hind petered out, but Aziza and I kept up our lessons.

Although Aziza had spent two years in Baghdad, she had lived the entire time in the carefully supervised college dormitory, so her knowledge of the big city was very limited. She knew enough, however, to want to know more, and she would question me by the hour; I had never seen such curiosity about the outside world before. Every session, whether we were discussing politics or religion or marriage or geography, always ended in the same way. "Tell me," she would say, "about the high life." By this she meant the kind of life she thought I led when I was not in El Nahra, in which women and men sat and talked together, went to restaurants and movies in fashionable suits and well-cut dresses, and danced, at one gala ball after another, under brilliantly lighted crystal chandeliers.

Aziza and I became friends, but we did not speak of our friendship. If we had, Hind would have felt affronted (after all, she had known me first) and Laila and Khadija would have complained bitterly. For, I discovered, friendships among women were much more important and much more intense in this segregated society than in our own. Where the men spend the major part of their time away from women, the women have to depend on each other for company, for support, and for advice. A man might be a devoted father or brother or a loving husband, but in El Nahra he was seldom, if ever, a companion. I never heard a woman discuss her emotional attitude toward her husband or her father or brother, but long hours were spent in debates about the fidelity or indifference of women friends. Naturally these friendships became most serious for women who were single or childless or widowed, but even married women with large families had close women friends for whom they composed poems or cooked special sweets. To a visitor in the sheik's harem, Selma once said, "Beeja is not Fatima's friend, she is Laila's friend," and when I protested, she said, "Yes, yes, you and Fatima like each other but you are the *friend* of Laila." And that was that.

20

An Excursion into the Country

Aziza and I kept up our lessons twice a week that autumn, but it was usually I who went to see Aziza. Therefore I was surprised to find her at my door after lunch one afternoon. Laila, who had been visiting, sprang up in delight, pleased that the teacher, a person of some importance, should appear when she was present.

"Come for a ride with me," said Aziza. "It is such a fine day."

"A ride?" I echoed.

"Yes," replied Aziza. "My cousin is here from Diwaniya with his car and his driver. They are going partridge hunting along the canal. I will sit in the back seat to look at the view and I thought you might like to come. Do come, Beeja!" she urged, clapping her hands together. "The country will be beautiful today."

"I would love to," I answered. An excursion away from my house and garden would be a real event. But I turned to my visitor Laila.

"Laila must come too," said the kindly Aziza, and Laila beamed. "But," she added, "are you sure that your father would allow you to go driving with my cousin?"

"Of course, of course," said Laila.

When I remember that afternoon, I wonder what gave it such a luster. It had none of the characteristics of autumn afternoons to which I was accustomed—no brilliant leaves, no crisp winds or changing skies. Perhaps it was the light, the sunlight in Mesopotamia which warms without burning, which adds subtlety to what is usually an elemental landscape. For fall here is really spring. The year's principal crops are planted early in October. By the end of the month the brown fields that have baked under the summer sun are fuzzed with green. This thin dusting of

green, the young barley and wheat and sesame plants, casts
a gentle haze over the flat land. Even the uncultivated
sandy sections develop shadows, and the sharp fronds and
spiny trunks of the date palms look softer in outline.
Gazelles race over the plains; the partridge nests in the
new grasses. This is the best season of the year, for the
heat has lifted and the icy muddy winter has not yet
come.

Aziza's cousin, one rifle in hand and a second rifle on
the seat beside him, rode in front with his driver. Both
men wore tribal dress, almost identical with the garments
worn by the men of the El Eshadda. For their tribe and
the El Eshadda were members of the same tribal confederation. The cousin spoke occasionally to Aziza, but he
was careful not to address Laila or myself. We sat silently,
wrapped in our abayahs, enjoying a marvelous sense of
release in the unexpected holiday.

We went as far as Seddara El Nahra, the point where
the sluice gates of the El Nahra canal are located. Here a
small rest house had been built in a large garden facing
the canal; I knew this little house and garden well, for
Jabbar, as irrigation engineer, had free use of the place
and often brought his sister Khadija, Bob, and me here
for picnics. Today, however, we passed on to a section of
canal that I could not remember having seen before, and
drove along for nearly half an hour until the cousin
stopped the car near a plowed but unplanted field. Aziza
indicated that we would get out and walk a little while
the men went on ahead to hunt. In this way they would
not intrude on our privacy while we strolled, and they
would return for us when they had bagged a brace of
partridge.

Strange as it seems to me now, I realized as we got out
of the car and breathed deeply the country air how long
it had been since I had had a chance to walk aimlessly
for pleasure. It was not the sort of thing that ladies in
El Nahra did; they were busy most of the day, and in their
leisure hours they hardly felt the need of more exercise.
Even if they had, they were expected to stay indoors with
their families and not wander about in public view.

The three of us struck out over the furrows of the field, clutching our abayahs up slightly above the ankles so that we would not trip on the uneven earth. We walked away from the road toward the bank of an irrigation canal no longer in use. The bank formed a fairly high ridge where Aziza had suggested we might sit for a better view; from there we could easily see the car when it returned.

"How lovely it is," said Laila. It was the first time she had spoken since we had left my house.

"It is good for the mind, the countryside and its scene," said Aziza to me, in her stilted not-quite-colloquial English.

I looked about me and agreed.

Brown and green, the flat land stretched away to the horizon, a horizon which seemed only a flat base for the arch of the sky. Over and above the ridge toward which we walked the camel-thorn grew, its spiny branches picked out clearly against the wide emptiness of that cloudless sky. A few small undistinguished birds rose from the brush and whirred over our heads toward the water of the canal, and as we neared the bank we heard a deep, pulsating note.

"It is the calling of the partridge," said Aziza, and began telling me the Arabic names of the birds and plants. Laila was not listening; she walked along with her head down, apparently deep in thought; I had never seen her so quiet.

Suddenly over the ridge three children appeared, two barefoot boys with shocks of black hair and a girl in a ragged abayah, carrying a baby on her hip. They stopped dead at the sight of us, as surprised to see us as we were to see them in this apparently empty place. Aziza spoke to them, but they did not answer. After a moment of intense scrutiny, one of the boys bolted down and across the hollow of the unused canal. We were close enough to the bank to be able to see now two or three mud huts clustered on the far side of the canal. A scrap of green, raggedly outlined, marked the garden and I guessed that these were water squatters who had settled near the old canal in the hope of getting moisture from it. When the rains came, the land would just sustain a small crop without further irrigation.

While we watched, the boy disappeared into one of the huts and reappeared with a man. Laila looked frightened and turned to run but Aziza held her ground. The boy pointed, the man started toward us, then seemed to change his mind, for he retreated into the hut again and a woman emerged and came toward us, the boy running ahead and pointing.

"Stand still, Laila," said Aziza. "Where are you going?"

"Oh," cried out Laila, "someone will recognize me and tell my father I have been out wandering!"

"Then cover your face, you silly girl," replied Aziza in her severest, most schoolteacherish tone.

Laila stood still, but she covered her face with her abayah and turned away as the woman neared us.

"*Salaam alaykum!*" called Aziza cheerfully.

The woman did not reply. She had paused on the bank above to stare down at us, three ladies, wearing respectable abayahs, out walking in a strange field. Every inch of her thin, tattered figure seemed to question our presence. She peered over our heads to see if we had escorts, and even I turned around to search for a sign of the cousin's Buick. The road was empty.

Finally she returned our greeting.

"We are out walking because it was such a beautiful afternoon," offered Aziza.

"Where do you come from?" demanded the woman.

"Don't tell her, Aziza," pleaded Laila. "Please don't tell her."

But Aziza recounted in detail the story of our outing while the woman and the tousle-headed children listened; even the baby did not make a sound. After Aziza had finished, there was a long silence before the woman, her old-young face already set into harsh lines of hunger or pain or fear, switched her tattered abayah about her feet ever so slightly and said perfunctorily (she would have been violating all of her social codes had she done otherwise, even in this situation) "*Ahlan wusahlan.* Come and drink tea with us."

We declined with thanks and moved off, murmuring "God be with you" and "Peace be with you," farewells which were not returned. After crossing perhaps half the distance between the ridge and the road, we looked back. The woman and the children still stood in a line against the sky.

When we reached the road, the Buick still had not appeared, so I offered to take pictures of the girls. Laila refused, but Aziza posed by the little arched iron footbridge which crossed the canal; then she climbed the bridge to pose again, leaning on the railing and looking into the water romantically.

The Buick roared up just before sundown and we clambered gratefully in. It was good to be rescued on the lonely road as night approached and the only human habitation for miles those unfriendly families in the mud huts. It was very cosy in the car. The lights were on in El Nahra and it was actually dark when we reached my door. On impulse, I asked the girls to have supper with me, as Bob was eating in the mudhif.

Over cold chicken and salad, watered yogurt and tea, Aziza became quite eloquent. The subject was tribal purity, and Laila supported her effusively on every point. Neither girl, it appeared, would ever dream of marrying a man not of her own tribe.

"It is—it is—" fumbled Aziza, looking desperately for an explanation which might appeal to my strange Western mind, "it is like the British royal family," she finished triumphantly. "They do not sully their bloodlines. Why? Because they are proud of their lineage. That is the way we feel."

"But if a man from another tribe were very handsome and very rich would you marry him?" asked Laila.

"I might like to, if I saw him and fell in love with him," said Aziza.

"I would, if my father asked me to," burst out Laila.

"Any girl would do whatever her father asked," retorted Aziza, "but my father would never ask anything like that. In our tribe we are very tall and we want to keep the tallness."

"Of course," said Laila politely, and then to make amends she added, "your cousin is very tall."

"Yes," said Aziza.

At that moment Mohammed called through the shuttered window to ask if he could speak to me privately. I was surprised, for Mohammed never interrupted or intruded when I had guests, especially women. I excused myself, and Aziza asked me as I went out whether Mohammed could walk her home, as she did not like to return to the school alone in the dark.

Mohammed waited in the kitchen.

"Sitt," he burst out without even a prefatory greeting, "something very bad has happened."

"What?" I cried, my mind jumping to a vision of Bob lying dead in a ditch out in the middle of the plain.

"It is Laila," he said.

"Laila?" I echoed, in some perplexity.

"Yes, Laila. Isn't she in your room now with the school-teacher?"

I nodded.

"Didn't you take her with you this afternoon?"

"Yes," I said, still not understanding.

"You should not have done that," said Mohammed solemnly. "In fact, you should never have gone at all without asking your husband."

My first reaction was one of irritation. What right had Mohammed to tell me what I must and must not do?

"Thank you very much, Mohammed," I said as calmly as I could, "but I am sure my husband would not object. After all, I was with the schoolteacher, whom everyone respects."

Mohammed brushed my reply aside with a gesture of impatience. I could hardly believe that this was Mohammed, who never spoke like this to anyone, and had never presumed to discuss my conduct with me. But he continued firmly, "Sitt, you are a foreigner and although you wouldn't, I should think, want to ruin your good name, you don't have to live here. The schoolteacher's cousin is a very bad man; he drinks and gambles and stays with bad women in Diwaniya."

I opened my mouth to interrupt but Mohammed held up his hand warningly.

"Laila is in great danger," he said. "If anyone"—he paused and repeated "—anyone were to know that she went riding with a strange unmarried man without men from her family present, she could be killed. Her father would have to do it to save the honor of the other women of the family. Do you understand?"

Yes, now I did understand, with the sickening realization that one has as a child of being caught in an act of serious wrongdoing, conscious that there will be no discussions or excuses, no opportunity to explain. It is done and one is to blame and waits for punishment.

"What shall I do, Mohammed?"

"You must deny that Laila was with you. Say it was a cousin of the schoolteacher. I know Laila went and so do some of the children who saw you go, but I will deny it and so will the children because they like Laila."

"But Mohammed, she is here now, eating supper with me. Everyone will know that, and will see her leave."

Mohammed paused. "You could say that she came after the ride to eat supper with you," he decided. "Perhaps you had better explain to the schoolteacher."

I went in to Laila and Aziza, where they sat chatting happily, and told them what Mohammed had said. "We must swear it was a cousin of yours in the car, Aziza," I finished, "and all stick to that story."

"Yes," said Aziza.

Laila's holiday manner disappeared as I talked; she now rose abruptly, knocking her half-full glass of tea all over her abayah. I pushed my handkerchief at her, but she did not take it.

"Never mind, never mind," she said and wiped ineffectually at the wet abayah with her hand.

"I must leave," she said, shaking our hands perfunctorily and going out quickly.

Aziza and I were left looking at each other. "I should have known better," she said. "I know how conservative these people are; after all, I grew up as Laila did. That is why I made a point of asking whether her father would allow her to go. When she said yes, I was too careless to press it further.

"We must say nothing," she added. "The least they can do is to beat her. Let us hope they do nothing worse."

Mohammed coughed discreetly outside the window where he was waiting to escort Aziza home. He would walk, as he walked with me, a few steps ahead to lead the way; and he would wait until the school gate had clicked shut behind Aziza and only then return.

Aziza took my hand.

"I'm sorry our lovely afternoon finished this way," she said.

My face must have shown what I felt, for she added quickly, "Don't worry, please. If no one will admit that she went with us, it will be all right."

When Aziza had gone, I sat appalled at the possible consequences of my thoughtlessness. I tried to busy myself tidying up our two rooms, but I had a bad hour, alternately imagining Laila weeping and beaten, or Laila thrown into the canal and drowned (would they tie her hands and feet?). There should be something I could do to help, but, alas, there was nothing. What I had done could not be repaired by any words or action of mine.

Bob's appearance was hardly reassuring. He had just spent an extremely uncomfortable half hour in the mudhif being scolded by Nour for his husbandly neglect in letting me go out alone. Poor Bob had been at a disadvantage, for he had been away from El Nahra the entire afternoon and knew nothing of what had happened.

"I covered you, I think," Bob said, "by saying that I had told you beforehand that you could go, but I didn't know anything about the sheik's women, fortunately. When they asked me who was in the car with you, I said quite truthfully that I had no idea. But I have never seen Nour so upset. He spoke very abruptly. He has never acted this way in all the time we have been here."

Bob was as upset as I.

"I'm afraid you've made quite a blunder," he said. "You might have asked me before you went. You've made me look foolish and compromised your friend."

"I know, I know," I wailed, "but what can I do?"

He thought for a moment. "I think you probably should stay here, but I had better go back to the mudhif and act as if nothing were wrong. Maybe I can find out what is happening."

We both knew this was unlikely. Whatever Laila's punishment, it would be administered behind the high walls of her house. What actually took place would be known only long after.

Bob on his return had little to report. Nour had seemed calmer, but had repeated his earlier strictures on Bob's conduct. "Nour is being overconscientious because Sheik Hamid is in Baghdad," Bob said.

"If only the teacher's cousin hadn't been such a rake," he added, "I have the feeling it might not have been so bad. Nour may be afraid that the cousin will gossip about Laila and you in the Diwaniya coffee shops. Then the tribe will lose face. This business of the good name of their women being the honor of the tribe is no joke."

Neither of us slept much that night. I reproached myself again and again for being so thoughtless. After all, Aziza had asked Laila and she, Laila, had made her own decision about going. It was not all my fault. But I knew that I should have been perceptive enough to realize that it was an almost unheard-of action for as sheltered a girl as Laila. I was older and, as a married woman, theoretically I was more responsible. On the other hand—and so I argued back and forth.

Mohammed, when he came in the morning, had not dropped his role of counselor-adviser. This must mean that the situation was still grave, but when I asked he said he did not know what had happened. He told me not to visit Laila's house but instead to visit the sheik's house. This seemed like a good way to appear unconcerned and a wise move in general, but I found it very difficult to walk up the path that morning, past Laila's house (what was going on inside?) and into Selma's courtyard. I sat down in the bedroom and prepared myself to face questioning. Selma and Samira sat with me, and Kulthum came in to drink tea. Several other women stopped momentarily, but an hour passed with no mention of yesterday.

Bob told me at lunchtime the men too had stopped talking about it in the mudhif. I asked Mohammed at nightfall if he had heard any news.

"Laila is all right, I think," he said, "but she hasn't been out of her house all day, and neither have her sisters."

At this I felt a great sense of relief, although Mohammed warned me again never to mention the episode to anyone. It would, he said, be all right for me to visit Laila the next day.

Laila greeted me cheerfully. I had just about decided Mohammed had exaggerated the seriousness of the whole affair when Laila left the room, and her three older sisters came in and closed the door. They proceeded to give me the politest, most cutting lecture I have ever received.

I was thoroughly embarrassed as the girls pointed out the damage I had nearly done.

"We know that you don't understand our ways," said Fatima.

"We realize you didn't mean any harm," put in Nejla.

"We just wanted you to understand . . ." Sanaa left her sentence unfinished.

None of the three actually mentioned the facts of the case, and when I put in, rather crossly, that after all Laila had come of her own accord, they merely looked at their hands.

Finally Fatima said, "Yes Beeja, we know she should not have gone. We have scolded her already, but she is young and silly. You are older and a married woman and have been to school. If our father knew for certain, he would beat her very hard. We were all so frightened for Laila last night."

The three girls stared at me in a somber way, while I felt they were willing me to imagine the things that might have happened to Laila. I dropped my eyes before that steady, virtuous, oppressive gaze, saying I was very sorry for the trouble I had caused.

Fatima caught me by the hand. "We will never mention this again," she said.

Gradually our pattern of visiting re-established itself, the men in the mudhif no longer discussed the question, and I thought the incident forgotten completely. But two months later I was drinking tea with Selma. We were discussing I don't remember what, when she casually asked, "Who was in the car with you, Beeja, when Sitt Aziza took you for a ride?"

"Aziza's cousin from Diwaniya," I replied promptly.

"What was her name?" inquired Selma, pouring a little hot tea into the saucer and blowing it.

"I've forgotten."

"Many people say that it was Laila in the car," said Selma, offering a little of the cooled tea to her three-year-old daughter, who sipped it noisily.

"They are wrong," I lied.

One of the women said, "But my daughter told me she saw Laila get into the car."

"So did mine," put in another.

My uneasiness was growing, but Selma cut the two women short.

"Didn't you hear Beeja?" she asked. "Are you calling our guest Beeja a liar?"

No more was said. But I began to realize that Bob and I would never be other than foreigners, even though our efforts to conform to the local customs might prove ingratiating. No one would seriously blame us for our lapses, but we had to recognize our responsibility when, on our account, other people were exposed to blame or shame or worse.

How little I really knew about the society in which I was living! During the year I had made friends, I had listened and talked and learned, I thought, a great deal, but the pattern of custom and tradition which governed the lives of my friends was far more subtle and complex than I had imagined. It was like the old image of the iceberg, the small, easily recognizable face on the surface of the water giving no idea of the size or shape or texture of what lies beneath.

PART V

21

Winter

Winter came down upon us with a sudden rainstorm. All day clouds had been gathering in the skies, the first time for months and months, and at sunset the rain poured onto the land. Everyone rejoiced, for an early heavy rain was good for the crops. We went to sleep that night lulled by the refreshing sound of rain beating on our roof after the dry heat of the summer.

At the end of the third day it was still raining. By now the road was a morass of mud, and I did not leave the house. Even at home it was difficult enough. Every time we went from one room to another or across the garden to the bathroom or the garbage pit, we would slip and slide on the mucky ground.

Mohammed was not so lucky. He still had to haul our water several times a day and bring food from the market, and he finally stopped wearing shoes altogether. He would hoist his dishdasha up and double his aba over his head against the rain, but his legs were always splashed with mud up to the knees when he finally arrived.

Our roof began to leak and we would wake in the middle of the night to feel the splash of rain on our faces, on the floor, the chairs and table. Until the sun shone again the mud roof could not be repaired, so I set pots and pans in strategic places on the floor and we covered our bed with a tarpaulin and our heads with raincoats when we slept.

By the fourth day, even Bob decided to stay indoors and work on his notes. Our diet had become very monotonous, for none of the farmers were bringing produce to market. The taxis from Diwaniya had stopped running, so no canned foods or jam or cigarettes came into El Nahra, and the supplies in the shops dwindled steadily. The post office was closed and the telephone line was out of order.

The Biblical story of the deluge, which is supposed to have taken place very near El Nahra, seemed very real. We were quite cut off. Who would have thought that rain would be a problem in the middle of the desert? But it was. Horses could make very little headway in the thick, deep mud, the cattle could barely walk, and everyone who could stayed indoors and tended the eroding mud walls and roofs. The men were worried about the crops, said Mohammed. The water table had been high to begin with, and too much rain at one time could easily drown the young shoots of grain. We knew now why Haji had built our little house on a slight rise in the garden. Mohammed, our only link with the other people in the settlement, reported that the floors in some houses were already wet. If the rain didn't stop soon, many people would be flooded out.

Fortunately, on the sixth morning, it did stop. We woke to bright sunshine and an unexpected amount of noise. At first we could not account for the burst of noise, and then we realized that the settlement, which had become quieter and quieter during the rain, was merely emerging from its enforced retreat. Children were running up and down the road again, servants were setting out for the suq, and the livestock, driven out of their enclosures for the first time in days, were mooing and braying with joy.

Mohammed came to say that Haji had invited us to lunch. To celebrate the end of the rains, Selma was making *faisanjan*, or Persian chicken, and Sheik Hamid wanted us to sample the special dish. At noon I put on my abayah and tried to pick my way up the road through the slimy mud and the deep puddles. Through Saleh the weaver's open door I could see Hathaya, his daughter, and his old mother laying reed mats over the muddy ground, to protect the wool which Saleh was stringing back and forth from the loom to the pegs at the end of the court. All the houses along the road had rows of fresh dung cakes spread out to dry for fuel on the wall tops; the housewives had been busy that morning.

Laundry was underway in Haji's house. The daughter

were hanging up clothes, children's dishdashas, sheets, towels and dresses on lines stretching all around the big central court. A pot of white clothes still boiled over an open fire and Amina, stirring with a long reed stick, nodded to me cheerfully as I came in.

From Selma's own apartment drifted an odor strong enough to drown the smells of wet dung, mud and laundry, a lovely odor which came from the kitchen. Here the chicken simmered on a Primus stove while Selma stirred and tasted.

Faisanjan was a worthy delicacy to celebrate our release from the rain. The preparation took hours. First walnuts were pounded and pounded in a mortar until nothing was left but the oil. The chicken was jointed and browned in the oil and then a little salt was added and water in which dried pomegranate seeds had been soaking. In this fragrant broth the chicken cooked slowly until the broth thickened to a nut-brown sauce and the chicken fell from its bones. Walnuts and dried pomegranate seeds and salt proved to be an unexpectedly delicious combination of flavors. I told Selma that it was excellent and she smiled.

"No one in El Nahra can make faisanjan like Selma," said Samira.

Selma did not protest.

Three days later, when no more rain had fallen, Mohammed said he thought it safe to repair our roof. Two men came from the suq with buckets and ladders. I watched from behind a half-closed shutter while they hauled up buckets of mud. I heard the sound of the mud being slapped on the roof and smoothed by hand. A few drops of mud plopped down past the window. The men climbed down and took away the ladders. Our roof repair (which would last for five years, they said stoutly) cost exactly $1.25, and had taken about an hour.

Sherifa, Mohammed's sister, had been ill for several days. Mohammed described her symptoms as fever, chills, coughing and vomiting. I asked whether I could visit her.

"After a day or two, when she is better," he suggested.

"Has she been sick like this before?"

"Oh yes, many times," answered Mohammed, "but it is worse in winter, the cough especially."

The day he came to announce that Sherifa was well enough to see me, I took some aspirins and fruit and went to her. But if today she was supposed to be better, I wondered what her illness had been before. The normally cheerful and always polite Sherifa made little attempt to greet me. From the mat, where she lay covered with a blanket, she raised a limp hand.

"I'm very sick," she said.

Her mother Medina was making tea over the tiny charcoal fire. I asked whether I could bring the doctor for Sherifa.

"No, no, I don't want him here," said Sherifa, raising herself slightly on one elbow. Then she was seized by a fit of hard, dry coughing and lay back on the mat and turned her head away from us.

Medina offered me tea, and Fadhila, who was mixing bread dough for the noon meal, came in to sit for a moment. Fadhila asked me to stay and watch her bake the bread; she seemed unmoved by the sight of Sherifa, who was now moaning continually.

"Poor Sherifa," I said. "What a pity."

"Oh yes," said Fadhila matter-of-factly. "She is always like this in winter, poor thing. But what can one do?"

"Bring the doctor."

Fadhila raised her hands.

"Why?" she asked. "If he came, which is quite unlikely, he would charge a great deal of money, which we don't have. And even if we could pay him, then he would prescribe many expensive medicines, which we can't afford to buy. God wills that poor Sherifa be ill, and he grants me, thank God, good health."

I still felt that, if necessary, we could bring the doctor for Sherifa, and asked Bob to discuss it with Mohammed. Mohammed said he did not want the ill-famed doctor in El Nahra to come, but that perhaps we could take Sherifa with us when we went to Diwaniya the next time. He had heard that the new woman doctor at the free government hospital was running a good clinic.

"Of course we will take her," said Bob. To me he added in English, "She probably has tuberculosis, you know, and what can we do about that?"

We had already heard of a death from tuberculosis that winter, a young woman from the market people. The incidence of tuberculosis was very high in El Nahra, the doctor had told Bob, but they did not know the exact figures, for the disease remained more or less quiescent through the hot summers, but flared up again when the cold rains began.

If anyone had reminded me, in the heat of September, that soon I would be shivering with the penetrating cold and that ice would form on the mud puddles outside our door each night, I would have laughed. Yet here we were again, wearing four or five layers of clothes all day long in the rooms where just two months ago we had sweltered in 120-degree heat.

That year we were grateful for our two Aladdin kerosene heaters, bought secondhand from friends in Baghdad. They made the rooms fairly comfortable and were a great improvement over our charcoal brazier, which had smoked so much that the fumes gave us headaches.

Everywhere I went to visit now, some member of the family was sick. The women put on heavy black sweaters or imitation black caracul jackets under their abayahs. Over their dishdashas the children put on sweaters and wrapped their heads up in wool scarves and caps.

"If one's head and neck are warm, all is well," Mohammed pronounced. He himself wore a wool tweed sport coat over his dishdasha, under his aba. It was secondhand but in good condition, bought from a big bundle of coats and sweaters which had arrived in the suq, Bob said, when the cold started. Some enterprising Lebanese businessman, we discovered, had begun buying up lots of used European and American coats in New York and London and selling them by the bundle in the small cities and towns of the Middle East.

But many people in the settlement could not afford such luxuries. They added another layer of cotton garments, warmed themselves on good days in the morning sun, drank glass after glass of hot tea and huddled around small charcoal braziers at night.

The cold deepened, and the price of charcoal rose higher and higher in the market. For us this was of minor importance, but I lay in bed at night listening to the rain and wondering about the families who went to bed at nightfall simply to keep warm. At least they would be warm there, I thought, remembering the pile of blankets that seemed to be the only major possession I had seen in many houses.

One morning I woke feeling very poorly indeed. By noon I had a high fever and by nightfall all the symptoms of severe bronchitis and flu had descended on me. Bob put me to bed and Mohammed brewed meat broth and mint tea. I could not remember when I had been so sick.

The next day Laila and Rajat came to visit. Laila had brought me four eggs; she and Rajat clasped my hand and murmured words of encouragement. They sat by my bed and watched me anxiously. When I coughed, Laila coughed; when I blew my nose, Rajat sniffed in sympathy. By noon I was exhausted from trying to talk to the girls, and wanted only to be left alone. When lunchtime came they left, promising to come back as soon as they could.

"Oh, it's not necessary, thank you very much," I said weakly.

"Beeja," Laila answered, "how can we leave you alone when you are sick?"

My protests were useless, and promptly after eating the two girls returned and sat down by my bed again. The rest of the day passed in a haze of fever. I finally could not even manage social pleasantries, and would doze off periodically and through my half sleep hear Laila and Rajat discussing my illness. I remembered the scene at Feisal's bedside when the crowds of women and children had assembled to keep him company while he fought typhoid fever. Someone had once told me that in this society loneliness was one of the greatest of misfortunes, for it meant that your family had deserted you, and you had no one sufficiently concerned for your welfare to stay with you. Where I felt I needed solitude to recover from an illness, my friends in El Nahra believed just the opposite. When a person is sick, they reasoned, he needs support from his friends and relatives even more.

I was touched by Laila and Rajat's concern, but when they told me, in finally departing, that Sherifa and Samira would sit with me tomorrow, I did not feel I could face it. I asked Bob to have Mohammed pass the word in the settlement that he, Bob, was going to stay home with me until I was well, knowing that this was the only way I could decently prevent the women from coming without hurting their feelings. Two days later I was ready to come out into society again.

About this time, through conversation in the mudhif, Bob became aware of a neighbor of ours whom we did not know, a blind man who seldom stirred from his house. His wife was dead and he had two sons, one nearly blind like himself. "How," Bob asked, "does he support himself?"

"It is very cold today," answered a man, moving closer to the small brazier of burning charcoal in the center of the mudhif.

"Yes, indeed," said another. "Thank God we have a fire and food and good company."

Bob told me he was at first totally mystified by the conversation, but with a little help from Mohammed he began to understand. The man, said Mohammed, was very poor. Haji gave him food, many people gave him food; as a matter of fact, this was the time of year when people gave him food or money.

Bob decided that it would be nice to "do something" for the man and said so.

A murmur went around the mudhif.

"Ah, but it is not necessary, as a guest, that you should do so," said Haji's brother Abdulla.

"Not necessary," echoed the men.

"But I insist," said Bob.

"Mr. Bob insists," repeated Abdulla.

"Ahhhh," commented the men.

"Yes," said Bob, stating his intention to buy a sack of

wheat for the man, the most practical gift he could think of. The tribesmen seemed to pay no attention, and Bob was puzzled.

Later that day he gave the money to Mohammed. "Go buy the grain and get a porter to deliver it," he said.

Mohammed looked uncomfortable. "This is a pound and a half," he said.

"Yes," said Bob. "What's the matter? Isn't that enough?"

"Let's just give him the money," suggested Mohammed.

"But why? He'll just spend it on cigarettes or something," Bob said, in a rush of annoyance, "and then starve the rest of the winter."

Mohammed looked carefully at the ground, then at Bob, then at the ground again.

"He is a man," he said. "Let him choose."

Poor Bob stared at Mohammed. "Take the money," he got out, "and give it to him and for heaven's sake don't say where it came from."

For a long time after Mohammed had gone, Bob sat at the kitchen table. I poured some coffee and we drank it slowly. Finally he said, a little wryly, that he wished he could have paid the money minus the personal embarrassment to learn what he had learned.

"To discuss a gift publicly here," he said, "is obviously in the worst possible taste. I knew that before. And a recipient of charity has just as many if not more rights than the donor. I knew that too. What's the matter with me?"

He was very annoyed at himself. "It's amazing how many ways we seek to gratify ourselves," he said.

"Don't be so hard on yourself," I answered. "You felt sorry for the man, you wanted to do something and you have. That old man is probably enjoying his first cigarette in months, even if he is cold."

"I hope so," said Bob. "I really hope so."

Winter was hard on us all in El Nahra.

Our winter depression was broken by word from the two American engineers in Diwaniya, who called Bob at the mudhif to say they would be out for dinner. This was cheering news. John Priest and his colleague, Tim Maestas, maintained a headquarters house which had often been a refuge for us in an emergency, when we missed the train to Baghdad or were stalled in Diwaniya awaiting a taxi to El Nahra. But we seldom saw the boys themselves, for they were out in the field for weeks at a time.

In anticipation of their arrival, Mohammed bought quite a fat chicken, and I baked a cake and some cinnamon rolls. But after lunch the rain began and at dusk we knew the road would be so bad the boys would never make it. The next day, however, it cleared slightly and that evening, as we were finishing supper, we heard the roar of a truck outside our wall. Mohammed ran to open the gate, and five minutes later John and Tim tramped up the path, bearing a case of beer! Tim produced a pack of cards. We were immediately jubilant at the prospect of a change of routine, which was even more welcome after our disappointment of the night before.

I brought glasses and the men opened beer cans with great gusto and hilarity. Bob fiddled with the radio, looking for gay music, but all we got was the Arabic news broadcast from Moscow.

"*May khallif,*" said Tim in execrable Arabic, "never mind, we'll sing for you. Didn't I ever tell you I was a boy soprano years ago in Oakland, California?" He began to warble, "O, a little bit of heaven fell from out—" and on the high note we dissolved into laughter.

"We've been out in the boondocks for ten whole days," announced John. "Truck bogged down, sunk to the axle in the thickest, gooiest damned mud I ever saw. And then of course it had to rain again and we holed up in the wet tent for two days; couldn't even try to get her out."

"The driver went to the nearest village for help," Tim put in. "And you know it took twenty, yes, twenty guys to budge her. The home office will never believe how much baksheesh it cost." He and John exchanged glances.

"Have another beer, boy," suggested John.

"I'll have another myself," said Bob.

The flame was burning merrily in our kerosene heater.

We settled into chairs around the table and Tim had already dealt cards when the doorbell sounded.

Bob and I looked at each other questioningly. Who could be calling at this hour? He went to see and returned to summon me.

"Women," he announced.

There at the gate stood a little cluster of women. I greeted them, puzzled to know the reason for this visit, since the women seldom went out of their houses after dark except during Ramadan and Muharram. They reached the house and paused by the lighted window of the living room. I rushed after them to warn against the presence of the men inside but a roar of raucous male laughter went before me. By the time I let them into the kitchen, the women were suppressing excited giggles behind their abayahs.

"We came to keep you company," explained Laila, her eyes bright. "My father heard the truck with the American men drive up, so he agreed we could come and sit with you so you wouldn't have to be alone all evening."

The women, exchanging smiles of virtuous complicity, now pulled chairs into a circle. At the full realization of what their visit meant on this particular evening, my face must have shown my disappointment.

"Why, what's the matter, Beeja?" cried Laila, starting up.

"It's nothing," I said. I lit our other kerosene heater and the women gathered around it. "I think," I added, "I think I—hear my husband calling," I finished, on inspiration.

"Now, don't go in the room," teased Laila. "Talk to Mr. Bob through the door so those men won't be able to see you."

Everyone laughed heartily.

And there I was, trapped by my own hand, so to speak. I stood out in the cold by the living-room window and called in to Bob, telling him of my predicament. And he laughed. Actually laughed. All three of them guffawed. I felt positively murderous.

"Bring us another ash tray, dear," he said, and I stomped

off furiously, hearing the glasses clink and the cards slap down on the table.

"At least they can't play bridge," I thought nastily.

But before the kitchen door I paused.

"Laila and Sherifa and Basima have come on an errand of mercy, they think," I told myself. "They feel sorry for me. How can I tell them to leave? I can't."

In another vein, I considered. "How could I possibly disillusion them? Could I tell them I'm going to sit in there with three men, two not even relatives, and drink beer and play cards?" I shocked myself at the vision of what that would have done to my carefully maintained image in the community.

At the sound of another roar of laughter from the living room, my resolution faltered. "Perhaps the women won't stay long," I thought unkindly, and opened the kitchen door.

But the ladies stayed and stayed—and stayed. They did everything in their power to amuse me. We sang songs, they wrote out poems, and Basima composed a couplet for the occasion which had a wonderful double play on the word "visitor". I made three pots of tea. When the men pounded on the wall, demanding glasses, clean ash trays, coffee, the women would pause in their merrymaking, look at me sympathetically and shake their heads in a "we know what it is to be a woman and suffer" look.

At eleven o'clock the women rose, apologizing profusely for leaving me while *they* (jerk of the head toward the wall behind which could be heard male voices) were still there.

"We've stayed out much later than we should anyway," explained Sherifa, "but we were enjoying ourselves so much the time seemed short."

She was right. It had been a good evening, though somewhat different from what it had begun to be.

The living room was thick with smoke.

"Have your friends gone home, dear?" Bob inquired sweetly. He was smoking a cigar.

"Did you say your wife was living in purdah?" asked John of Bob.

"Yes, and a good thing too," put in Tim. "Best way to start a marriage. Train 'em up early."

"Of course, of course," said Bob, as though he had planned it all.

Naturally there was no beer left.

22

Jabbar Becomes Engaged

Jabbar had become one of Bob's best friends in El Nahra. In the beginning it had been understandable that Bob should see a lot of him, since Jabbar was the irrigation engineer and Bob was interested in the local irrigation system. But as the months passed, their relationship, despite certain very real obstacles, developed into a deeper friendship. Jabbar held violently anti-Western political views and hence for a long time was highly suspicious of Bob's motives in settling in El Nahra. But he was also a naturally friendly person with a lively mind and a good deal of intellectual curiosity. Like most Iraqis, he had the gift of separating his political views from his personal judgments about people, and gradually he came to realize that Bob's work in El Nahra was truly that of a graduate student doing research for a degree, and had no ulterior political basis.

I, too, saw Jabbar fairly often, for he continued to attempt to bring his sister Khadija out of seclusion; to go on short excursions with us or to eat with us was a good way of accomplishing this. I had always liked Jabbar. He was kind, he was gay and amusing, he had the clean-cut boyish good looks (dark curly hair, regular features) that are attractive to almost everyone. He was much admired and respected in El Nahra, a real achievement in an area where the representatives of the central government were always viewed with some distrust and suspicion. The ancient enmity between town and country still prevailed throughout most of Iraq, and El Nahra was no exception.

True, the tribesmen disapproved of Jabbar's card playing and drinking, but they respected the way in which he administered the irrigation office. Water, quite simply, was life in El Nahra, and the irrigation engineer, in accordance with instructions from Baghdad, decreed when the sluice gates were opened and shut, allowing or stopping the flow of water from the Euphrates into the El Nahra canal. The times of flow were generally set in Baghdad, but there were many day-to-day situations (one farmer complains he is not receiving water because his neighbor upstream is illegally damming a canal) in which Jabbar had to exercise his own personal judgment. In a lesser man this judgment would usually have been used for personal gain, but Jabbar was not that sort of man. He listened to all complaints and adjudicated disputes, often calling on Haji or the mayor to help him in making a decision. In this way he bowed in both directions: to the mayor, who like himself represented the new control of the area by the central government; and to the sheik, the traditional adjudicator of such disputes before the central government had taken over.

Jabbar believed firmly that Iraq needed a revolution to throw out the Nuri Said government, which had been set up by the British. He thought that the feudal estates should be redistributed equally among the people. He knew that Iraq had far to go before it could achieve the technological accomplishments of the West, which would, he thought, provide every Iraqi with a high standard of living. Only under a socialist government, he felt, would technological development be accomplished as quickly as possible. To him, socialism represented the application of science to the problems of society.

Bob would point out that the West's level of technology had been reached very gradually, over a period of years, and that "efficiency" in achieving social change often had very disagreeable consequences for the people who were supposed to benefit.

"We haven't time to wait," Jabbar would reply. "Look at the fellahin. The people are hungry, they need doctors, they need food. What can I tell them about democracy?"

As an engineer, with scientific training, Jabbar was much impressed by the Marxist argument that social change took place automatically and logically. One just established the framework and everything moved along according to scientific plan. Schools, factories and hospitals were built, people automatically accommodated themselves to the changes and the society adjusted to meet the new challenges.

One day Bob told Jabbar about an experience he had had in a distant clan settlement, thinking that it might jar Jabbar from his preoccupation with the Marxist line.

Far out in the middle of the plain, miles from the nearest village, a tiny clan had settled. The two brothers who ruled the clan jointly had received Bob and the sheik's son Nour, who had ridden up on horseback, and had entertained them in their mudhif. Talk turned to politics.

"Why," said the tribesmen, "has it taken Russia only forty years to accomplish what it took the West a hundred and fifty years to do?"

Bob questioned this. He talked about the advantages and disadvantages of authoritarian governments, and mentioned the help Russia had received from America and Europe, who had gone through a long slow process of industrialization and democratization.

"No," the tribesman said, "you people could have done all Russia has done in forty years too if you had had Marx to guide you."

When Jabbar heard this story, he simply said, "Perhaps the man oversimplified the matter, but he is basically right."

So went the argument between Bob and Jabbar, day after day. But politics was not the only subject of their conversation. Jabbar wanted to marry. He was handsome and intelligent and many mothers of his cousins had sought him as a husband of their daughters. But Jabbar had modern ideas, and he wanted to marry a girl who was also modern, who had been educated and who would be his partner in helping to build the new Iraq. As he had cast behind him the families through whom he would have normally negotiated for a bride, he was obliged to turn for help to college friends, especially Naji, a Baghdadi of a middle-class family. More than a year ago Jabbar had told Naji that if he heard of a suitable girl, he should begin negotiations in Jabbar's name.

Late one winter afternoon Bob received a message from Jabbar: "The news from Baghdad is good. Please come over immediately." Bob went. I waited and waited supper and finally went ahead and ate alone. At eleven o'clock I heard the click of the gate latch.

"What happened?" I asked, consumed with curiosity.

Bob sat down and put his feet up. He looked tired and exhilarated at the same time.

"It's quite a story," he said. "I asked him what the news from Baghdad was, but Jabbar said, 'I see, Bob, that you are in a hurry.' I protested, and said that whatever he had to tell me was more important than anything I had to do at the moment. He seemed to debate with himself, and finally I couldn't help it and burst out, 'Are you engaged?'"

"I don't know," Jabbar had replied. "It's very strange really; let's have a drink."

And this is Jabbar's story as he told it to Bob:

My mother, Khadija and I went to Baghdad because Naji had made an appointment for us with the uncle of a very fine girl. The uncle is an inspector in the Ministry of Education, and Naji said the girl was young and pretty, had been to school and came of good family. Naturally I was interested. My mother and Khadija waited at Naji's house while I went alone to visit the uncle.

We drank tea and the girl's uncle said to me, "Your work is finished. Everything is arranged so that you will move to Baghdad immediately."

At this I became angry and said, "I didn't come here in order to be transferred to Baghdad. I came to be married."

The uncle said, "But I thought you agreed that my niece, who is only seventeen, should finish her last year of secondary school."

I said I had agreed to this, that I considered her education very important, but she could finish secondary school in Diwaniya.

However, I felt I had to explain that I was not

ready to move to Baghdad. My present salary would
not permit me to live comfortably there, for rent
alone would take half my wages. I told him I had
bought land in Baghdad and hoped to build a house
there in the future, but that all of this took time and
planning.

The girl's uncle seemed to agree, and when we
parted he said, "Tomorrow I want you to meet the
girl's mother's brother; he is Khalid Amma, the Minister of Foreign Affairs." I was very surprised to hear
this, for Khalid Amma is probably the second man
in Iraq after the Prime Minister. I had known the
girl's family was a good one, but I had not known that
it was so important. I was not too sure I wanted to
marry into this family for fear it might be beyond
me.

My mother and Khadija visited the girl and her
mother. Afterward my mother told me that the girl
was very nice and pretty, but that her mother would
not agree to her daughter's leaving Baghdad. "It
would be best if Naji's mother or some other neutral
person were to discuss the situation with her," she
suggested.

Naji's mother talked to the girl's mother for a very
long time. Sometimes the mother seemed to agree to
let her daughter leave Baghdad and sometimes she
changed her mind. Finally she said she wished to talk
to her sister, and Naji's mother understood that the
girl's mother did not want to decide that day. The
way the situation stands now, Naji will call me as
soon as he knows their answer. . . .

At this point Bob interrupted. "So, Jabbar," he said,
"you're going to marry into a rich and politically conservative family! You and your liberal ideas!"

But Jabbar had just laughed, and said, "When the revolution comes they will be glad to have me in the family."
He continued his story:

The same night after I had seen the girl's uncle,
Naji and I met in a restaurant Abdul Razzak, an old

friend of ours from the engineering college. I was
happy to see him, for he and Naji and I had been like
brothers in college; since I am not often in Baghdad,
I had not seen him for several months. After dinner
Abdul Razzak said he had to speak to me in private
and suggested that we go back to Naji's house.

Naturally I wondered what Abdul Razzak had to
say to me that was so private he could not mention
it before Naji. But Naji is very understanding. He
went away and left us alone in his sitting room. As
soon as the door was closed Abdul Razzak said,
"Would you marry a girl who was twenty-five?"

At first I thought he was joking, because he knew
that Naji had been negotiating with a girl's family
for me and that I was practically married already.
But then I saw that he was not joking and I replied,
"I would marry a girl if she appeared twenty-five exactly or younger. Why do you ask?"

"There is this girl," said Abdul Razzak, "and she
is very wonderful. She is not married because for
seven years her mother had cancer and she was needed
at home. Many men asked for her hand but she refused. Two months ago her mother died."

I was very much surprised, for Abdul Razzak is
not married himself and it is not usual for a bachelor
to know such things about an unmarried girl. "How
do you know about her?" I asked.

"She is my sister," he said.

Then I could not say a word, because according to
our custom a man never talks about his sister to unmarried men, even his closest friends.

Abdul Razzak said, "You are like a brother to me,
Jabbar, and I want you to have my sister, whom I
love very much. I know you and I think she is better
for you and you are better for her than anyone else
could be."

I was very much moved that Abdul Razzak should
trust me in this way. I said, "I am honored that you
speak to me of your sister. I will come to see you tomorrow before leaving."

After Abdul Razzak had gone, I told Naji what he had said. Without hesitating for a moment, Naji advised me to leave the first girl and marry Abdul Razzak's sister. Again I was surprised, for remember, Naji had made all the arrangements for me to marry the first girl and had gone to a lot of trouble for me. I finally confessed to Naji that I did not know what to do.

"But it is a great thing for Abdul Razzak to break with custom so he can be sure his sister will be happy," pointed out Naji.

"Yes," I replied.

"You should be honored."

"I am."

The next morning I telephoned Abdul Razzak and said that if his sister accepts me, I am agreeable.

And that is the end of my story, concluded Jabbar.

"But what about the first girl?" interposed Bob.

"Well," said Jabbar, "her family is very important, but I do not know it well. If Abdul Razzak's sister will have me, it is better that I marry into that family."

"But," said Bob, "won't the first family be angry with you if you break off your arrangement with this girl now?"

"We will never say no exactly," said Jabbar. "When they give their message to Naji, he will find he cannot reach me until he has heard the answer from Abdul Razzak's family. Then if Abdul Razzak's family agrees, my mother will have to postpone several times going to the house of the first girl to hear their answer. And in this way they will know without our saying anything."

"I hope everything will turn out as you wish," said Bob.

Jabbar laughed. "God willing," he said, "but I'm not sure I know what I want. For four years I have had no prospects for marriage and now in a single day I have two."

By the end of the week Abdul Razzak's family had agreed, but the girl, also infected with the new progressive ideas she had picked up in school, had said that she wanted to meet Jabbar before she personally would consent.

At this news Abu Saad, the conservative mayor of El Nahra, said to Jabbar, "You are making a modern marriage, Jabbar; be careful. I don't agree with your methods, but I still hope for your sake that the marriage succeeds."

Jabbar explained to Bob that Abu Saad was older and did not understand that times were changing. Then he went off to Baghdad and stayed for four days. I was almost as impatient as Bob for his return so we could learn the outcome of his suit.

What finally had occurred was completely unexpected. The sister had not liked Jabbar and he did not like her.

"She was too tall and bossy," he said to Bob, "not warmhearted, too intent on her own ideas." The match had been called off, by mutual agreement, and Jabbar was now engaged to the first girl. Late summer had been set for the wedding date.

"Are you happy?" said Bob.

"Well, I don't know," said Jabbar again. "In a way it is too bad about Abdul Razzak's sister, because it would have been a good thing to break with a custom like that. The first girl is very nice, and her family a good one, but yet . . ."

Bob felt, and I agreed with him, that the engagement, which had been conducted in traditional fashion, lacked luster for Jabbar, who thought of himself as a pioneer, a man willing to dare great things in the name of progress. This aspect of his personality cried out for a dramatic gesture to demonstrate his position to the world, a gesture which the marriage to his friend's sister would have been. His present bride-to-be would no doubt prove to be ideal eventually, but at the moment his soul still yearned after the other match, which carried with it, in addition to the untraditional aspect, an aura of romance and friendship and sacred honor.

23

Death in the Tribe and in the Town

A high, keening wail startled me one cold morning, a
wail which was coming nearer and nearer to our house.
I left my cooking, dragged a kitchen chair out to the mud
wall, climbed up and peered through the screen of camel-
thorn. A funeral procession was passing. The coffin,
wrapped in a red-patterned rug, bobbed only a few feet
below the top of my wall, carried aloft on the shoulders
of several men. I wondered who had died, for the sheik
himself and his older brother Abdulla were among the
pallbearers, followed by a large slow-moving crowd of men
and boys. Behind them came the women, their faces
covered with abayahs, wailing as they walked. Their piercing cries rose above all the other sounds of the winter
morning, as though the whole settlement heard and
waited.

While I watched, one of the pallbearers, a very old
tribesman with a short white beard, stumbled and the
coffin bobbed slightly. A boy ran up to steady the old
man at the elbow and the procession turned along the
canal to town, heading for the center of El Nahra where
a taxi would be waiting to take the body to Najaf. Two
men, Bob had said, always accompanied the body to Najaf,
the holy city where all pious Shiites hope to be buried,
staying to see that burial rites were carried out properly,
the body wrapped in its rug to be placed in a tomb or
grave near the mosque. The coffin would return to be used
again.

I could see, from my kitchen chair, people on the canal
road stopping and waiting in silence as the procession
passed by. Halfway to the bridge the women from the
settlement paused and let the coffin continue its slow
journey without them. But, crowded together shivering on

the bank, they continued to wail. I could not see the coffin loaded onto the roof of the taxi, but I knew when it left El Nahra, for the wailing rose higher and higher and then stopped. The women dispersed to their houses in twos and threes. I stayed to watch until the men, too, returned to the settlement, conversing in quiet voices as they passed my wall. A little girl skipped along the path, carrying a bar of soap and a paper funnel full of tomatoes. The grain mill, silenced during the funeral procession, began its strident *wheet-wheet-wheet*, and the sounds of the settlement resumed. It was an ordinary morning once more.

Who had lain in the coffin? Someone important enough to be carried on the shoulders of the sheik of the tribe. Bob said at lunchtime that it had been the wife of Hamid's father, the crippled little old woman had been living in the sheik's compound.

Further details were supplied by Laila, when she came that afternoon with her bag of embroidery. "See, Beeja, we have a set of sheets and pillowcases to do for a girl who is to be married soon. They will pay well for it, almost a pound."

"What about the old woman?"

"Yes, well, she was very old. She just stopped breathing this morning. You remember at the Iid she could hardly sit up to eat her lunch. She was Sheik Abdul Emir's second wife, not Haji's mother; but when the last of her children died about ten years ago, Haji offered her a room in his house. They say she was a very good woman; her mother was from the Bedouin."

"So she wasn't related to Sheik Abdul Emir?"

"Oh yes," said Laila. "Her father was a brother of Abdul Emir's father, so she was his bint-amm. But her mother was from the Bedouin."

There was no ceremony for the old woman beyond the procession. Within a fortnight another death took place and official mourning ceremonies were announced. The mother of Um Saad, the mayor's wife, had died far away in Baghdad after a long illness. When Um Saad returned to El Nahra, her mother had been dead nearly three weeks, and

Um Saad had gone through the ritual mourning period in Baghdad; she was destined to go through it for five days more. Everyone was expected to call at the house of Um Saad and offer condolences. On the third day I put on my darkest clothes under my abayah and set out.

The servant who answered the door at Um Saad's neat house gave me a strange look as I entered. Could Um Saad not be at home? I wondered. Was someone sick? The servant said no, no one was sick, Um Saad was at home. She hesitated a moment, then simply told me to keep my abayah on, and ushered me into the living room.

I was unprepared for what met me. Since Um Saad and I had so much in common, I assumed that our attitudes toward death might also be similar, that this condolence call would be much like the ones I had paid in my own country. I was quite, quite wrong.

All of Um Saad's Western-style furniture had been pushed against the wall, and two lengths of carpeting covered with pillows had been laid out in parallel lines on the floor. Seated cross-legged on these pillows were ten or twelve women, clad in black. Um Saad herself sat at the head of one of the rows; she, too, wore black, and not her smart black suits or dresses, but a long, loose garment. Her hair, usually arranged so fashionably, was bound up in the traditional head scarf and chin scarf. Her face was worn and red-eyed from weeping, and she clutched an abayah around her shoulders. I hardly recognized her, she looked so much like the women who surrounded her.

I hesitated at the entrance, still unsure. Should I go up to Um Saad, take her hand and offer my sympathies? Apparently the answer was no. The servant pointed to the rows of shoes at the door. I took mine off, was guided to an empty pillow and sat down. There were no greetings. The women opposite stared at me in silence and I stared back. After a moment or two one of the women said something, half to herself, half to the group, which I understood as a generalized eulogy of motherhood. The woman seated next to me took it up.

"What is there to replace one's mother? Nothing, nothing," she chanted. "Nothing, nothing."

"True, very true."

"There is nothing to replace a mother."

My neighbor rocked back and forth on her heels and moaned, "Nothing can ever take the place of your mother, Um Saad." She sniffled, sniffled again, and burst into tears.

At this, every woman present began to cry systematically. Most of them threw their abayahs over their heads and sobbed in private, but the woman directly across from me sat impassively while tears ran down her cheeks.

My initial uneasiness had gradually given way to melancholy at the sight of poor Um Saad and the somber grief-stricken women, and I was close to tears when the weeping began to subside. Faces were uncovered, the women dried their eyes and blew their noses, and a silence fell once more on the room.

I sat and waited.

Um Saad began to talk about her mother's illness. It sounded like cancer to me and had gone on for years, she said. The story of the woman's suffering, her rallies and relapses, her sorrow at the death of one son, the departure of another for studies abroad, her courage in the face of great pain were recounted, between sobs, by her daughter.

"And I," finished Um Saad, "was far from her when she needed me most. I could only be there when she was ready to die." She broke down, and the women covered their heads again and wept with her. This time I did, too, covering my head with my abayah and sobbing without restraint. I felt sorry for Um Saad, sorry for her mother, sorry for myself even, far from home and my own mother.

An hour passed. Women rose, one by one, went up to Um Saad, pressed her hand, and departed. Um Saad begged me to stay and have a cup of coffee. Her husband's niece was with her, the dietitian for the teacher-training school dormitory in Diwaniya.

The three of us, over our cups of coffee, held what seemed to me a surprisingly ordinary conversation in view of the wake in which we had just participated.

Um Saad began to talk about the ceremony. She admitted she was near exhaustion. "But it is better this way," she told me. "One must have some time alone after a death, and also time with one's friends and relatives. Time to mourn is necessary, but when this is over I shall be ready to return to work, to everyday things."

24

At Home in El Nahra

After the wake, I was away from El Nahra for more than two weeks; Peter, the third son for our missionary friends in Hilla, was born in late January and I went to stay with Joyce until she was strong enough to manage her household again.

Before I had been home twenty-four hours, Laila came to inquire after my friend and give me all the news.

"How is the American lady? Did she have a boy?"

"Yes."

"El hamdillah," said Laila. "Boys are really the best, Beeja; they can take care of their mother when she's old. What good are girls?"

I was shocked. How could Laila talk like this, with her eight devoted and hard-working sisters? I said so.

"Well, naturally we love each other but we'd all like to have a brother. Wouldn't you?"

I nodded.

"So," said Laila, "and how big was the boy?"

"Seven pounds."

"Seven pounds! That's very small. The child won't live," pronounced Laila.

"What do you mean, Laila?" I retorted, in some heat. "Very small—seven pounds isn't very small! Of course the child will live; it's a very normal size for a child."

Laila looked at me and smiled mischievously. "Don't be so nervous, Beeja—I was only teasing you. Probably," she said, "American babies are smaller than ours if all American ladies are thin like you."

"Probably." How could Laila go on like this, when she knew nothing about it? But I also knew she had long ago spotted my vulnerable areas and, when she was feeling lighthearted, felt no compunction about twitting me. For although she liked me, Laila still thought of me as a protégé with a great deal to learn. Teasing was a good way of exposing my prejudices and sharpening my wits at the same time.

"Don't you want to hear the news?" asked Laila. "Selma is pregnant again."

"Selma?"

"Yes, and she's not too pleased either, but Haji is. If she has a boy, it will be his eighth son. And remember Sahura, who was married last summer? She's home."

"What's the matter with Sahura?" I asked, bringing in a tray with two glasses of tea.

"She had a miscarriage, and was so sick her husband got frightened and brought her all the way home across the plain on horseback. Even my father told my mother he shouldn't have done that, because the long ride made Sahura much worse and maybe she won't be able to have any more children. She just lies on the mat in her mother's house and doesn't want to get up."

I offered Laila a glass of tea. "I'm afraid my visit causes you a great deal of trouble," she murmured dutifully, and I had to offer the tea again before she would take it.

I smiled to myself, thinking that as many times as Laila had drunk tea with me, the custom of protesting was so strong she could not drink tea without exercising that custom.

"We had a fine celebration when Abdulla's youngest boy was circumcised—the three-year-old who is Bassoul's son. The Bedouin second wife. The doctor came from Diwaniya to do it. His father bought him new shoes and a white dishdasha and a brown sweater." Laila paused to put three teaspoons of sugar in her glass, stirred and sipped her tea.

"Bob tells me Ahmed is here," I contributed. Ahmed, Abdulla's oldest son, was in college in Baghdad and was often spoken of as the sheik's successor, especially since Haji's own eldest son Nour had poor health and might not be strong enough to assume the duties of the sheik-ship.

"Yes," said Laila. "He came because Khariya, his

mother, is sick. I think I told you long ago that Khariya sold all her gold jewelry to pay for Ahmed's college expenses."

Ahmed himself had told Bob of his mother's sacrifice. "If it were not for my mother," he had said, "I would never have been able to go to college. Oh, my father is proud of me now, now that I'm an effendi and have an education, but when I finished primary school in El Nahra and wanted to go on, he refused to give me a single fils."

Laila was saying that Ahmed was going to take his mother to the woman doctor in Diwaniya.

"Bob says Ahmed is a very bright boy," I remarked.

"I think he'll probably marry his bint-amm, Haji's daughter Samira, then he will be sure of being sheik," predicted Laila. She dipped an English biscuit carefully into her second glass of tea.

"I've saved the most exciting news for last," added Laila, "but I really shouldn't tell." She sat back and her eyes twinkled. "In fact, I *can't* tell you." She nibbled on the biscuit unconcernedly.

"Oh please, Laila," I begged. Laila was always the bearer of news rather than the subject of it. Looking at her thin little body, the head of fine black hair marred by a certain awkward tilt, the plain face with its intelligent but small eyes, the mobile too-wide mouth, I felt perhaps the Book of Stars was right in telling her she would not marry. She had energy and talent and moderately good health and could support herself. But she had little gentleness and no beauty to make a man draw in his breath at his good luck when he raised her veil on her wedding day. She was too sharp, too curious, too stubborn, difficult as well as plain. She would grow into the role she was beginning to assume already, a small pillar in the women's society, a fountain of gossip and good talk, a woman whose emotion would be expended in bitter enmities as well as deep friendships —with other women.

As I had thought, Laila could not keep this secret with which she had been taunting me. But she evidently felt it worth while to be cautious, for she leaned over and whispered.

"You must not tell anyone, but Haji's son Ahmar, the clerk in Diwaniya, has written to my father and asked for my sister Sanaa's hand in marriage."

"How did you find out?" I asked, surprised that a daughter as young as Laila would be taken into her father's confidence in such a matter.

"My father reads Arabic, but he doesn't write it," explained Laila, "and so he had to ask Basima to write the letter to Ahmar, asking him to wait. And Basima told me in bed last night."

"That's wonderful! But why did your father ask him to wait?"

"Haji is against this marriage. He wants Ahmar to marry one of Abdulla's daughters."

"But Ahmar obviously wants to marry Sanaa."

"Yes," answered Laila patiently, "but my father doesn't want to offend Haji just now. Our land is getting salty and my father may have to buy some of Haji's land before too long."

I offered Laila another glass of tea and thought of Sanaa. Was she destined to be an old maid like her sisters, to sit in her house year after year while her beauty faded? I hoped not. But if land was at stake as well as the uneasy peace among the sheik's brothers, her chances of happiness would not be considered very seriously.

"Promise you won't say a word, Beeja, even to Mr. Bob."

I promised.

All the next week was spent visiting women I had not seen during my absence. Selma certainly did not look happy at the prospect of another child. She seemed listless and her movements were already slow, though she was only four months pregnant. We sat down together on a mat in the sheik's bedroom and Selma produced a small dish of pumpkin seeds.

"It's so hard for me to bear children, Beeja," she said. "Everyone said it would be easy, because I have big hips" (she slapped one broad thigh) "but it wasn't. Then my mother said it would get better with each child, but it hasn't. It's awful every time."

"You must rest after the baby comes," I suggested.

"Oh yes, rest, that's what everyone says." Selma nodded her head. Her usually good-natured face looked bitter for a moment. "Well, I stay in bed for two days after the birth and that's all."

"Only two days?" I echoed foolishly.

"Yes, and even then I have so much work to do when I get up." She closed her eyes.

I touched her knee. "I'm sorry, Selma. I too had always heard it got easier."

Selma opened her eyes and sighed. "And then the midwife has to come and cut my breasts so the milk will come. That's almost worse than having the child."

I was appalled. "Cut your breasts? But why?"

"I don't know, but it's the only way. Otherwise I can't nurse and then what would the baby live on? It would die."

At this I felt completely inadequate, and did not know what to say in sympathy. Now I realize that poor Selma must have had inverted nipples and the midwife was doing the only possible thing, painful though it must have been, to free the milk supply.

Selma looked at my stricken face. "Never mind," she said, trying to smile, "God is good. Maybe it will be easier for you. The children are worth it, el hamdillah. How is your friend in Hilla?"

Two days later I took a present of cloth and went to sit with Sahura, who tried to rise when I came into the small mud-bricked room, but grimaced with pain and lay down again on the mat.

"She shouldn't have lifted those big sacks of grain," said her mother Sheddir in a scolding voice. She sat beside her daughter, spinning wool. "How could you be so stupid, Sahura?"

I glanced at Sheddir in surprise and saw that there were tears in her eyes.

"She is a good girl, wanted to help her husband; she didn't know any better," said Sheddir; she took up from the floor of the room the wooden spindle she had put down when I entered and resumed her spinning. "It was a boy," she said, looking down; her hands moved quickly, rubbing the threads of wool together and moving the spindle so that the thin strand of yarn grew longer and longer.

I walked to Khadija's house, and she told me that Jabbar was bringing his bride Suheir home from Baghdad in July. "You won't be here," she said.

"No, I guess not," I replied. "Come," I suggested to change the subject, "let's go visit the schoolteachers."

Little girls in their white-collared black uniforms were streaming out of the school gate when we arrived. Hind and Aziza were going from room to room gathering up the day's records while the janitor swabbed the floors of the halls. We were taken into the teachers' office and Hind ordered coffee.

Aziza looked thin and tired. Remembering her animation and enthusiasm when she had arrived in El Nahra last fall, I wondered. Had she been ill? Had life been too hard on her in this lonely village?

Hind, always quick to sense a mood, had seen me look at Aziza. "Beeja," she announced, "this girl works all the time. She doesn't have the faintest idea of how to play." She laughed, not pleasantly, but Aziza did not join her. I knew Aziza was a hard worker and a serious girl. Hind, on the other hand, managed to take life very lightly and do with it just about what she pleased. Had the frivolous headmistress and the serious junior teacher clashed head-on, and the junior come out the loser, unable to take the mocking and the ridicule? From Aziza's set face, it seemed so.

"How are your sisters in Diwaniya?" I asked Aziza.

She turned and gave me all her attention. "I haven't seen them for a long time, but I can imagine what they are doing. It is time to think of spring. My mother always had us take out all the blankets and our woollen clothes and air them carefully. Afterward we would sit together and mend everything, and then we would put the woollens away with cloves in each layer, to keep out the moths. I remember mother made anise tea for us to drink while we mended," she added wistfully.

"Come, come, Aziza, don't talk as though your poor

sisters were dead," teased Hind, and Khadija laughed
obligingly. "Tell us about Jabbar's bride, Khadija—is she
pretty? What kind of gold pieces did she choose for her
wedding jewelry?"

By the end of the afternoon Aziza had begun to relax
and Hind produced a book from under a pile of papers on
her desk. It was a volume of modern Iraqi poetry and
Hind chose some of the love poems to read aloud. She
read very well. Suddenly she slammed the book shut.

"Read my fortune in the coffee cup, Aziza," she said.
"Tell me when I shall marry."

The next morning Hussein's wife Sajjida came to see
me. Her oldest girl had been sick for a long time with
cough, but was better now. I went in the evening to Mohammed's, where Sherifa made lemon tea and we sat
around the charcoal brazier telling stories about the past.
Sherifa had a two-week-old lamb which she had bought to
raise and sell in springtime. Bleating, it tottered about the
room on fragile legs until Sherifa persuaded it to settle in
her lap, where she fed it milk from an old medicine bottle
with a nipple. Afterward Sherifa and Medina took down
the lantern and walked me home. Soon, however, we blew
out the lantern, for a full moon rode high in the wide,
clear sky. Against that sky the palms were cut out dark and
clear, and the camel-thorn topping the walls became a
strange, intricate pattern of decorative filigree. Pale light
dappled the mud houses, and when we turned from the
alley toward my house the moon was reflected, like a
watery balloon, in the still waters of the canal.

That night I sat in my kitchen and wondered at the
changes in me. We were scheduled to leave El Nahra
within a month, and I found I was avoiding the thought.
During the last year and a half my life had slowly but
surely become intertwined with the lives of my women
friends, and I was surprised at the depth of my feelings.

When Bob came in from the mudhif, I told him. He
looked at me quizzically. "I feel the same way," he said,
"but I have always thought, from the beginning, that our
situation here had much more to offer me than you. We

have to go, though, because I have lots of library research to do in Baghdad before we leave for home in June."

"Yes, I understand."

"We could come back for the big feast in May, if you like," suggested Bob, "the Iid after Ramadan. Why don't we? By that time we'll both be more accustomed to the idea of going, and it'll be easier to say our last goodbyes after we've been away for a while."

"That's a fine idea." The more we talked of it, the better we felt, and by bedtime we were already planning the presents we would bring back with us.

The truck had drawn up outside the gate and men were carrying our bags and baskets and bundles out the door. The little house was stripped almost clean, as bare as when we had arrived more than a year and a half ago. In the kitchen in lonely splendor sat the refrigerator, our hospitality present to Sheik Hamid. The furniture he had lent us was still in the living room, but the big wardrobe with the double mirror now reposed in Mohammed's house, our contribution to Mohammed's wedding savings. The stove and the plastic chairs and the aluminum folding table were tied on top of the truck. Children streamed in and out of the open garden and Laila stood beside me holding a present, a two-kilo can of rice, cleaned rice. I looked at the rice, trying to figure just about how many hours of patient labor it had taken the girls to pick out the straw and chaff and tiny particles of dirt. I said I could not think of a nicer present.

Laila wiped her nose. "You won't come back for the Iid," she said accusingly.

"Oh yes I will. Mr. Bob says we will and so we will."

"No, you won't." She wiped her nose again and I held my breath, afraid of what she or I might do next. At that moment Sherifa arrived with another present, a can of sweets—her mother's specialty, made with milk and pistachio nuts.

"Well, if you do come for the Iid," went on Laila importantly, "you must stay at our house, not at Haji

Hamid's." She launched into a long account of the comforts of her house as compared with that of Haji's.

Sherifa and Laila and I checked the two rooms once more to make certain nothing had been left behind. A pile of pumpkin-seed husks in one corner of the living room was all that remained of my party the night before. I had told Laila to spread the word that Bob would be in the mudhif that last evening and I would welcome any woman who might come. It had been a gay party; we had consumed several kilos of pumpkin seeds, five packages of cigarettes and countless glasses of tea.

"Come on, B.J., the driver is waiting," Bob called from the gate. At the sound of his voice, Laila and Sherifa instinctively covered their faces.

Mohammed came running up the path; he was coming to Baghdad to work for us until June. His freshly pressed kaffiyeh and his agal seemed set at exactly the right angle, but being Mohammed, he could not resist adjusting them once more. "*Yallah,*" he said. "Everything is now ready."

There was no time for extensive farewells. I climbed up beside Bob in the driver's seat. We had hired an entire truck and I saw that it was full not only with our possessions, but with townspeople and tribesmen taking advantage of a free ride to Baghdad. The sun was bright and the children ran after us, shouting, as the truck turned the corner and swung out of town along the gleaming canal.

PART VI

25

Back to Baghdad

We settled in Baghdad with a friend who was doing research in Middle Eastern history. She had rented a *mushtamal* or garden cottage in the southern residential area of Baghdad. Since the mushtamal was two stories high, we were able to divide space fairly well and sharing rent and food expenses was a saving for all of us.

Mohammed did not stay after all. For the first two or three days in Baghdad he walked around in a constant state of contained excitement. Everything was new and wonderful to him. He went twice to pray at the shrine of Khadhimain. But gradually he became more and more glum. We knew he was lonely without friends or relations, but there was nothing we could do about it. When we sent him shopping, he would come back without the things we wanted, complaining he didn't know the suq and couldn't be sure which merchants were honest. He got lost several times trying to find our house. After living all his life in a place where he was related to many of the residents and knew everyone else, to be cast adrift in a strange place where no one recognized or cared about him was a frightening experience for Mohammed.

At the end of the second week he asked if he might go home. Bob gave him a month's wages, helped arrange for him to get an official work permit for future use, and wrote a letter to Jabbar asking him to remember Mohammed if any jobs arose in the near future within the bureaucracy of El Nahra. The morning he left, Mohammed was a new man. He had bathed and wore a clean aba and kaffiyeh; I had seen him ironing the kaffiyeh the night before. "I don't know where the ironing man's shop is," he had said defensively. Now his few belongings were tied in a bundle and he could hardly wait to go. El Nahra had little to offer him economically, but there at least he knew who and where he was.

Abdulla's son Ahmed was finishing college in Baghdad, as was Hadhi, Sheik Hamid's son. Hadhi and Sheik Hamid had quarreled over politics and were barely on speaking terms; Hadhi's mother Bahiga, like Ahmed's mother Khariya, sent him money. Perhaps this common bad experience with their fathers had drawn the boys together. At any rate they were close friends, and they took Bob to dinner one night. Bob came home in a bemused state.

"The two boys were really going at it politically," he told me. "Hadhi sounds as if he has been given the treatment by the local Commies. A bright boy. I wonder what will happen to him. Ahmed is bright too but not so interested in politics. He knows he's being considered for the sheikship, but he has rather mixed feelings about the position. Says he's going to get a job teaching and stay in Baghdad. On the other hand he talks about getting married to one of Sheik Hamid's daughters—Sabiha, I think he said her name was. Which one is she?"

"Not Sabiha," I said immediately. "He must mean Samira."

"Samira, Samira," repeated Bob. "No, that wasn't the name, I'm sure."

"It must be, because Samira is the really beautiful daughter, the one with the two marvelous braids of black hair. Without her head scarf and chin scarf, with her ruddy skin and those black braids, she looks like the daughter of Pocahontas. But Sabiha—Sabiha is silly."

Bob thought a moment. "Who has the lighter skin?" he asked.

"Sabiha, but—"

"Ah-ha," said Bob. "That's the reason. A matter of prestige."

I exploded. "That's ridiculous, Bob. Samira has everything: beauty, a warm heart, intelligence. Sabiha may be light-skinned but she certainly has nothing else to offer."

"Well, that's the most important thing to Ahmed, apparently."

"But if this system of marriage weren't operating, if Ahmed could meet both girls, I'm sure he'd—"

"He'd do exactly the same thing," finished Bob. "You forget he grew up with the sheik's children, and knew both Samira and Sabiha very well until they were eleven or twelve. He knows what he wants and that's that."

I still felt annoyed at Ahmed, but I knew it was mostly for Samira's sake. If Ahmed did marry Sabiha, this eliminated one of the best marriage possibilities for Samira, who, as a sheik's daughter, had a very narrow range of acceptable husbands.

Jabbar came to Baghdad whenever he could to see his fiancée Suheir. The couple was allowed to see each other and enjoy a brief period of courtship, for the official betrothal ceremony, the "signing of the book," had already taken place. Although the consummation of the marriage was yet to come, Jabbar and Suheir were now legally man and wife, as only under extremely unusual circumstances was a marriage contract broken after the signing of the book.

One weekend he brought his sister Khadija to Baghdad and we lunched together at a fairly secluded upstairs restaurant. Neither girl wore the abayah and Khadija was very nervous. She sat self-consciously at the table, picking at the buttons on her coat, and every so often casting sidelong glances at Suheir or me to see how we were handling the food.

Over kebab and *tikka*, flat bread and pickles, Jabbar and Bob discussed politics. Suheir displayed a gold bracelet, a gift from Jabbar, which they had bought together that morning in the gold market on River Street.

A plump, pretty girl well aware of her charms, Suheir teased Jabbar constantly and unmercifully. Occasionally he would actually blush and Khadija would clap her hands in amusement. Khadija seemed fascinated by Suheir, and Suheir was working hard to ingratiate herself with Khadija —wisely enough, since the two women would be living in the same house before long. Khadija apparently was won over, but knowing the moods of this unhappy, uncertain girl, I wondered.

Suheir, by a single gesture, commanded the conversation. "Shall we tell them, Jabbar?" she asked.

"Tell them what?"

"About our plan." She blinked her eyes coquettishly.

"Oh yes," replied Jabbar. He looked suddenly delighted. "Suheir is going to educate the women of El Nahra away from the abayah." He laughed aloud.

Khadija looked shocked. "You mean she is not going to wear the abayah?"

"That's right, I'm not," answered her future sister-in-law. "And you can take it off too. We'll show those villagers won't we, Jabbar?" She leaned forward and almost, but not quite, touched his hand.

Jabbar sat back in his chair and pulled hard on his cigarette. "You see, Bob," he said, "here is a true daughter of modern Iraq. Together we will destroy these outmoded customs."

Bob and I glanced at each other. We seemed to be thinking the same thing, that this, at last, was the dramatic gesture Jabbar had been seeking, the gesture of defiance and pride which had been lacking in the traditional marriage arrangements.

Jabbar had eyes only for Suheir, who was leaning forward whispering something to him. He laughed again. I smiled to myself, thinking that probably he would be happy with Suheir, and then I caught sight of Khadija who was eyeing the couple, a stricken and unpleasant look on her face, the look of a frightened rabbit. At that moment I hoped fervently that Jabbar would not insist on his shrinking little sister's assuming the freedom he was willing to give her. Khadija's daughter perhaps might be comfortable without the abayah, but I doubted that Khadija ever would be.

Sayid Muhsen also came to Baghdad. One of Bob's close friends, he was the leader of a clan settlement an hour or more away from El Nahra. It was Sayid Muhsen who had built the school in his settlement and personally petitioned the Ministry of Education for a teacher. It was in Sayid Muhsen's school that boys and girls attended classes to gether. Sayid Muhsen had other modern ideas. He had had four children in four years and felt it was time to stop, or he would be unable to provide a decent living for his family. Accordingly, he had taken his wife to a Diwaniya doctor and asked for contraceptives; the doctor had given his wife a device to wear, he told Bob, but it had not worked, since she had had a fifth child recently. Besides, his wife complained that the device was very painful to wear. Also it had been expensive, five Iraqi pounds.

At this Bob had become very angry at the cavalier way his friend had been treated, and told Sayid Muhsen that if he came to Baghdad with his wife, Bob and I would personally take them to the American Hospital to see the resident woman doctor.

Accordingly, one sunny April day we went trooping to the hospital. Bob and Sayid Muhsen and five of his male relatives sat on one side of the long, white-walled waiting room. I sat on the other side with his wife, who was heavily veiled from head to foot. Whether the five male relatives were there for Sayid Muhsen's moral support, or whether they came as an honor guard for his wife, we never knew.

Fortunately the woman doctor at the American Mission Hospital was a sympathetic and understanding person as well as a competent physician. She spoke very little Arabic and had an Iraqi nurse to interpret. I explained the situation first and she asked to see the expensive device. When Sayid Muhsen's wife produced it from some inner fold of her voluminous abayah, the doctor's eyes widened and she, too, began to look very angry.

"That is an instrument for examination purposes only," she said. "You mean you actually wore this thing?" she asked, turning directly to Sayid Muhsen's wife and forgetting she knew no English. The Iraqi nurse hurried to translate.

"I wore it for several months," answered Muhsen's wife. "The doctor told me to. But it didn't help, because I had another baby anyway."

After this had been translated, the doctor opened and shut her mouth. She cleared her throat and began a little

talk about the principle of contraceptives, the nurse inter-
preting as she went along. "Now," she said to me, "would
you mind leaving?" I explained to Sayid Muhsen's wife
that I would be outside the door.

I waited for a good quarter of an hour, while the men
opposite shifted uneasily in their seats and I, watching
them, grew restless myself. Eventually the doctor came out
and asked me to have the husband come in. I signaled to
Bob and he brought Sayid Muhsen over. Sayid Muhsen
disappeared into the doctor's office. In another quarter of
an hour the couple reappeared and we left together.

At the door we parted in some confusion and without
a word. The male relatives went ahead, Sayid Muhsen
shook Bob's hand, was uncertain what to do about me
since we had never spoken before, did nothing therefore
but turn on his heel, say goodbye to Bob and indicate that
his wife was to follow. She turned her heavily veiled person
vaguely in my direction, as though she were about to say
something but thought better of it since Bob stood beside
me and there was no uncertainty at all in her mind
about him. She turned and fled. Later Bob told me that
Sayid Muhsen had been impressed with the efficiency and
politeness with which the affair had been conducted, as
well as with the reasonable size of the bill. He had paid
only two pounds for everything.

When Sheik Hamid came to town for the spring session
of Parliament, Bob went to see him in his hotel. He returned with an invitation. Haji had expressed a desire to
take us to dinner at the Auberge, a fancy and expensive
Baghdad night club.

"I've inquired," he told Bob, "and I've been told that
this is a very reputable place. You don't need to worry
about taking your wife there."

Sheik Hamid would never have taken any of his own
wives or daughters to a night club or to any public gathering. He would take me, but only if the place was respectable. I was touched by the sheik's consideration, and
relieved to find that he would accept our foreign ways in
this new setting.

That evening the sheik's driver called for us in the Oldsmobile. When we climbed the steps of the Auberge, we found the sheik and his oldest son Nour already present in the small, well-appointed but still empty bar.

Sheik Hamid was in good spirits. Having spent his summers in Lebanon, he was, I think, pleased to be able to show us that he was conversant in many of the ways of the West. He ordered fresh lemonade all around, and afterward a dinner of soup, roast beef, potatoes, green beans and salad. He took a table on a slightly raised platform which was somewhat removed from the big dance floor and its surrounding tables. This way we were not inordinately conspicuous to the rest of the clientele, which at that early hour was still small. A trio played softly in the background and I had settled down to enjoy our meal when I became aware of how excruciatingly embarrassed Nour was. It occurred to me that not only had Nour probably never been in a restaurant like the Auberge before, but also that this was one of the few times he had eaten with his father and perhaps the first time he had eaten with any woman, much less a Westerner, since he had been a child at his mother's side. His father confirmed this in the next moment.

"It's time Nour learned some foreign ways," said Sheik Hamid, "well enough to get along, anyway, don't you think?"

Nour smiled dutifully. "Yes, Father," he said, although he could hardly have felt more at ease by having his lack of experience pointed out to us.

Being with his father, Nour was duty-bound to be silent except when spoken to, a duty which he fulfilled that evening to the letter. But he seemed totally bewildered by the food and table service and kept glancing at Bob to see what was to be done with the array of spoons, forks and knives arranged in an unknown pattern around his plate. I kept comparatively quiet myself, Bob volunteered a few jokes and Haji responded with some of his own.

The dinner passed in relative calm and we were relaxing over coffee when the trio finished and a large dance band came on. As we ate, more and more people had slowly been filtering into the Auberge and now many of the small tables around the dance floor were occupied. When the band started off, brassy and loud, a few couples ventured out to dance, in rapid succession, a rhumba, a waltz and a slow fox trot. A Charleston retired most of the dancers, but three active couples remained and Haji laughed uproariously at their antics.

"You see," he pointed out to Nour, "that's the sort of woman you find in Lebanese night clubs. You can always tell a woman of that type by the kind of clothes she wears." He glanced briefly at me, and then jerked his head in the general direction of the dance floor.

Nour followed his father's gaze and his eyes widened. I, too, followed Haji's eye, from my own reasonably conservative dress (high neck, three-quarter sleeves) to the décolleté cocktail dresses on the dance floor. And suddenly seeing through the eyes of Sheik Haji Hamid the couples gyrating frenziedly around, the women in tightly fitted low-cut dresses kicking and twisting in time to the music, I was embarrassed for my countrywomen. I was embarrassed partly because they appeared ridiculous and partly because of what I knew the sheik was thinking of them.

We could never have explained to Sheik Hamid that the majority of those lightly clad, madly pivoting women on the dance floor were respectable married women dancing with their husbands, or proper embassy secretaries out on a date. He simply would not have believed us. Just how firmly fixed his ideas were we learned by his attitude toward us in relation to the activity on the dance floor. It did not occur to him that we might want to dance, or that Bob and I were ever participants in merrymaking of this sort. He talked to Bob and Nour in confiding tones, as though he were an old roué introducing his sons to the fleshpots of Monte Carlo.

I suppose I was flattered, for I had apparently shown, by my restrained conduct in El Nahra, that all Western women were not, per se, wanton, but I had done this by generally observing Hamid's own customs toward women. How many years would it have taken, I wondered, to con-

vince Sheik Hamid that I was a respectable woman if I
had not worn the abayah in El Nahra, if I had sat with
the men in the mudhif, ridden horseback in blue jeans
and wandered through the suq and the village as I pleased?
How many years would it take, I wondered, before the
two worlds began to understand each other's attitudes to-
wards women? For the West, too, had a blind spot in this
area. I could tell my friends in America again and again
that the veiling and seclusion of Eastern women did not
mean necessarily that they were forced against their will
to live lives of submission and near-serfdom. I could tell
Haji again and again that the low-cut gowns and brandished freedom of Western women did not necessarily
mean that these women were promiscuous and cared nothing for home and family. Neither would have understood,
for each group, in its turn, was bound by custom and background to misinterpret appearances in its own way.

At this moment Haji Hamid leaned over and nudged
Bob, indicating a particularly curvaceous blonde in black
who was being whirled around by a young Iraqi somewhat
shorter than herself.

"There," he said, "look at that." From his tone, he might
as well have said, "Look at that tart and her client."

To my horror I recognized a girl Bob and I both knew
well. Her partner was also an acquaintance of ours.

The gulf that divided us from Haji Hamid never seemed
greater to me than at the moment when I realized that
we could not introduce him to our friend. He had already
made up his mind about her, and the fact that we knew
her would detract from our reputation, not improve hers.

The sheik must have caught a hint of my consternation,
although I tried very hard to act as though nothing had
happened. Yet I was terrified that the girl would come
over, to confront us, as it were, with the absurdity of our
position. Perhaps I could do what such a situation demanded, but I was not sure; I was afraid that our evening
would be ruined and something else indefinable spoiled
forever.

"I think your wife is tired, Bob," said Haji. He consulted
his gold wrist watch. "We should go home."

Home we went, avoiding the dance floor on the way to the door. We were not noticed. The Oldsmobile delivered us to our mushtamal, where with many thanks and a great sense of relief we bade Haji Hamid and Nour good night.

We talked until very late that night. The dinner party had dramatized, a little more effectively than we might have wished, the difference between the sheik's world and ours. It had also made us realize that our presence in El Nahra had done little to resolve those differences. We admitted to each other that we had both had somewhat irrational and idealistic notions of being examples, of bridging the gap between one set of attitudes and another. Now, of course, we knew we had not basically changed anyone's attitude, except perhaps our own. With our friends in El Nahra we had established personal ties, as individual human beings. This was all we should have hoped for, and perhaps it was enough.

26

Leave-taking

We were on pilgrimage ourselves, back to El Nahra to celebrate the feast with our friends. Instead of the knocking train, we had allowed ourselves the luxury of a taxi ride from Baghdad, and the car sped through a countryside that was shorn and green, for the harvest was nearly finished. In a few fields we passed, clouds of chaff still rose into the air from the threshing circles, where the fellahin led their strings of donkeys around and around to trample the wheat and the barley. We knew that the harvest was finished in the area around El Nahra, because Nour had written Bob that the annual division of grain between Sheik Hamid and his sharecroppers had already taken place. The yield had been good this year. It was May 1958. In Baghdad, pundits declared the undercurrents of revolution stemmed by the news from the countryside. In a good year, revolution was less likely. But we did not think much about revolution that late spring morning. After three months of hard paper work in Baghdad, the prospect of a holiday with the tribe in the peace of El Nahra was very inviting.

The problem of accommodations had been neatly solved, and what I had feared would become a quarrel between Selma and Laila did not even develop. Laila wrote to say that since we were guests of the tribe, it was only right that we stay with Sheik Hamid and his family. She and her sisters would expect me for lunch. Bob would sleep in the mudhif and I was to be housed in the harem —but where, I wondered? The apartments of Bahiga and Kulthum were too small, and they could not put me in Selma's own rooms because that was where Haji slept.

"Are you looking forward to going back?" asked Bob.

"Of course." I spoke more sharply than I intended and he looked down at me.

"You don't have to be so snappish," he said. "I just wondered how you felt. After three months of city living, it'll be quite a change. You haven't forgotten how scared you were when we came down the first time, have you? I was really worried about you."

"No, I haven't forgotten." But it seems so long ago, I thought, when I was somebody else and hardly knew Bob. I looked back at my old self patronizingly, mentally patting that frightened bride on the head. Poor thing. She certainly had been worried and unsure of herself. I could still recall vividly my overpowering embarrassment as I had sat without abayah in the Diwaniya station and people had pointed at me. The frustration of not being able to understand what was said to me. That circle of unfriendly women in Selma's quarters, whispering behind their abayahs and giggling—at me? Sheik Hamza goggling. Sheddir spitting out my good bread on the floor. And the chastening realization that the women had pitied me. Pitied *me*, college-educated, adequately dressed and fed, free to vote and to travel, happily married to a husband of my own choice who was also a friend and companion. The idea of a husband as friend had never occurred to my friends in El Nahra, and as for the rest, none of it meant much beside the facts.

"Poor girl," Kulthum had said, summing it all up. No mother, no children, no long hair, thin as a rail, can't cook rice, and not even any gold! What a sad specimen I must have seemed to them. I smiled again at my image. What kind of charity combined with compassion had persuaded them to take me in?

Bob spoke again. "What are you thinking about?" he asked.

"Only that the first trip seems ages ago," I answered. "It seems quite natural to be going back. I've missed my friends."

Bob put his arm around me. "I feel the same way," he said.

By the time we reached Diwaniya, the wind had come

p and the clear sky was darkened by a fine cloud of rolling
ust and sand. A strange brown pall hung over the country-
de. Shopkeepers in Diwaniya were slamming down their
etal shutters and animals were being herded home
rough the streets, ominous signs that this would be a
ig storm.

"What a shame," said Bob, echoing my own thoughts.
The feast will be ruined."

We transferred to another taxi and for the last time
eaded out across the plain to El Nahra. The shrine of
bu Fadhil was shrouded in a mist of dust, and the hori-
on was gradually disappearing as the wind strengthened
nd raised more and more sand. In an hour, when we
eared El Nahra, the clump of palms at the edge of the
llage was only a vague dark mass in the moving swirling
louds of dust. We drove down the main street just in
me to see the fluorescent lights turned on, although it
as scarcely four o'clock in the afternoon. The canal was
urky in the dulled light. Few people were out by the
me we turned the last corner and passed the wooden
ate in our wall, locked and double-locked against intrud-
rs, I saw in sorrow. We were deposited in front of the
udhif; here sand beat against the taxi like fine hail and
ehind the huge arch of the mudhif the shadowy palms
ere tossing back and forth on slender trunks.

"We're going to get the full blast of the storm here,"
id Bob. "The wind has a clear field all the way across
om the desert. I hope it lets up soon. Oh look, there's
Jour coming down from the mudhif. I'd better go."

"Have a good time," added Bob, and he was gone, run-
ing back with Nour to the shelter of the mudhif.

Ali, the old gardener, helped me out of the taxi and for
e first time the full force of the wind hit me, whipping
y abayah around my legs and flinging sand into my face.
pulled my abayah close for protection, Mohammed took
y bag and I was ushered into the compound.

"She's come!" shouted a figure, whom I recognized in
e dimness as Amina. She dashed forward. "Beeja is
ere!" she called.

"Ahlan wusahlan," said a voice. Samira, I thought.

"*Ahlan, ahlan,*" another called. Bahiga.

"Beeja," cried Laila and took both my hands. She stoo off and looked me over quizzically. "You came back."

"Of course I came back," I said, trying to be matter-o fact and smiling at that sharp sidelong look of Laila's.

Fatima shook my hand. "We told you, Laila," sh chided.

Kulthum's voice was heard scolding. "What are yo standing out there in the wind for? Can't you see tha Beeja has come a long way in this awful dust and is tired Bring her inside." She emerged, smiling all over he wrinkled face, the three blue tattoo dots still clear in th cleft of her chin. "Come, my dear," she said, taking me t the arm and leading me through the court.

I sat down in Haji Hamid's bedroom, the same pir satin bedspread covering the gilt four-poster, the neat folded bedding piled to the ceiling, the oil painting c the mosque in sunlight, photographs of Sheik Hamid an Sheik Abdul Emir, and of King Feisal I on horsebac with the Iraqi flags crossed above him. It seemed ve pleasant and very familiar.

"She did come back," repeated Laila.

"Well, we thought you'd *want* to come back," Kulthu said, "but we knew you couldn't come unless Mr. Bc brought you, so we couldn't be sure."

Selma bustled in out of breath and wrung my han violently. She was very pregnant and very fat; the sean of her ordinarily loose dress appeared to be at burstir point.

"See how big Selma is! Her baby should be enormous Medina had followed Selma into the room and rapped h smartly on the behind. The company laughed delighted and Selma turned and tweaked Medina's abayah.

"Have some respect for pregnant women," she sa lightly.

"*You* have some respect, my girl," retorted Medina, "f old age. I'm so old I can say anything I want. Ah me, bu I'm tired, I have to admit it." She advanced into th room, erect and graceful still, carrying herself so that h rusty black garments billowed behind her like a cou

train. She sat down and took my hand. Hers was bony
and warm. "How are you, Beeja?" she asked.

"Ya Selma," she called, "ya wife of Sheik Hamid," in-
flecting her words in such a way that one could not help
but laugh, "do you think the house of your illustrious
husband is bounteous enough to offer me a cigarette?"
Selma threw one to her, took one herself and sat down
with us.

"Where's Sherifa?" I asked.

"She'll be coming as soon as she's milked the cow. She
knows you're here."

"Tea, Amina," said Selma, "and then, Beeja, we'll show
you where you're to sleep."

Amina brought a huge tray. The little glasses in their
china saucers clinked and tinkled as we stirred the sugar.

"I'm very glad to be back," I said.

After tea the group escorted me to my quarters, the
storeroom just off Selma's court which had once been
Bahiga's bedroom, when she was still bearing children for
Haji. Clean mats covered the floor, and furniture had been
moved in, a bed and a cupboard, a washstand, a table
and an armchair. Samira walked around the room, touching each piece of furniture and telling me where it came
from, while the company in admiration kept exclaiming
"Al-lah!" Laila pointed out that it was our old bed they
had brought in for me.

"So you'll be more comfortable," explained Kulthum.
"Nour thought of the table, because he knows you write
letters and do things like that. Samira and I brought the
mirror, and Selma said they should bring the armchair,
too." She turned to me expectantly.

For a moment I did not know what to say. I was moved
by the women's thoughtfulness and concern for my comfort. I was also struck, for some reason, by the armchair.
How I had fought, long ago, to sit on the floor with the
women rather than in that lonely armchair in Haji's
room. My friends, in trying to provide for my needs, had
again pointed up the basic dissimilarities in habits which
would always exist between us. But now it no longer mat-
tered. I felt they had prepared the room and made it

comfortable for me out of mutual respect and affection, and beside that reality, our differences seemed unimportant.

My hesitation was misinterpreted. Selma said anxiously, "What's wrong? Is there something we've forgotten?"

"Oh no, it's lovely, thank you all." I paused, and decided to blurt it out. "I didn't say anything because I couldn't."

Blank faces greeted me.

Oh no, I thought, let us not have our communications break down now. I rushed on, "I mean I'm so glad to be with you again that I couldn't speak for a moment."

Still no comprehension. I began to feel quite desperate as I searched the faces of my friends. It was Selma, as she had done so many times before, who saved me. She had narrowed her eyes suddenly and I saw that she had grasped the sense of what I was trying to say. She spoke quickly to the women and they turned back to me smiling.

"*Ahlan wusahlan*," they said. "*Ahlan. Ahlan.*"

A sudden gust of wind whipped the door open and distributed a swirl of sand about the room. The women rushed to slam the door shut. "You'll be much more comfortable than Mr. Bob," Laila pointed out. "The mudhif is full of dust." She settled herself with the other women beside me on the mat-covered floor. Shut in from the storm, we felt safe and well tended.

"*Shlonich*, Beeja, how are you?" asked Alwiyah.

"Well, thanks be to God. And how are you?"

"Well, thanks be to God."

"I'm afraid I cause trouble by my presence," I offered.

"No, no, we are honored to have you visit us," returned Alwiyah.

"*Shlonich*, Beeja?" asked Samira, and so we went, reestablishing our relationship in the formal phrases of custom and ceremony.

"Do you remember the bird that hit you in the head?" Laila giggled.

I nodded.

"Has Mr. Bob seen any birds like that in Baghdad?"

Laila watched me, winking and nodding at the other women.

"Not yet," I smiled, "but maybe there are some there, who knows? Have you seen any here, Laila?"

Laila was taken by surprise. "Who, me? I'm not even married." The women whooped. Laila looked at first disconcerted, but gradually her expression changed to one of pleasure, and she sat nodding happily, presumably, I thought, in satisfaction at my good performance.

Nothing had changed. I might never have been away. We talked, as we had talked before, of children and marriage, of cooking, of things that had happened while I had been gone; they were gradually easing me back into my old life here.

I was awakened by the sound of children laughing. At first I couldn't imagine where I was—gray mud walls high around me, unfamiliar quilts and embroidered sheets, closed wooden shutters admitting thin bars of daylight through the cracks. Then I remembered and rose, a muddy taste in my mouth from the dust that had sifted in during the night, under the door and through cracks in the shutters and walls. The smell of it was still thick in my closed room. Bob had probably had a miserable night lying in the near-open in the mudhif.

It was the first day of the feast. When I opened my door, the wind had died and the sun was shining weakly through the dust that still drifted gently in the air. In the court all of the children of the compound were frolicking, gay in their new clothes. A crowd had gathered around a baby gazelle which one of the boys was coaxing to drink from a bottle; Selma's son Feisal picked up the milk-white kid and brought it over. He set it down on its gangly legs and the kid's eyes, brown and much too big for its small pointed face, focused uncertainly on me.

"Abdulla found it in the bush," Feisal said.

"Its mother was dead," explained Abbas. "Abdulla heard the baby crying when he was out hunting."

Amina advanced with a tray. "Out of the way, out of

the way," she hollered at the children. "Do you want me to slop the Sitt's breakfast tea?"

Grinning, she set the tray on the wooden table, wiped her hands on her dusty abayah and held them out to me. "*Ayyamak sa'ida*, Beeja," she said.

"*Ayyamak sa'ida!*" More of my housemates were entering the room, dropping their clogs on the doorstep as they came forward to shake hands for the feast.

Selma said, "*Enshallah walad*, Beeja [God willing, you will have a boy]."

"Do, Beeja," urged Laila. "After all, you've been married two years now. You don't want Mr. Bob to divorce you, do you?"

"When she gets back to America and is with her mother, then she'll have a boy, *enshallah*," pronounced Kulthum. She patted my knee.

To turn the attention away from myself, I said, "Selma, it is you we're thinking about. *Enshallah* you will have a boy."

"It'll be another girl," put in Selma quickly. "Just because Haji especially wants a boy this time."

"No, no Selma, don't talk like that," the women shouted.

Selma raised her heavy bulk from the floor with some difficulty. "Time to get back to work," she reminded the group.

Soon the women were busy with preparations for the gigantic noon meal to be served in the mudhif. The butcher had come and gone while I slept. Kulthum sat in her old place, cutting up the slippery meat while the younger daughters pared vegetables and the children ran errands between the compound and the mudhif. Laila and I went up on the roof again to watch the gathering of the tribesmen. I could see Bob, looking a bit rumpled from his night in the mudhif, standing with Sheik Hamid and Nour. The men of the El Eshadda circled in the figures of the hosa, paused to chant their poems of praise to the sheik and to the tribe and raised their rifles for a salute. The shots rang out in the hot, dusty air. In a few minutes we were called down to help load the trays, and then we returned to the roof to watch the procession to the mudhif, men balancing on their heads the heavy trays of rice, meat, stew—enough food for two hundred people.

The next day I lunched at Moussa's house and here I felt even more at home, slipping along the dark passageway into the open court where the sisters had assembled to greet me. I turned toward the sewing room, where we had sat so many times together, but the girls ushered me into their mother's sitting room where Um Fatima herself waited to lead me to a pillow.

After lunch, Um Fatima conveyed the momentous news that Basima would enter the girls' secondary school in Diwaniya the following autumn. She would live with a cousin of her father's and come home weekends.

"That's wonderful," I said sincerely. "In a few years she'll be a teacher like Sitt Aziza, maybe even a principal."

"*Enshallah*," said Basima modestly, but I could tell by the look in her eyes that she agreed with me.

"Our father says that Rajat will go too, when she finishes primary school here," added Fatima. The shy Rajat dropped her head in embarrassment.

"Sitt Aziza said Rajat is doing very well in her studies," put in Sanaa. Rajat dropped her head even lower.

We discussed Basima's fall wardrobe. Laila was making her three dresses.

"That won't be nearly enough," said Basima. "I've heard that the girls in Diwaniya wear a different dress every day. I can't buy that many, but I must have at least five, and a jacket." She was quite self-important about it, and her mother spoke sharply.

"You are lucky to go to school at all, Basima," she said, "and you'll be lucky to have one dress, let alone three."

This seemed a good moment to bring out the small presents I had bought in Baghdad—perfume, cloth, sweets —something expected from anyone coming home from a trip.

After tea I professed weariness, but Laila would not listen. "You can sleep in America," she said. "Let's not waste these days. This afternoon we are going to see

Salima. The teachers are in Diwaniya for the feast, but I promised Salima we'd come."

So went the feast. Next day we visited Sherifa and Medina and Fadhila, Mohammed sitting with us and smiling constantly while we drank lemon tea. "Send me a charm from America so I can have a child, Beeja," said Fadhila, "and so Sherifa can marry again." From Mohammed's house we went on to Ali's and that afternoon Hussein took me down the canal to his clan settlement. Sajjida was pregnant again. "*Enshallah walad,*" I offered. "*Enshallah,*" she rejoined. The little girls looked on solemnly. In the evenings the women came to my room in Haji's compound, and I spent all the money in my purse on cigarettes and pumpkin seeds. Amina brewed tea with cloves. One morning a very old woman I had never seen before entered the room. "*Ayyamak sa'ida,*" she said in a cracked voice. I rose to greet her in return and added, almost without thinking, "*Enshallah hejjiya* [God willing you will make the pilgrimage]."

The old lady settled herself, groaning and grunting with the effort, on the floor, and then peered at me. "How long have you been here?" she asked.

"Almost two years."

She pursed her lips and nodded slowly. "She's coming along all right," she announced to the rest of the women.

"See, Beeja," said Kulthum, "you're learning. Stay one more year and you'll be just like us. Ask Mr. Bob to bring your mother and then you'll never have to leave us and go back to America."

The moment was broken by the arrival of Feisal with a note from Bob. "Since there seems to be no other way of meeting," he wrote, "I have arranged that you and I are to take a walk and look at the fields behind the palm grove. After lunch, when everyone is napping, come to the door of the compound and I'll be waiting nearby." I laughed, recalling all the abduction-from-the-seraglio melodramas I had ever read.

"What is it? What's so funny?" clamored the women.

"Have you no manners?" Selma asked. "It's not polite to ask." Then she laughed herself. "But what is it, Beeja?"

"My husband wants to see me after lunch outside the compound."

"He must miss you," teased Laila.

"Doesn't like to sleep alone," Amina squeaked.

"*El hamdillah!*" pronounced Kulthum firmly over the raucous remark which Amina was adding to a giggling audience. Feisal snatched up my written reply and ran.

The sun was still high when Bob and I stepped out together along the edge of the palm grove. The children could not resist following, and we had a small band running along behind, but keeping a reasonably respectable distance. Before us stretched a network of canals, their banks making a tracery, hillock-high, which marked off the tiny plots of farmland like squares on a checkerboard. Only harvest stubble was left in the ground, but there was still water in the canals so we picked our way along the uneven ground of the banks.

"I've never been this far out before," I said.

"You haven't, of course—I never thought," Bob answered. "I wanted to talk to you and this seemed the easiest way. How's it going?"

"I don't look forward to leaving, if that's what you mean."

"I don't either," he replied, "though I wouldn't mind being out of the dust."

"It's not so bad now the wind has died."

We walked steadily along. Crows rose from the harvested fields and when we looked back, the mudhif was hidden by palms. Where the big canal turned, a thick clump of camel-thorn grew out and over the water, creating a fairly large shaded area on the bank.

"This must be where the women come in summer to take baths," I told Bob. "They've told me about this place; it's hidden from the mudhif and they have a little shelter from the camel-thorn."

"How do they take baths? In the canal?"

"Yes, they wait till sunset and come in groups. They bathe in the canal with all their clothes on, then go home and put on clean clothes. Quite ingenious."

"Are the women curious about your life in Baghdad?"

"Not at all," I answered. "It seems as though I haven't been away."

We were skirting the settlement, heading back along a roundabout road which, Bob said, led to the big bridge spanning the El Nahra canal. The children had dropped behind long ago.

"Mr. Bob, Mr. Bob," someone was shouting. Two tribesmen were running and gesticulating at us. Bob walked toward them and I stood with my back to the men, gazing out at the long, flat brown landscape, cut into tiny squares by the canal banks, the enormous sky dwarfing it and yet protecting it as well. The winds came from the desert and blew away the loam in the spring, but some sank into the canal and was thrown up again as silt in the fall. The sun burned the earth till it cracked, but the winter rains filled it until it could live again. Every fall the fellahin planted grain in the square plots, and the Euphrates River water, piped into these small canals, watered the grain and the people lived for another season. Thus it had been for more than five thousand years. The women were part of it, too, part of an enduring and traditional way of life that had developed in response to conditions in the valley, a way of life in which the women were secure and generally content.

They had never envied me, only made me fit, as well as I was able, into their patterns. I had done so, learning something about myself along the way. It had been a rewarding honeymoon, I thought, if not precisely what the bridal consultants in Chicago would have advised. But then their view of marriage, like that of my friends in El Nahra, was a limited one.

I turned to Bob, but he was already speaking. Never mind, I would tell him another time.

"I'm sorry," he said, "but I have to get back. There are guests from Baghdad in the mudhif and Sheik Hamid wants me."

We parted at the compound.

That night Laila appeared after supper. "You must come to us," she said. We sat together in the sewing room, the sisters and their cousins from across the alley, and ate fruit and drank tea. Suddenly there was a furious pound-ing on the door, and a figure in man's clothing advanced threateningly upon us, striking the air with a huge stick.

"Here, you silly girls, why are you sitting idle when you should be working?" shouted a thickly disguised voice. "Have you finished cleaning all that rice?"

The heavy stick swung above us, and while we all paused uncertainly, Basima tugged at the kaffiyeh cover-ing the figure's face and her sister Nejla was revealed, chok-ing with laughter.

"You were scared, Beeja. You didn't know who it was."

"Nejla is very good," said Laila.

"Yes, very good indeed." For a second I had been un-sure.

"Do Abdulla," suggested Fatima.

Nejla's stance changed. She stood straight and tall and appeared suddenly thin as she walked proudly around the room, swinging the stick slightly, the man's aba flowing behind her; it was a remarkable imitation.

Once more there was a pounding on the door. Basima rose to open it. Alwiyah and Samira and Selma stood there.

Fatima exclaimed in surprise. "Selma!" she said, strik-ing her forehead with the back of her hand in mock amaze-ment. "To what do we owe this honor? You haven't been in this house since your last daughter was born, three years ago. Girls, look what we have here, the favorite wife of our esteemed uncle, Haji Hamid!"

"We heard that Nejla was entertaining," answered Selma flippantly. "We wouldn't dream of missing that. Besides, isn't Beeja leaving tomorrow?" She threw off her abayah, wrapped it round her knees and sat down in the center of the group, which moved aside to make way for her.

"Yallah, Nejla, do Mr. Bob," she said with a glance at me, and Nejla obliged, imitating Bob's long strides and rapid pace while everyone clapped. She then gave us a very bitter, accurate imitation of Dr. Ibrahim, followed by a bit of buffoonery that was obviously Ali, the aging gardener.

"Now Mohammed," and Nejla mimicked Mohammed's shambling gait, a mixture of dignity and humility, and his eternal gesture of adjusting his agal and kaffiyeh, to such perfection that his sister Sherifa shrieked with laughter.

When Nejla sat down to drink tea, the talk turned to Basima's plans to go to secondary school. Selma thought it a good idea, but said that many women in the settlement did not feel the same way.

"You must expect that, Basima," she counseled.

"Many families don't like to see us going out and getting an education to better ourselves," offered Fatima.

Selma looked disdainful. "That isn't it at all. It's whether it is proper for Basima to live in the house of her cousin, where there are unmarried men her own age."

Fatima's eyes blazed. "What do you mean, is it *proper?*"

"You know perfectly well what I mean," answered Selma, quite loudly.

The tempers of the two women, usually so balanced, seemed about to explode into violence, and I could not see that the words which had passed between them were that important. Basima, who had been sitting quietly during this interchange peeling an apple, now cut the apple in half and held out a piece to each of the angry women. Selma looked down at the proffered fruit, distracted for a moment, and then in a sudden furious gesture struck the piece of apple from Basima's hand. Fatima drew in her breath in a long, quivering hiss. The company became very still. It was Nejla who saved the situation. Picking up the discarded piece of apple from the floor and taking the second from Basima's hand, she began to eat them alternately.

"The reason I am so good-natured and healthy," she said, winking at me, "is that I never let good food go to waste."

Someone snickered, but Selma and Fatima remained tight-lipped.

"Now you, Selma," continued Nejla, "you're fat enough, it's true, but Fatima needs to gain weight or she will never marry."

She munched the pieces of apple and we all laughed obediently. Selma turned her head and began to talk to Medina. Then I remembered the ancient, still unresolved feud between the men who were heads of the households represented by Fatima and Selma. Moussa and Hamid had split many years ago over the question of the succession to the sheikship. Sheik Hamid had not wanted his son Ahmar to marry Moussa's daughter Sanaa, although Ahmar had asked specifically for Sanaa's hand. Selma's sister had eloped with another son of Sheik Hamid, the one who was to marry Fatima. In El Nahra, as in any small community, there were conflicts between families, resentments and bitterness which were buried deep but which were always ready to flare up in situations such as this.

I thought, it will not be easy for Basima until she finishes school, but when she is finally a teacher like Hind and Aziza, the women of the settlement will forget their jealousies in mutual admiration of her status as an effendi. Even Selma will not be able to resist showing off and talking about her educated relative.

To change the subject, Laila began to talk of my impending departure, which was the last thing in the world I wanted to discuss that evening.

"Will you write to us?"

"Of course I will," I said.

"No you won't." Laila sniffed.

"How is the garden?" I asked firmly. "Tell me."

"I don't know," said Laila, wiping her nose ostentatiously. "It's been locked up since you left."

"Maybe if I asked Haji," I suggested, "he would open it up and we could sit and have Coca-Cola there tomorrow morning."

The women looked pleased but doubtful.

"Don't you ask Haji," Selma counseled. "Ask Mr. Bob to ask him."

Bob was successful. Ali, grumbling, unlocked the gate, and we swept in, Laila, Fatima, Rajat, Sherifa, Samira, Alwiyah and I. Rajat brought Coca-Cola and we sat in a circle on the uncut grass, under the shade of the bitter-orange tree. Because it seemed impossible that I should be leaving my friends forever, I did not mention the subject; nor did they. We talked of the past and always when conversation flagged, we talked of Basima's going to school in Diwaniya. She was the first girl of the El Eshadda to go.

"Will you wear an abayah there?" asked Alwiyah.

"Of course she will wear the abayah," retorted Fatima. "Every woman in Diwaniya wears one."

"The woman doctor at the hospital doesn't wear one," Sherifa said. "I saw her when I went to have my chest X-rayed. You remember, Beeja. She seemed to be a good doctor."

"Sitt Aziza says that she and Hind don't wear the abayah when they're in Baghdad," volunteered Laila.

"But that is haram," Fatima announced. "It is written in the Koran that all women must wear the abayah."

"You're wrong, Fatima." It was Basima, younger sister, contradicting older sister. We all stared at her. "It is not in the Koran at all. Sitt Aziza says so. And how would you know anyway, since you can't read the Koran?"

All things change with time, and in the silence of Fatima as she looked at her impertinent and yet chosen younger sister Basima, the past seemed to hang in balance with the present. But it was Fatima who gave in.

"I will ask the mullah," she said, but her tone was unconvincing.

"Let's see if Beeja's house is locked," suggested Laila. I had no desire at all to inspect my mud house, but there seemed no alternative as the women rose and we mounted the path past the palms and the oleanders to the two wooden doors. They were not locked and we swung them in. The rooms were empty—even the reed mats had been taken up from the dirt floors. It was no longer my house. But as I turned to leave, I heard a faint twittering and some feathers floated down from the roof beams onto the earth.

I smiled to myself. "The birds have come back," I said to Laila, and started to explain. Before I had finished, someone began banging steadily on the gate.

"It's Ali," called Fatima. "The taxi is waiting outside the mudhif."

My bag had already been passed out to Mohammed and stored in the trunk. The women had gathered at the door of the compound, and I, determined to be gay, had started down the line to shake hands, murmur traditional farewells and thanks for their hospitality. When I came to Selma, heavy and clumsy with the child she was carrying, she smiled politely in a set way and then as I smiled back, her face changed and she threw her arms around me and cried aloud. At this my own reserve broke and I found myself weeping, passing from one abayah-clad figure to another in a welter of embraces and tears.

"Go, go, Mr. Bob is waiting," hissed Ali from the other side of the doorway, and I flung myself out the door, past the mudhif where the tribesmen stood and into the taxi. I had only a glimpse of Bob's startled face, of Nour bending to shake his hand, before the door was closed, the taxi started, and I heard behind me, echoed in my own sobs, the sound of a swelling cry of ululation. It came from the compound. In that high wail, the expression of joy or excitement or grief which is inherently the women's own, they were bidding me goodbye.

Post Script

My husband has just returned from a brief business trip to Iraq, the first visit either of us has made since leaving in 1958. Bob went back to El Nahra, wondering apprehensively how our friends had fared during the revolutions which have taken place in the six years we have been gone. He found the village much the same. Sheik Hamid has weathered the political storms fairly well; the life of the tribe seemed substantially unchanged. The mudhif still dominates the settlement, but the sheik has also built himself a modern brick guest house, behind the harem and near the palm grove. A regular bus service links the village with Diwaniya and the old mud road has been raised and graded. A new intermediate school for boys has been built. Otherwise, except for the ease and speed of his trip from Baghdad, Bob said he felt as though he had been away from El Nahra for six months, not six years.

Naturally Bob did not see my friends the women, but just before he left, an extraordinary bundle was delivered to him, together with three letters for me. The bundle contained gifts: from Moussa's house came a large plastic bag, carefully stitched together at both ends on a home sewing machine. Inside was a cotton skirt made by Laila, a pink embroidered blouse from Fatima and Basima, and lengths of material for my children from Um Fatima. The women of Mohammed's house, Sherifa, Medina and Fadhila, sent a hiriz, a charm of gold set with tiny turquoises, "to hang from the hair of your youngest child and protect her from the Evil Eye, as is our custom here." Selma sent a lovely gold ring, set with five delicate seed pearls.

The letters were full of news, which supplemented the information I have received over the years in letters from Laila.

Sherifa, the deserted wife, has been divorced and has married again, "to a good man this time," she writes. She has a son.

Mohammed is in the Iraqi Army, an officers' orderly.

Abad, the boy who used to study his lessons under the street lamp, is doing well in his last year of secondary school in Diwaniya.

Jabbar and his new bride Suheir were both tragically killed in an auto accident on the Baghdad-Diwaniya road, only five months after their marriage.

Hussein, our guard, has a construction job in El Nahra. His wife Sajjida has at last borne a healthy boy.

Ahmed, Abdulla's son, married Haji Hamid's fair-skinned daughter Sabiha and works in a bank in Diwaniya.

Laila herself is still unmarried and sews at home.

Sanaa did marry Haji Hamid's son Ahmar. She has a son.

Nejla got her fat man, a rich merchant in Diwaniya. "She can eat all the rice she wants," reports Laila, "and she has a very sweet daughter."

Basima is now Sitt Basima, principal of a girls' primary school in a nearby village.

Selma has had three children since I left, one a boy. Bob saw this little son of Selma's dressed up in an American cowboy suit Sheik Hamid had brought back from Lebanon; he pronounced him the best-looking of all of Hamid's good-looking boys. "Dear sister, Um Laura Ann," begins Selma's letter. (Since I am a mother now too, she greets me as the mother of my oldest child.) "My dear, I was very much pleased to see the pictures of your children which Mr. Bob brought. I pray they are in good health. When will you be coming to see us? All of the family send our love and we are kissing the eyes of your children. Your sister, Um Feisal."

Cairo, 1964

GLOSSARY OF ARABIC TERMS

aba — a long cloak worn traditionally by Iraqi men.

abayah — the long black cloak worn traditionally by Iraqi women.

abu — father.

agal — a dark rope which holds an Arab tribesman's head scarf (*kaffiyeh*) in place.

ahlan wusahlan — welcome.

ahl-es-suq — people of the market.

Allah wiyach — God be with you (feminine form).

asha — woman's head scarf.

ayb — shame.

ayyamak sa'ida — May your day be happy (a greeting used on feast days in Iraq).

baksheesh — a tip.

bayt, byut — house, houses.

bint-amm — female cousin, father's brother's daughter.

bint-khaal — female cousin, mother's brother's daughter.

chobi — a line dance performed by men or boys.

dabka — a man's line dance.

dafna — burying ceremony.

dishdasha — the basic garment which is part of the street wear of both sexes in Iraq; a long garment made like a nightshirt.

diwan — reception room.

effendi — originally a Turkish civil servant; now generally an educated man who wears Western clothes.

el hamdillah — thanks be to God.

enshallah — God willing.

faisanjan — a Persian chicken dish, with walnut oil and the juice of dried promegranate seeds.

fellah, fellahin — farmer; farmers.

fiimaanila — goodbye; literally, "go with God's blessing."

fils — a coin worth about three cents; 100 fils make up the Iraqi sterling pound or dinar, worth $2.85.

foota — scarf; used by Iraqi women to mean chin scarf.

gaymar — the butterfat remaining on top of water-buffalo milk after it has been boiled and cooled.

ghee — clarified butter.

haji, hijjiya — terms of address for the man or woman who has completed the pilgrimage to Mecca.

hajj — the pilgrimage to Mecca.

halal — ritually permissible, as opposed to haram.

haram — ritually forbidden; sin.

hashmiya — a loose gown worn by southern Iraqi women on ceremonial occasions.

hilwa — attractive (fem.), *hiluu* (masc.).

hiriz — a charm or amulet.

hosa — a tribal war dance of southern Iraq.

ibn-amm — male cousin, father's brother's son.

ibn-khaal — male cousin, mother's brother's son.

Iid el-Fitr — the feast of fast-breaking, following Ramadan.

Iid el-Adha — the feast of sacrifice; the feast of the tenth day of the month of pilgrimage.

imam — a religious leader; may also refer to the shrine or the tomb of the religious leader.

kaffiyeh — the head scarf worn by Arab tribesmen.

khubuz — flat wheat or barley bread.

khubuz laham — flat bread with meat and spices baked into it.

kohl — powdered antimony, used as eye make-up.

kraya — a religious reading, common in Shiite communities.

kubba — a dish common throughout the Middle East: a paste of rice, or of meat and cracked wheat, is filled with meat, onions, spices, raisins, then fried or baked.

leban — in Iraq, yogurt mixed with water.

maasalaama — farewell; literally, go in safety.

mashallah — what wonders God hath willed; i.e., wonderful!

may khallif — never mind.

minbar — the niche in the mosque which faces toward Mecca.

mudhif — tribal guest house in southern Iraq.

muezzin — the man who, from the minaret of the mosque, calls the Moslem faithful to prayer.

Muharram — month in the Islamic lunar calendar during which Hussein and Ali, the grandsons of the prophet Mohammed, were slain.

mukhtar — title given to the man in charge of the market.

mullah — Moslem religious teacher, man or woman.

mushtamal — garden cottage in town.

muwadhifin — government civil servants.

nitwanness — we are here to enjoy ourselves.

oud — a stringed instrument, like a lute.

patcha — Middle Eastern dish, made by boiling the sheep's feet, head and stomach.

purdah — an Indian term generally meaning the seclusion of women in separate quarters.

Ramadan — Moslem month of fasting.

salaam alaykum — peace be unto you.

sammoon haar — hot bread.

Sayid — a descendant of the prophet Mohammed.

serifa huts — rough makeshift houses built of mud and mats.

shabih — passion play.

Shiite — a sect of Islam; the followers of Ali.

shlonich — how are you? (feminine form)

sirdab — summer cellar; a room dug into the ground for greater coolness.

Sitt — term of polite address used for an educated woman.

Sunni — the largest sect of Islam.

suq — market.

sura — a chapter or section of the Koran.

taaziya — mourning ceremony, including a procession of young men who ritually flagellate themselves during the Shiite commemoration of Ashur, the tenth of Muharram, day when Hussein and Ali were slain.

tamurhindi — a datelike fruit from India; used in Iraqi cooking and to make a cold drink.

tiji daayman — come often.

tikka — grilled lamb meat.

um — mother.

yallah — let's go.

Note:

Following the suggestion of the publisher, any Arabic words which appear in Webster's Unabridged Dictionary are spelled accordingly.

To simplify the problem of transliterating Arabic, I have omitted, in the Glossary and throughout the book, most of the diacritical marks usually used to indicate special Arabic sounds which do not occur in English. The "kh" sound is roughly equivalent to "ch" in the German "ich"; "gh" to the "gh" in "Ugh"; "ch" is hard, as in "church"; "dh," as in "mudhif," is close to the "th" sound in "the."

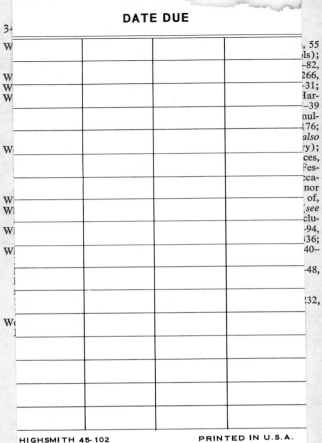

DATE DUE

34

HIGHSMITH 45-102   PRINTED IN U.S.A.

71453